MW01093965

Leibniz & Arnauld

R. C. SLEIGH, JR.

Leibniz & Arnauld

❖❖❖❖❖❖❖❖❖❖❖❖❖❖❖❖❖❖❖❖❖❖❖❖❖❖❖❖❖❖❖❖

❖❖❖❖❖❖❖❖❖❖❖❖❖❖❖❖❖❖❖❖❖❖❖❖❖❖❖❖

A COMMENTARY ON THEIR

CORRESPONDENCE

Yale University Press ❖ New Haven & London

Designed by Jill Breitbarth
and set in Ehrhardt type by
Tseng Information Systems, Inc.
Printed in the United States of America by
BookCrafters, Inc., Chelsea, Michigan.

Library of Congress Cataloging-in-Publication Data

Sleigh, R. C., 1932–
Leibniz and Arnauld : a commentary on their correspondence / R. C.
Sleigh, Jr.
p. cm.
Includes bibliographical references.
ISBN 0–300–04565–4 (alk. paper)
1. Metaphysics—History—17th century. 2. Leibniz, Gottfried
Wilhelm, Freiherr von, 1646–1716—Correspondence. 3. Arnauld,
Antoine, 1612–1694—Correspondence. I. Title.
B2599.M7S53 1990
193—dc20 89–38107
CIP

1 3 5 7 9 10 8 6 4 2

For Phyllis

Contents

❖❖❖❖❖❖❖❖❖

Acknowledgments

Research for this book began at the Institute for Advanced Study during academic year 1982–1983; a draft of the manuscript was completed there in academic year 1986–1987. I thank the institute, its then director, Harry Woolf, and the faculty of the School of Historical Studies, particularly my mentor there, Morton White. I am grateful for financial support during those two academic years to the institute, the National Endowment for the Humanities, and the University of Massachusetts. I appreciate, in particular, the support of Murray Schwartz, dean of its Faculty of Humanities and Fine Arts, and Michael Jubien, head of the Department of Philosophy.

The research involved in this book required the services of various libraries. I am indebted to Anke Holzer of the Manuscript Department of the Niedersächsische Landesbibliothek in Hannover, the library of the School of Historical Studies at the Institute for Advanced Study, Firestone Library of Princeton University, Baker Library of Dartmouth College, and Sigfried Feller, Edla Holm, and Richard Talbot of the University Library of the University of Massachusetts. I thank the members of the Seventeenth-Century Study Group for their help, particularly Robert Adams, Martha Bolton, Vere Chappell, Edwin Curley, Willis Doney, Daniel Garber, Michael Hooker, Ruth Matern, Fabrizio Mondadori, and Margaret Wilson.

I have benefited from comments offered at various colloquia where parts of the work in progress were presented: chapter 4 at Georgia State University, the University of Arizona, Arizona State University, the University of California at Berkeley, the University of Southern California, the University of California at Irvine, and Dartmouth College; chapter 5 at the University of Georgia, and to the Leibniz Society of America; chapter 6 to the New Jersey Philosophical Association and at the University of Texas at Austin; chapter 7 to the Spindel Conference on Rationalism at Memphis State University, and at the Fourth International Leibniz Congress in Hannover.

For help in seeking out manuscripts and ascertaining their probable dates, I am indebted, as Leibniz scholarship generally is, to Albert Heinekamp, director of the Leibniz-Archiv in Hannover, and to Heinrich Schepers, director of the Leibniz-Forschungsstelle of the University of Münster.

I am grateful to graduate students at the University of Massachusetts who have taken part in seminars on Leibniz that I have offered there regularly since 1972—in particular Andrew Black, David Cowles, Gregory Fitch, Carol Gabriel, and Del Ratzsch. I also thank the head secretary of the Department of Philosophy, Susan Holden, who typed numerous versions of this manuscript.

Hector Castañeda explained to me the rationale for concentrating attention on the texts of a limited time period in the life of a great philosopher. Over the years, he has encouraged my studies of Leibniz, for which I am grateful.

The idea for this specific project formed in the summer of 1981, when I was rescued from academic administration by the members of a National Endowment for the Humanities Summer Seminar, entitled "Leibniz among the Rationalists." I am indebted to every member of that seminar. The bibliography contains items that developed out of work done there by Lynn Baker, Georges Dicker, and Alan Hart.

I also thank the following scholars who provided helpful comments on work in progress: John Boler, Martha Bolton, David Blumenfeld, Daniel Garber, Glenn Hartz, Nicholas Jolley, Mark Kulstad, Christia Mercer, Walter O'Briant, Morton White, Frederick Worms, and John Wright.

I owe a great debt to Reinhard Finster of the Leibniz-Archiv in Hannover, who generously furnished me with copies of his transcriptions of the Leibniz-Arnauld correspondence, including a number of unpublished drafts of letters from Leibniz to Arnauld.

I am grateful to members of the Leibniz group at the 1988 NEH Summer Institute on Early Modern Philosophy, sponsored by the Council for Philosophical Studies and held at Brown University. Members of the Leibniz group offered suggestions for improvement in a penultimate draft of the book. Specific points are credited in the footnotes to Gregory Brown, Daniel Fouke, Daniel Garber, Mark Kulstad, Christia Mercer, Steven Nadler and Donald Rutherford. No doubt others are deserved. Steven Nadler and Donald Rutherford also helped with points of translation. Careful readings of a penultimate version of chapter 4 by Donald Rutherford and David Cowles generated significant revisions.

During an extended and delightful visit to the University of California at Irvine in 1989, I received useful suggestions from Ermanno Bencivenga, Dale Brant, Paul Graves, and Alan Nelson.

I thank my editor at Yale University Press, Harry Haskell, whose efforts improved the manuscript significantly.

Melvin Village, N.H.

A Note on Translations and Citations

❖❖❖❖❖❖❖❖❖❖

All quoted passages are given in English. The following method of citation is employed for published material, except for citations to the Leibniz-Arnauld correspondence: each quoted passage is followed by a reference to a source containing the passage in the original language (for the most part, French or Latin) and, in some cases, by a reference to a source containing another translation of the passage into English. In some cases the translation given here differs from the translation cited. Citations to unquoted material follow the same format.

Citations to the Leibniz-Arnauld correspondence are more complicated. Two distinct versions of Leibniz's letters to Arnauld exist. Those best known to students of Leibniz are copies retained by him and revised from time to time with an eye to possible publication. These are published in C. J. Gerhardt, *Die philosophischen Schriften von Gottfried Wilhelm Leibniz*, volume 2; the standard translation into English is H. T. Mason's *Leibniz-Arnauld Correspondence*. Fortunately, Mason's translation contains Gerhardt's pagination in its margins. I employ the abbreviation "LA" for simultaneous reference to Gerhardt and Mason. Versions of the letters as received by Arnauld are published in *Lettres de Leibniz à Arnauld d'après un manuscrit inédit*, edited by Geneviève (Rodis-) Lewis, abbreviated "RL." Citations in the form "LA———" refer to a draft of one of Leibniz's letters or to one of Arnauld's letters. In the case of letters from Leibniz to Arnauld, if the material cited is substantially the same in both the version sent and the version retained, or if it occurs only in the version retained, the designation "LA———" will be used. If there is substantial difference between the two versions, the designation "LA———(RL———)" will be employed. And if the material occurs only in the version sent to Arnauld, then the designation will be in the form "RL———."

Unfortunately, some of the material relevant to my enterprise has never been published in a format available publicly. In referring to Leibniz's unpublished correspondence I have used the designation "LBr" to stand for the relevant letter as catalogued by Bodemann (in *Der Briefwechsel des Gottfried Wilhelm Leibniz*), followed by the revelant folio number, according to Bockmann's pagination. Leibniz's unpublished manuscripts receive analogous treatment; they are designated "LH," with appropriate references to Bodemann number and pagination (see Bodemann, *Die Leibniz-Handschriften*).

I have quoted liberally from sources not previously available in an English translation. Where such translations are available, I have leaned toward reference by citation alone.

Abbreviations

A   German Academy of Science, ed. *Gottfried Wilhelm Leibniz: Sämtliche Schriften und Briefe*. Darmstadt, Leipzig, and Berlin, 1923—. Cited by series and volume.

AT   C. Adam and P. Tannery, eds. *Oeuvres de Descartes*. Paris, 1897–1913. Reprint. Paris: J. Vrin, 1964–1975. Cited by volume.

C   Louis Couturat, ed. *Opuscules et fragments inédits de Leibniz*. Paris, 1903. Reprint. Hildesheim: Georg Olms, 1966.

Confessio   G. W. Leibniz. *Confessio philosophi*. Cited by page number in A/6/3.

CSM   *The Philosophical Writings of Descartes*. Translated by John Cottingham, Robert Stoothoff, and Dugald Murdoch. 2 vols. Cambridge: Cambridge University Press, 1985.

DJ   James Dickoff and Patricia James. *The Art of Thinking*. Indianapolis: Bobbs-Merrill, 1964.

DM   G. W. Leibniz. *Discourse on Metaphysics*. Cited by section numbers as in G, vol. 4. Translated by Peter G. Lucas and Leslie Grint. Manchester: Manchester University Press, 1961.

Doney   Nicholas Malebranche. *Entretiens sur la metaphysique* (Dialogues on metaphysics). Edited by Willis Doney. New York: Abaris Books, 1980. Original French with translation into English.

FC   G. W. Leibniz. *Nouvelles lettres et opuscules inédits*. Edited by Louis Alexandre Foucher de Careil. Paris, 1857. Reprint. Hildesheim: Georg Olms, 1971.

G   *Die philosophischen Schriften von G. W. Leibniz*. Edited by C. J. Gerhardt. 7 vols. Berlin, 1875–1890. Reprint. Hildesheim: Georg Olms, 1965. Cited by volume.

General Inquiries   G. W. Leibniz. *General Inquiries about the Analysis of Concepts and Truths*. Cited by page number in C.

General Notation   G. W. Leibniz. *General Notation*. Cited by page number in Grua.

GM   G. W. Leibniz. *Mathematische Schriften*. Edited by C. J. Gerhardt. 7 vols. Halle, 1849–1863. Reprint. Hildesheim: Georg Olms, 1963. Cited by volume.

Grua   G. W. Leibniz. *Textes inédits*. Edited by Gaston Grua. 2 vols. Paris, 1948. Reprint. New York and London: Garland, 1985.

L   G. W. Leibniz. *Philosophical Papers and Letters*. Edited and translated by Leroy E. Loemker. 2d ed. Dordrecht: D. Reidel, 1969.

LA   Leibniz-Arnauld correspondence. Cited by page number in G, vol. 2.

La logique   Antoine Arnauld and Pierre Nicole. *La logique, ou L'art de penser*. Edited by Pierre Claire and François Girbal. Paris: J. Vrin, 1981.

LBr   Eduard Bodemann. *Der Briefwechsel des Gottfried Wilhelm Leibniz in der Königlichen öffentlichen Bibliothek zu Hannover*. Hannover, 1895. Reprint. Hildesheim: Georg Olms, 1966.

LH   Eduard Bodemann. *Die Leibniz-Handschriften der Königlichen öffentlichen Bibliothek zu Hannover*. Hannover, 1889. Reprint. Hildesheim: Georg Olms, 1966.

LO   Nicholas Malebranche. *The Search after Truth/Elucidations of the Search after Truth*. Translated by Thomas M. Lennon and Paul J. Olscamp. Columbus: Ohio State University Press, 1980.

MK   Kurt Müller and Gisela Krönert. *Leben und Werk von G. W. Leibniz: Eine Chronik*. Frankfurt am Main: Vittorio Klostermann, 1969.

ML   André Robinet, ed. *Malebranche et Leibniz: Relations personnelles*. Paris: J. Vrin, 1955.

MP   G. W. Leibniz. *Philosophical Writings*. Edited and translated by Mary Morris and G. H. R. Parkinson. London: Dent, 1973.

Necessary and Contingent Truths	G. W. Leibniz. *Necessary and Contingent Truths.* Cited by page number in C.
New Essays	G. W. Leibniz. *New Essays on Human Understanding.* Cited by page number in A/6/6. The Remnant and Bennett translation employs the Academy edition pagination (*New Essays on Human Understanding*, edited and translated by Peter Remnant and Jonathan Bennett [Cambridge: Cambridge University Press, 1981]).
OA	*Oeuvres de Messire Antoine Arnauld, Docteur de la Maison et Société de Sorbonne.* 43 vols. Paris, 1775–1783. Reprint. Brussels: Culture et Civilisation, 1967. Cited by volume.
OM	*Oeuvres complètes de Malebranche.* Edited by André Robinet. 20 vols., plus *Index des citations* and *Index général.* Paris: J. Vrin, 1958–1984. Cited by volume.
P	G. W. Leibniz. *Logical Papers.* Edited and translated by G. H. R. Parkinson. Oxford: Clarendon Press, 1966.
Primary Truths	G. W. Leibniz. *Primary Truths.* Cited by page number in C.
RL	Geneviève (Rodis-) Lewis, ed. *Lettres de Leibniz à Arnauld d'après un manuscrit inédit.* Paris, 1952. Reprint. New York and London: Garland, 1985.
Schmidt	G. W. Leibniz. *Fragmente zur Logik.* Edited and translated by Franz Schmidt. Berlin: Akademie Verlag, 1960.
Schrecker	G. W. Leibniz. *Monadology and Other Philosophical Essays.* Translated by Paul Schrecker and Anne Martin Schrecker. Indianapolis: Bobbs-Merrill, 1965.
Specimen	G. W. Leibniz. *A Specimen of Discoveries about Marvelous Secrets of a General Nature.* Cited by page number in G, vol. 7.
Systema	G. W. Leibniz. *Theologisches System.* Translated by Carl Haas. Tübingen, 1860. Reprint. Hildesheim: Georg Olms, 1966. Original Latin with translation into German.
Theodicy	G. W. Leibniz. *Theodicy.* Cited by section number as in G, vol. 6. Translated by E. M. Huggard as *Theodicy.* New Haven: Yale University Press, 1952. Reprint. LaSalle, Ill.: Open Court, 1985.

Chapter 1

❖❖❖❖❖❖❖❖❖

INTRODUCTION

In early February 1686 a blizzard brought operations at the silver mines in the Harz mountains to a halt. Before the blizzard, Gottfried Wilhelm Leibniz had been fully engaged in supervising the installation of windmills he had designed that would provide a uniform water supply for use in the mining operations. Leibniz used his unanticipated free time during the blizzard to write what has come to be called the *Discourse on Metaphysics*. On completion of the *Discourse*, Leibniz wrote to Landgrave Ernst von Hessen-Rheinfels on 11 February 1686:

> Being at a place where for some days I had nothing to do, I have composed a small discourse on metaphysics, about which I would be very pleased to have the opinion of M. Arnauld. For the questions of grace, the concourse of God and creatures, the nature of miracles, the cause of sin and the origin of evil, the immortality of the soul, ideas, etc., are touched upon in a manner that seems to open up new possibilities for elucidation of very great difficulties. I have enclosed the summary of the articles it contains, for I have not yet been able to have a fair copy made. I therefore beg your supreme highness to have this summary sent to him and that he be requested to give it a little consideration and to state his opinion. (LA 11)

Ernst and Arnauld both did as requested, and the Leibniz-Arnauld correspondence was under way. The *Discourse* and the correspondence mark a crucial epoch in the development of Leibniz's mature metaphysics, as he himself stated on a number of occasions. His first published presentation of this metaphysics, the *New System of Nature* (1695), begins: "It is now some years since I conceived this system, and entered into communication about it with several learned men, and in particular with one of the greatest theologians and philosophers of our time" (G/4/477 [MP 115]). Leibniz thought of publishing the correspondence with Arnauld as early as 1695 and as late as 1708.[1]

In this commentary I focus on the *Discourse* only to the extent that it illuminates the discussion in the correspondence. There is less connection between the *Discourse* and the correspondence than one might expect. The evidence is nearly conclusive that Leibniz never sent the complete *Discourse* to Arnauld, and that Arnauld had no more to go on than rather sketchy summaries. Leibniz does not mention sending the *Discourse* to Arnauld, nor does Arnauld mention receiving it. No copy has been found among Arnauld's papers. Furthermore, Arnauld's copy of Leibniz's long letter of 14 July 1686 closes with a summary of an argument presented in section 17 of the *Discourse*; Leibniz's copy contains no such summary. Thus it is clear that, five months into the correspondence, Arnauld still had no copy of the *Discourse*.

1. HISTORICAL METHODOLOGY

In an important paper on Leibniz's treatment of modality, Benson Mates wrote:

> It seems to me that there are two quite different kinds of studies
> that fall under the heading "history of philosophy." The first consists of
> attempts to discover and set forth, as accurately, objectively, and com-
> pletely as possible, the philosophical views of various historical figures.
> In studies of this kind there are, by general consent, a number of well-
> defined sins to be avoided. One must not "read in" to the author views
> that he did not expressly state, and must not ignore relevant statements
> that he does make, especially when these are incompatible with those
> of his statements upon which one is placing emphasis. In other words,
> one must remain very close to the text. The second kind of historical
> study, which Bernard Williams has aptly called "history of philosophy
> philosophy," has a different set of rules. Here the goal is not so much
> that of setting forth the plain facts about what an author thought and
> said, as of finding in that author ideas for the solution of a philosophical
> problem in which one is interested.[2]

Mates went on to note that "perhaps it would be better not to speak in this connection of *types* of historical studies but rather of *tendencies* or *moments* in historical studies, these tendencies being combined in different proportions in different instances." Perhaps so, but I agree with Mates that a useful distinction can be drawn between what I will call "exegetical history" and "philosophical history." It may be helpful to specify the distinction ostensively. The following are recent examples of first-rate contributions to philosophical history: Mates's article "Individuals and Modality in the Philosophy of Leibniz," from which the above passages are quoted; J. L. Mackie's *Problems from Locke*; and Jonathan Bennett's studies of Kant, the British Empiricists, and, most recently, Spinoza. I pick Mates, Mackie, and Bennett in part because each says up front that he aims at philosophical, not exegetical, history. As outstanding examples of recent exegetical history concerning Leibniz, I would cite Robert Adams's article "Leibniz's Theories of Contingency" and Daniel Garber's "Leibniz and the Foundations of Physics: The Middle Years."

In the Anglo-American tradition, exegetical history has been on the defensive in this century, at least until quite recently. Yet the primary purposes of exegetical history, pedestrian as they may be, are reasonably clear. In my view, the same cannot always be said for philosophical history. At least two distinct strategies are often connected with philosophical history. Although these strategies are not difficult to characterize, it is sometimes difficult to associate a clear purpose with their exemplars. One strategy consists in attempting to set out a philosophical theory utilizing *some* doctrines associated with a historical figure, but intentionally introducing revisions where that figure's views are deemed unacceptable. Of course, the resulting theory is not attributed to the historical figure, or indeed to anyone. It merely demonstrates how so-and-so's doctrines work out when modified in such and such a fashion. This modification often involves some contemporary philosophizing, frequently employing fashionable technical apparatus. Sometimes this approach yields illuminating results; but sometimes it is nothing more than an exercise in a priori reasoning to no clearly defined end.

A second strategy often connected with philosophical history consists in discussing some philosophical topic "in the company," to use Jonathan Bennett's words, of some historical figure. In the hands of a master like Bennett this approach sheds light simultaneously on both the philosophical problem and the historical figure. In less capable hands it degenerates into closet metaphysics (or whatever). It allows the author a front for probing philosophical problems, presenting arguments, even reaching conclusions, without being held to current standards of rigor. In my opinion, the effort attendant on philosophical history is often not justified in terms of the purely philosophical product. This outcome is not entirely surprising. If you want to work on the problem of personal identity, it is useful to read John Locke's writings, but it is more important to read Sidney Shoemaker—in part, of course, because Shoemaker has incorporated Locke's insights in his own work. If you are interested in making a contribution to the metaphysics of modality, it does no harm to study Leibniz, but Kripke is really more to the point. Philosophy is not related to its history in the way physics is to its history, but there *is* progress in philosophy, and it is not necessary to study the history of a philosophical problem in order to make a fundamental contribution toward the understanding, perhaps even the solution, of that problem.

On the other hand, philosophical history at its best contributes to the most exciting aspect of exegetical history. Recall Mates's characterization of what I am calling exegetical history as an attempt "to discover and set forth, as accurately, objectively, and completely as possible, the philosophical views of various historical figures" and to "set forth the plain facts about what an author thought and said." This is one component of exegetical history. A second, equally significant and often more exciting, component consists in an effort to explain *why* the philosopher under scrutiny thought and said what he did. Useful exegetical history, then, has both a fact-finding component and an explanatory component.

The fact-finding component. With respect to a given author (say, Leibniz) on a given topic (say, substance), we want a *surface account* of our author on the topic in hand: an account of what the author himself, at some fixed time, would have said he believed with respect to the matters in hand, given time for due reflection, a sober mind, and no grounds for duplicity. The reference to some fixed time is important. We want an account such that at some time in his philosophical career our author would have accepted it, not a system averaged out, so to speak, over his entire philosophical career. As Hector Castañeda has noted, one serious problem here is "to determine what counts as an appropriate exegetical unit."[3] In Leibniz's case this is a particularly delicate matter. Its resolution frequently requires detailed knowledge of both the dating of various versions of a text and of related Leibnizian texts written at approximately the same time.

Thus, an account of many of Leibniz's doctrines in the *Discourse on Metaphysics* will be diminished if the historian is not familiar with relevant logical doctrines, devised by Leibniz at approximately the same time, in the *General Inquiries about the Analysis of Concepts and Truths*. Furthermore, by a surface account I do not mean a cut-and-paste job. It is not a matter of collecting sentences (or translations thereof) written by our author. Rather, the goal is to formulate the author's central views on the topic in hand in sentences such that *we* know what propositions those sentences express and those propositions are the very ones our author accepted. Think how often exegetical history fails at this task. Most accounts of Kant's transcendental deduction serve as examples—lucid where Kant is lucid, degenerating to mere paraphrase just where one most wants help. In fairness, it should be said that the goal is elusive. I am aware of numerous places in this book where it seems to have eluded me. Still, from time to time in the heat of interpretation I have pulled back and asked myself: What would G. E. Moore think of that sentence? I believe that is a good thing for historians of philosophy to do.

Diverse interpretations of an author's meaning often appear equally plausible at the fact-finding level. Sometimes the explanatory component—a theory about the rational basis of the philosophical system under scrutiny—will tip the scales in favor of a particular interpretation. There is a delicate balance between data and theory, so to speak, that reaches the level of a fine art in the hands of the best historians.

An additional complication is prominent in Leibniz's case. More than most of his contemporaries, he tailored his presentation to different audiences, real or imagined, producing writings which have suggested to many that he had two quite distinct philosophical systems. Bertrand Russell put the view clearly in the preface to the second edition of his masterful study of Leibniz: "He had a good philosophy which (after Arnauld's criticisms) he kept to himself, and a bad philosophy which he published with a view to fame and money. In this he showed his usual acumen: his bad philosophy was admired for its bad qualities, and his good philosophy, which was known only to the editors of his MSS., was regarded by them as worthless, and left unpublished. . . . I think it probable that as he grew older he forgot the good philosophy which he had kept to himself, and remembered only the vulgarized version by which he won admiration of Princes and (even more) of Princesses."[4]

All things considered, I see almost nothing to be said in favor of Russell's idea that Leibniz had two philosophical systems. Leibniz did employ various styles of presentation, although no useful distinction can be drawn in this regard between work that he published and work that he circulated privately or not at all. These alternate styles of presentation create problems in interpretating our texts, particularly with respect to determining Leibniz's intended ontological commitments. The problem is exacerbated by the extent to which he employed various forms of reduction, enjoying the privilege of referring to entities to which he claimed no ontological commitment based on a scheme of reduction often not even noted in the text in hand. It is as if A. J. Ayer had suppressed the passages in *Language, Truth and Logic* in which he explicitly asserts the doctrine of phenomenalism. The remaining text would be puzzling, containing numerous sentences that appear to express propositions entailing the existence of material objects, others asserting the existence of sense data, and others asserting that in some philosophically significant sense the universe does not contain material objects in addition to sense data. We might invent various hypotheses to explain the puzzle; with good sense and good luck our hypothesis might be that Ayer held to the doctrine of phenomenalism.

In Leibniz's case matters are even more complex. Often a close reading of a text will suggest the hypothesis that Leibniz was therein presupposing some variety of ontological reduction, although it needs to be settled what is intended to be reduced to what, and by what means. Fortunately, Leibniz employed certain standard linguistic cues when he was about to formulate matters at the philosophically ultimate level, that is, when he was prepared to accept the prima facie commitments of his discourse as genuine ontological commitments. When he was ready to put his metaphysical cards on the table, Leibniz noted that he spoke "in Metaphysico rigore," or "dans la précision metaphysique," or "à la rigueur metaphysique." Linguistic cues help, but problems of distinguishing levels of commitment in Leibniz's discourse will loom large in what follows.

The explanatory component. Determining what a philosopher said is important; explaining why he said it is a more difficult, and surely more exciting, task. In part, the why will be provided by the philosopher himself in terms of the surface structure of his reasoning. But there is almost always a residual problem, that of explaining the rational basis for the most fundamental assumptions employed by the philosopher in question. I emphasize the rational basis; psychohistory is not part of exegetical history as I construe it.

That there is almost always a residual problem concerning the philosopher's most basic assumptions is not a simple, trivial consequence of the fact that reasoning has to begin somewhere. Usually, many aspects of the intellectual setting that bear on philosophical theses ultimately accepted by our philosopher go unstated. Motivations stemming from the then current intellectual setting need to be reconstructed by the exegetical historian. We need to provide a rational reconstruction of something like what Mandelbaum calls a philosopher's primary beliefs, including his theological and scientific beliefs, where relevant. By a rational reconstruction I mean a unified hypothesis about motivations, patterns of inference, and principles employed, but not stated, by our philosopher. The claim accompanying the hypothesis is not that the philosopher in question should have thought this way or might have thought this way, but rather that he *did* think this way. It is just here that philosophical history provides a useful aid to exegetical history. The problem, of course, is to strain out the "should haves" and "might haves" in order to arrive at a decent conjecture about the way it was.

Leibniz employed two types of basic principles. On the one hand are those that he explicitly called "first principles," what we might call "first principles per se." On the other are basic principles that guided his metaphysical reasoning, which he stated only on rare occasions under extreme provocation of the sort Arnauld could induce. However, he never called these tenets "principles," first or otherwise; they express an attitude as much as the content of some intellectual belief. These I call "attitudinal first principles." The distinction may be vague, but what matters to me is this: There are first principles that Leibniz employed and called "first principles," for example, the law of contradiction and the principle of sufficient reason. But there are attitudes at work, which can be formulated as principles, to which he rarely referred, but which must be recognized in order to grasp his reasoning—for example, a commitment to a form of substance/mode ontology, a commitment to real causation as opposed to mere constant conjunction, a commitment to the principle "no real entity without identity" and its variant "no real identity where convention is required." Much will be made of these attitudinal principles in what follows.

These brief remarks are intended to set forth my goals in this commentary. They are not intended to be contentious. I am not arguing that exegetical history is preferable to philosophical history. I am simply more comfortable with and, I believe, more competent at exegetical history. Even there, I have regard for my considerable limitations. The *via negativa* has always come easier to me. It seems to me extraordinarily difficult to make out just what Leibniz is up to in the texts under study here. I hope that I have raised a number of the questions that deserve attention, even if the answers I recommend may be off the mark.

2. THE TEXTS

The primary texts for this study are the *Discourse on Metaphysics* and the ensuing correspondence with Arnauld. I will also deal with other related philosophical work in the period 1685–1688.

The *Discourse* and the correspondence were first published in 1846 by C. L. Grotefend in *Briefwechsel zwischen Leibniz, Arnauld und dem Landgrafen Ernst von Hessen-Rheinfels aus den Handschriften der Königlichen Bibliothek zu Hannover.* Grotefend's edition, based on handwritten material in Hannover, includes the correspondence, the *Discourse*, an early (1671) letter from Leibniz to Arnauld, and some related correspondence between Leibniz, Foucher, and Fardella. Most subsequent editions of the *Discourse* and correspondence are based on Grotefend's edition. Anyone who has viewed the handwritten material—with its tightly scribbled line, numerous erasures, and inserts within inserts within inserts—will appreciate the magnitude of Grotefend's contribution, as well as the temptation of subsequent editors to follow him rather than return to the source. The standard edition, on which currently available translations into English are based, is that of C. J. Gerhardt, as contained in *Die philosophischen Schriften von Gottfried Wilhelm Leibniz*, published in seven volumes between 1875 and 1890. The *Discourse* is in volume 4, the correspondence with Arnauld in volume 2. The Gerhardt edition is based on the same handwritten material as Grotefend's. It contains some corrections, but also repeats some errors.

Two major textual finds in this century concern this project. While carrying out research on Leibniz's theological writings, Henri Lestienne discovered among the handwritten material a piece catalogued under the title "Traité sur les perfections de Dieu." It was the autograph version of the *Discourse*. The handwritten version on which Grotefend and Gerhardt based their texts is a fair copy made by a secretary, with corrections in Leibniz's hand. Presumably, the autograph copy is Leibniz's first crack at the *Discourse*; the fair copy, as emended, a later version. They differ in important and instructive ways, as I will discuss in chapter 5.

The Lestienne text contains the autograph version, the complete version prepared by a secretary, with corrections in Leibniz's hand, as well as two distinct partial versions. It also includes apparatus indicating erasures, emendations, corrections, and the like. Since my concern is with what Leibniz actually believed concerning the philosophical topics in hand at the time in question, 1685–1688, all of this matters to me. Nothing comparable exists in the case of the correspondence.

In 1952 Geneviève Rodis-Lewis published Leibniz's letters as received by Arnauld, copies of which she discovered in the national archives at The Hague. These letters indicate what changes Leibniz made at various times in preparing his copies of the correspondence for publication. Grotefend and Gerhardt based their editions on the copies retained by Leibniz; both included the same material, and, curiously, both excluded the same material.

There are interesting drafts for three of Leibniz's letters to Arnauld that have never been published. Moreover, except for isolated instances, neither Grotefend nor Gerhardt employed apparatus indicating the erasures, emendations, and corrections with which Leibniz's letters and drafts are replete. Through the generosity of the Leibniz-Archiv in Hannover, and in particular its director, Albert Heinekamp, I have had access to excellent copies of all the correspondence available in Hannover, that is, the material catalogued by Bodemann under the designation "16. Arnaud Ant." Trying to make out Leibniz's scrawl (in French) brought home to me the difference between knowing a language and really knowing a language. Fortunately, Dr. Reinhard Finster has kindly allowed me to use his transcriptions of the Hannover holdings, which he has made in preparation for a full presentation of the texts of the correspondence, together with a translation (into German), to be published by Felix Meiner Verlag. The texts of Lestienne's edition of the *Discourse* and Finster's transcriptions of the correspondence may be regarded as definitive, reaching the standards of the Academy edition.

There have been numerous translations into English of the *Discourse* and the correspondence. The best available translation of the entire *Discourse* is that of Peter G. Lucas and Leslie Grint. It is based on Lestienne's edition and, like it, details the important variations between the autograph copy and the fair copy, as well as the two incomplete drafts that Lestienne discovered. The Lucas and Grint version is the basis of the translations from the *Discourse* used in this book. (Appendix B contains a few suggested emendations, mostly trivial.) Citations to it will be not by page number, but by the number of the article from the *Discourse*. The best available translation of the correspondence is that of H. T. Mason. Here, too, I have a number of emendations to suggest in Appendix B. In some cases Mason translated Gerhardt's text flawlessly, but Gerhardt's reading of Leibniz's handwriting is faulty. Where Leibniz's emended copies of his letters differ from the letters as received by Arnauld, our purposes sometimes are better served by consulting the Rodis-Lewis edition.

So much for primary texts. Many of the related texts of concern to us bear on logical doctrines or the problem of God's freedom in creation. Between 1679 and 1686, Leibniz made remarkable progress in developing systems of logic. Fortunately, many of the relevant texts are located in Couturat's *Opuscules et fragments inédits de Leibniz*. Translations of many of the crucial texts are in Parkinson's edition of the *Logical Papers*, and in Parkinson and Morris's edition of the *Philosophical Writings*. The texts presented in the Couturat volume form the basis for his masterful study *La logique de Leibniz*. The fundamental thesis of Couturat's study—that Leibniz's metaphysics is implied by his philosophical logic—lifted Leibniz studies out of the doldrums at the beginning of this century. Many of the texts bearing on the problem of God's freedom in creation are located in Grua's edition of *Textes inédits*.

Unfortunately, some of the relevant secondary texts from our time period are not publicly available in published form. A significant portion of the texts in this category have been disseminated to scholars in the *Vorausedition* to a forthcoming Academy edition of the *Philosophische Schriften*. However, since this is not available in bookstores or libraries, I will refer to these texts by their Bodemann numbers, although the *Vorausedition* is my real source.

The amount of textual material involved in this study is relatively small. But it is dense, difficult, often frustratingly obscure, yet fascinating and worth the effort required to grasp Leibniz's thought, because of the incredible power, originality, and penetration of his mind.

Chapters 2 and 3 are intended to set the stage for an analysis of Leibniz's views, insofar as they can be gleaned from the correspondence with Arnauld. The heart of the matter begins in chapter 4.

In the preface to the first edition of his classic study *A Critical Exposition of the Philosophy of Leibniz*, Bertrand Russell noted that he first read the *Discourse on Metaphysics* and the correspondence with Arnauld while preparing lectures on Leibniz for Lent Term in 1898. "I felt—as many others have felt—that the *Monadology* was a kind of fantastic fairy tale, coherent perhaps, but wholly arbitrary. At this point I read the *Discours de metaphysique* and the letters to Arnauld. Suddenly a flood of light was thrown on all the inmost recesses of Leibniz's philosophical edifice. I saw how its foundations were laid, and how its superstructure rose out of them. It appeared that his seemingly fantastic system could be deduced from a few simple premises, which, but for the conclusions which Leibniz had drawn from them, many, if not most, philosophers would have been willing to accept."[5]

It is now difficult to imagine what it would be like to study the *Monadology* without benefit of the *Discourse* and the correspondence with Arnauld. There is no doubt that Russell's brilliant work has greatly enhanced our understanding of Leibniz. But surely there is some hyperbole in claiming that the *Discourse* and correspondence throw a flood of light "on all the inmost recesses of Leibniz's philosophical edifice."

In a paper published seventy-two years after Russell's book, Benson Mates summarized an illuminating discussion of one recess in the Leibnizian edifice: "Looking for an intuitive basis for saying that Adam would not have been the same individual if he had had any attributes other than the ones he does have, we have thus chased the quarry through thickets of Leibnizian terminology down to the point where the problem seems to be this: Is there any intuitive basis for Leibniz's notion of the complete individual concept?"[6] I have found my task much more like chasing an elusive quarry through thickets than like recording the details of the recesses of some structure standing perfectly illuminated before me.

It may seem excessive to devote an entire book to a single correspondence that lasted only a few years. I don't think so. The *Discourse* and subsequent correspondence constituted a seminal episode in Leibniz's philosophical life, as he himself said. Furthermore, Arnauld's probing questions forced Leibniz, on occasion, to dismount from his metaphysical high horse and explain himself. And such explanations are sorely needed. Because of the length of this book and its relatively narrow focus, I have refrained for the most part from commenting on relevant items in the secondary literature. Items of the secondary literature that were particularly useful to me are listed in the third section of the Bibliography.

3. SUMMARY OF THE DISCOURSE

Leibniz intended the *Discourse on Metaphysics* as a piece in a larger scheme. The larger scheme was the securing of reunion among the various Protestant denominations and, ultimately, reunion between Protestants and Catholics. The *Discourse* was intended to provide a philosophical framework within which the leading theological disputes might be resolved. Chapter 2 of this study is an effort to locate the *Discourse* in this context. The structure of the *Discourse* displays this purpose: it begins and ends with God. It opens with an account of God's perfection and a philosophical account of creation, including a discussion of the application of the principle of sufficient reason to God's choice of one among infinitely many possible worlds. It closes with a discussion of the relation of finite spirits (including human persons) to God. In between comes the metaphysics. Leibniz reached the metaphysics by asking how we are to distinguish the actions of God from those of individual substances created by God. Leibniz reasoned that, in order to answer this question, we need a clear grasp of what an individual substance is. He noted that the traditional doctrine—that a substance is an entity to which other entities are attributed, without it, in turn, being attributed to anything—was correct, but relied on an unanalyzed notion of attribution. In order to provide such an analysis, he introduced the concept-containment account of truth, that is, the doctrine that a categorical, affirmative proposition, whether singular or universal, is true just in case the concept of its predicate is contained in the concept of its subject.

Leibniz purported to derive a theory of the nature of individual substance from the concept-containment account of truth. The theory, which I will call the complete-concept theory of substance, appears to be this: an entity is an individual substance if and only if its concept contains all and only the concepts of those entities that may be attributed to it. All of the metaphysics so far summarized occurs in section 8 of the *Discourse*. Section 9 begins: "There follow from this several notable paradoxes." In fact, the "paradoxes" are regarded by Leibniz as sober metaphysical truths, indeed, many of the doctrines by which his system is identified: the identity of indiscernibles, the doctrine that substances can only begin by creation and end by annihilation, and the doctrine that each substance expresses the entire universe.

Three questions arise about the contents of these two sections of the *Discourse*. First, what led Leibniz to accept the concept-containment account of truth? After all, it sounds very much like saying that a proposition is true if and only if it is analytically true, a doctrine that would seem to lead to the disastrous conclusion that truth and necessary truth come to the same thing. Second, what on earth suggested to Leibniz that the concept-containment account of truth implies the complete-concept theory of substance? The connection is not at all obvious; indeed, at first blush it looks like an obvious mistake. Third, what connection did Leibniz see between the complete-concept theory of substance and the "notable paradoxes," the various theses about substance that give content to Leibniz's metaphysics? Again, at first glance there seems to be no connection.

In sections 10, 11, and 12 of the *Discourse*, Leibniz drew what he took to be a crucial consequence from this theory of substance—namely, that extension cannot constitute the essence of any substance, and that, if there are extended substances, their essence must consist in having a substantial form. This doctrine is discussed in detail in the correspondence and in chapters 5 and 6 of this book. I hold that Leibniz's views on this topic developed in significant ways during the correspondence. It is important to ask just what view about the nature and reality of extended items Leibniz reached at the close of the correspondence. How close was he then to his final view —the view that the ultimate individuals of the universe are nonextended, soul-like entities—monads—and that what we take to be extended items are appearances of collections of monads?

In sections 14, 15, and 16, Leibniz claimed to draw further consequences from the complete-concept theory about the nature of individual substances and the relations holding among them. These further consequences include: the thesis of *spontaneity*, that each state of a substance is a consequence of its preceding state; the doctrine that each created substance is like a "world apart," that no created substance is a real cause of the state of another substance; and the doctrine of "marks and traces," that the present state of a substance contains marks of all it will be and traces of all it has been. Also included among the further consequences are the main ingredients of what Leibniz later called the "pre-established harmony." In section 33 Leibniz applied that theory to explain what he called "the commerce of the soul and the body." Arnauld had difficulty seeing the difference between the pre-established harmony and occasionalism, a theory Leibniz took to be distinctly inferior to his own. These matters are discussed in chapter 7 of this book.

In sections 17 and 18 of the *Discourse*, Leibniz argued that a correct account of the physics of free-fall supports his metaphysical analysis of extended items, as opposed to that of Descartes. Arnauld did not rise to the bait here; we will. After a discussion of the utility of final causes in physics (sections 19 through 23), Leibniz attempted to offer a solution to the debate between Arnauld and Malebranche concerning the nature of ideas and their place in our knowledge (sections 23 through 29). Arnauld let it go; so will I.

In sections 31 and 32 Leibniz drew the consequences from his theory that are relevant to his reunion project. Specifically, he set out to show that the framework previously established—the notion that God created by choosing among an infinity of possible worlds, each world characterized in terms of the complete concepts of the substances composing it—provides the tools for resolving outstanding and divisive theological questions.

In section 30 Leibniz had argued that, contrary to initial appearances, there is no incompatibility between accepting the framework described above and attributing freedom to some of the created individual substances, for example, human beings. An analogous disclaimer is the subject of section 13. There Leibniz argued that there is no inconsistency between claiming that the concept of each individual substance is complete and that, nevertheless, some substances act freely and, hence, could have had attributes other than those they did have, that is, other than those contained in their concepts. Here Arnauld did rise to the bait. He thought that what Leibniz held was inconsistent with God's freedom. He thought this breach so serious that he asked rhetorically: "Would it not be better if he [Leibniz] abandoned these metaphysical speculations, which cannot be of any use to him or to others, in order to apply himself seriously to the greatest business he can ever have, the assurance of his salvation by returning to the Church?" (LA 16).

Freedom and contingency are discussed in chapter 4. Two of the difficult problems of explanation considered there have to do with Arnauld. The first half of the correspondence ends dramatically with what appears to be a concession by Arnauld: "It was more than enough to make me confess to you in good faith that I am satisfied by the way you explain what had at first shocked me regarding the concept of the individual nature. . . . I see no other difficulties remaining except on the possibility of things, and on this way of conceiving God as having chosen the universe that he has created among an infinite number of other possible universes that he saw at the same time and did not wish to create" (LA 63–64). The problems are these: what induced Arnauld to concede on the main point at issue; and what was his problem with the framework of possible worlds? Note that, given my account of Leibniz's larger scheme—the reunion project—Arnauld's concession must have been bittersweet to Leibniz, since the framework Arnauld so casually brushed aside was an essential component of the larger enterprise.

Leibniz had important things to say in our time period on freedom, both divine and human, that appear in neither the *Discourse* nor the correspondence. In discussing human freedom, Leibniz introduced what came to be his favored account of the difference between contingent and necessary truth, what I shall call the doctrine of infinite analysis. Roughly, the doctrine comes to this: a proposition p is necessarily true if and only if there exists some analysis of the concepts contained in p, in virtue of which p is reducible to an identity in a finite number of steps. Analysis is here conceived as a process of substitution based on definitional equivalence. An identity is a proposition that is true in virtue of its form, for example, A is A. A proposition p is contingently true if and only if there is no analysis in virtue of which p is reducible to an identity in a finite number of steps, but there is an analysis of p that approaches some identity q as a limit. The doctrine surfaces in a number of important logical works that Leibniz wrote in our time period. Perhaps the most significant of these is the working draft *General Inquires about the Analysis of Concepts and Truths*, dated by Leibniz 1686. I will say something about the doctrine of infinite analysis in chapter 4. Given that Leibniz regarded infinite analysis as a genuine breakthrough, the obvious question is, why is it not mentioned in the *Discourse* or the correspondence?

In the *Discourse* Leibniz maintained that the principle of sufficient reason applies to God's choice of a world to create. In the *Discourse* he considered, and brushed aside, the claim that such an application of the principle of sufficient reason is inconsistent with God's freedom (see, for example, section 3). But in other writings in our period Leibniz took the problem more seriously. What is the problem? It is natural to suppose that God is good of necessity and that it is necessary that if God is good then God chooses to create the best possible world. And it is also natural to assume that whatever possible world is the best, is so of necessity. But these assumptions seem to imply that whatever world God does create exists of necessity, and that, hence, God is not free in his choice. Leibniz wrestled with these problems much of his life, suggesting early on that the necessity involved is not inconsistent with divine freedom, and later arguing that we ought to reject one or more of the necessities involved (although he vacillated as to which). In order to comprehend what Leibniz did say in the *Discourse* and correspondence on freedom, we need to know what he was thinking about this problem at the time.

It will be noted from this summary of the *Discourse* that I intend to concentrate on those aspects on which Arnauld commented, thus giving less attention to some items of acknowledged importance to the development of Leibniz's mature system, such as the influence of his physics on his metaphysics. Perhaps the fact that this work is a commentary on the correspondence is justification enough for this restriction. In any case, I am most comfortable with those topics in the *Discourse* (or, at any rate, its summary) which piqued Arnauld's interest. Leibniz made some efforts to direct Arnauld's attention to points of physics. He sent Arnauld a copy of the *Brevis demonstratio erroris memorabilis Cartesii* with his letter of 14 July 1686, to which Arnauld responded somewhat haphazardly in September (LA 67–68); Leibniz responded to these remarks at some length (LA 78–81). Arnauld replied: "I grant you, Sir, that I have no ideas about the rules of movement clear and distinct enough to make a good judgment of the problem you have put to the Cartesians" (LA 89).

There is no question that Leibniz wanted Arnauld to reflect on the support his physics provided for his metaphysics. Consider this entreaty in Leibniz's letter of 14 January 1688: "I wish with all my heart that you might find the time to ponder for a half-hour my objection to the Cartesians. Your learning and your sincerity assure me that I would make you grasp the point, and that you would recognize in good faith what is involved. The discussion is not long, and the matter is of great importance, not only for mechanics but also in metaphysics" (LA 133). Still, Leibniz knew what he was getting when he selected Arnauld, a metaphysically inclined theologian, to be his correspondent with respect to the *Discourse*. On 8 December 1686 he wrote: "I indeed suspected that the argument taken from the general nature of propositions would make some impression on you; but I also admit that few are capable of appreciating truths so abstract and that perhaps anybody else but you would not so easily have perceived its force" (LA 73–74). Admittedly, these remarks occur in response to Arnauld's startling concession, previously mentioned, which surely put Leibniz in a warm frame of mind toward him. But beyond that I think they accurately reflect Leibniz's estimate of Arnauld's metaphysical talents and help to explain the metaphysical orientation of the correspondence.

Chapter 2

❖❖❖❖❖❖❖❖❖

THE INTERMEDIARY

Although the title of this book mentions only Leibniz and Arnauld, the correspondence was a three-cornered affair. The intermediary was Ernst, the landgrave of Hessen-Rheinfels. He and Leibniz corresponded concerning church reunion, containment of Louis XIV, the political state of the Holy Roman Empire, and related matters, beginning in May 1680 and continuing until the Ernst's death in 1693. One reason Leibniz sent the landgrave his letters intended for Arnauld was that Ernst knew Arnauld's current address; Leibniz did not. But there is much more to it than that. Leibniz's correspondence with Ernst and Arnauld played a significant role in his intellectual life. By making use of a friendly Catholic nobleman, he hoped to gain a sympathetic hearing for his views from a Catholic theologian. Arnauld would then vouch that Leibniz's thoughts about fundamental questions in dispute between Protestants and Catholics were not heretical from the Catholic point of view.

Leibniz and Arnauld had previously been linked with two other prominent Catholic noblemen: Johann Christian von Boineburg and Johann Friedrich von Braunschweig-Lüneburg (Hannover). Boineburg, Johann Friedrich, and Ernst had this in common: each was a convert from Protestantism to Catholicism. Leibniz worked in various capacities for Boineburg (or Boineburg's sometime employer, Johann Philipp von Schonborn, bishop and elector of Mainz) from 1668 until 1673. Boineburg died in December 1672, von Schonborn in February 1673. Almost immediately (on 26 March 1673) Leibniz wrote to Johann Friedrich:

> The famous Arnauld is a man of the most profound and wide-ranging thought that a true philosopher can have; his aim is not only to illuminate hearts with the clarity of religion, but, further, to revive the flame of reason, eclipsed by human passions; not only to convert the heretics, but, further, those who are today in the greatest heresy—the atheists and libertines; not only to vanquish his opponents, but, further, to im-

prove those of his persuasion. His thoughts, then, come to seeking how, so far as it is possible, a reform of abuses, frankly wide-spread among dissidents, would overcome the cause of the division. In this design, on several points of importance, he has made the first step and, as a prudent man, he goes by degrees. I am distressed that we have lost von Boineburg just when I have struck up an acquaintance with Arnauld; for I had hoped to bring these two minds, so similar in their honest soundness, on the road to a closer agreement. The Church, as well as the Fatherland, has sustained a loss with this man. (A/1/1/487–488)

With this letter Leibniz began to put together the Johann Friedrich triad, which came to fruition in 1676, when Leibniz accepted a position as counselor and librarian to Johann Friedrich at the court of Hannover. A good description of the three triads in which Leibniz and Arnauld were involved is contained in a letter Leibniz wrote to Johann Friedrich in the fall of 1679, on the occasion of a trip during which Johann Friedrich died:

The departure of your serene highness and the conjunction of the times oblige me to touch on a matter I have weighed carefully. But times and opportunities lost do not return, as I have already discovered from another occasion; and motives of piety and the public good must take precedence over all other considerations.

Hence, your serene highness should know that I frequently examined in a fundamental way controversies with the late Baron Boineburg where it was found finally that the Council of Trent can be accepted in its entirety without difficulty, except for three or four passages that, it seems to me, in order to avoid opinions involving a contradiction, must necessarily be given an interpretation that is not contrary to the words, nor to the doctrines of the Catholic church, I believe, but that is rather far removed from the opinions common to some scholastic theologians and, especially, the monks. Since these men have a great ascendency over minds (witness the difficulty that they have given to Galileo), I told him frankly, and in order to proceed with candor, and without any reservation, that I would have no difficulty in submitting to this and publicly avowing it, if a public declaration from Rome could be obtained for me, saying that these interpretations, which seem to me truths, are at least tolerable and contain nothing heretical or contrary to the faith. That being done, I would set out forcefully to put all this in such a clear light that, perhaps, my work could contribute something in time to reunion.

The late Boineburg was delighted with this proposal, and when I journeyed to France he gave me a letter of introduction to Arnauld, for he believed that his opinions could be of great weight. But as I proceeded with all possible circumspection, in order not to be viewed as inopportune, the death of the Baron occurred unexpectedly, which removed my hope of succeeding along these lines. So I did not explain myself to Arnauld, and from that moment on I thought of your serene highness, in as much as I knew that Boineburg had had the intention of speaking about it for reasons yet more particular, which I shall give in their place.

Now supposing these declarations obtained from Rome, I had formed the plan of a work of the first importance, which Boineburg marvelously approved, whose title was *Catholic Demonstrations*. It was to contain three parts: the first, demonstrations of the existence of God, of the immortality of the soul, and of all natural theology. In fact, I have some surprising ones. The second part was to be about the Christian religion, or revealed theology, where I wanted to demonstrate the possibility of our mysteries and to meet all the difficulties of those who claim to show absurdities and contradictions in the Trinity, in the Incarnation, in the Eucharist, and in the resurrection of the body. For the proofs of the Christian religion are only moral, since it is not possible to give another kind in matters of fact. Now every proof that carries only moral certainty can be overthrown by stronger contrary proofs, and, consequently, it is also necessary to respond to objections in order to satisfy ourselves entirely, for a single impossibility proved with respect to our mysteries would overthrow the foundation. The third part was to treat of the Church, where I have very convincing proofs that the hierarchy of the Church is of divine right. . . .

But in order to lay the foundations for these great demonstrations, I plan to preface them with the demonstrative elements of true philosophy, in order to aid the understanding of the principal work. There must be a new logic, so that we can know the degrees of probability, since this is necessary in order to judge of proofs concerning matters of fact, and of morals. . . . It is also necessary to push metaphysics further than has been done so far, in order to have true notions of God and of the soul, of a person, substance, and accidents. And, unless we have a more profound insight into physics, we cannot answer the objections that are formed against the story of creation, the deluge, and the resurrection of the body. Finally, true morality must be demonstrated, in order to know what justice is, as well as justification, freedom, pleasure, happiness, and the beatific vision. (A/2/1/487–489 [L 259–261])

An outline of the *Catholic Demonstrations* is to be found at A/6/1/494–500, with various parts thereof, completed in the period 1668–1671, located at A/6/1/489–493; and at 501–559 (with important critical apparatus located at A/6/2/569–582). The outline, and the completed parts, are just as limned in Leibniz's letter to Johann Friedrich of 1679, quoted above. Now that A/6/3 is available, covering Leibniz's philosophical work during the Paris period, it is clear that, although Leibniz devoted much intellectual energy to mathematics from 1672 until 1676, he also wrote widely on topics that fall under the outline of the *Catholic Demonstrations*. Particularly worthy of note is the *Confessio philosophi*, probably written in the fall and winter of 1672–1673 (A/6/3/115–149), and various components of the *De summa rerum* (A/6/3/461–588), a number of short essays containing what Leibniz took to be his major contribution to the ontological argument: a proof that the concept of a being having every perfection is consistent (see A/6/3/ 571–583).

It is probable, although not certain, that Leibniz was referring to a section of *Confessio philosophi* in paragraph 211 of the *Theodicy*, where he noted: "While in France, I communicated to Arnauld a dialog that I had written in Latin on the cause of evil and the justice of God. . . . This principle that I sustain here, namely, that evil has been permitted, because it has been included in the best plan of the universe, was already employed there; and Arnauld did not appear shocked by it."[1] It may seem odd, bordering on inconsistent, for Leibniz to write to Johann Friedrich that he "did not explain [him]self to Arnauld" in this regard, and yet to suggest that he presented Arnauld with the *Confessio*. But there is a plausible explanation. When Leibniz said that he did not explain himself to Arnauld, what he probably had in mind is that he did not outline the total reunion project for which the triad was to be utilized. The *Confessio* primarily concerns an attempt to justify the goodness of God, given the evil to be found in the world, a problem that does not discriminate among Christians of varying persuasions, and hence is not directly and immediately related to Leibniz's ultimate ends regarding reunion.

Nonetheless, assuming that Leibniz did present the *Confessio* (or, more likely, a part thereof) to Arnauld, it may seem surprising that there is no mention of it in the two men's correspondence after Leibniz wrote the *Discourse on Metaphysics*. Perhaps Arnauld had forgotten having read the *Confessio*; perhaps he never read it. Assuming that it is the *Confessio* to which Leibniz is referring in paragraph 211 of the *Theodicy*, Leibniz said about it: "Arnauld did not appear shocked by it"; nonreading could account for lack of shock. But is it not surprising that Leibniz did not refer to it? I do not think so. Arnauld was plainly shocked by what he found in the summary of section 13 of the *Discourse*, claiming that the doctrine therein formulated involved an unacceptable necessitarianism. If anything, the doctrine of the *Confessio* appears more reprehensible on the same score. Suppose that at the time of the correspondence Leibniz had come to reject the doctrines of the *Confessio* that appear to lead to necessitarianism; then he would have had good reason not to recall the *Confessio* to Arnauld's attention. I will examine the relation of the *Confessio* to the *Discourse* in chapter 4.

With the death of Johann Friedrich in December 1679, Leibniz took the first opportunity to construct a new triad—the last including Arnauld—with Ernst von Hessen-Rheinfels. In May 1680 Leibniz began a correspondence with Ernst that endured for thirteen years. Ernst was a natural choice. After his conversion to Catholicism, he circulated copies of a privately printed work, *The Sincere and Discreet Catholic*, among his friends, including Boineburg and Johann Friedrich. Indeed, in his first letter to Ernst, Leibniz wrote that he had been unable to find Johann Friedrich's copy of *The Sincere and Discreet Catholic* in the library at Hannover in order to return it to Ernst, as requested.[2] In a letter to Ernst of October 1680, Leibniz summarized *The Sincere and Discreet Catholic* as formulating two overriding obligations related to reunion: on Protestants, to seek with all their power to overcome the obstacles to reunion with the Catholic church; on Catholics, to remove the abuses in the Church that were associated with the division of Christianity.[3] Much of Leibniz's extensive correspondence with Ernst deals with how these obligations could be fulfilled.

The correspondence with Ernst moved slowly toward a statement of Leibniz's basic project. In an important letter of 3 November 1682, Leibniz broached a basic subject.

Most of the objections that can be made against Rome regard the practice of the people rather than the dogmas, and if this practice were disavowed publicly, these objections would cease. . . .

With respect to dogmas, in my opinion, the principal difficulty concerns transubstantiation. This transubstantiation implies a contradiction, if the philosophy of the moderns is true, who claim that the essence of body is to be extended and occupy a certain space. I see that the philosophy of the Gassendists and Cartesians has the advantage even in France, and I do not understand how those who believe it can be Catholics in good faith.

Since this same philosophy destroys no less real presence, I applied myself to this issue sometimes and I found certain demonstrations, dependent on mathematics and the nature of motion, which gave me great satisfaction on these matters, and I even believe that the possibility of transubstantiation can be deduced from them. . . . However, I would like to know if the manner in which I explain it could be accepted in the Roman Church, although it seems to me to agree sufficiently with the principles of scholastic theology, something the explication of the Cartesians does not do. After the correction and disavowal of evil practices I do not see anything that is more important for reunion than to be able to answer the apparent absurdities of transubstantiation. For all the other dogmas conform much more with reason. (A/1/3/272–273)

Here Leibniz reveals one part of the project of the *Catholic Demonstrations*, in a manner consistent with the project he outline to Johann Friedrich in the previously quoted letter of fall 1679. Subsequent letters to Ernst make clear that transubstantiation is not the only dogma of the Catholic church that Leibniz believed required a philosophical interpretation, conjoined with a proof of possibility. Leibniz outlined the project in an important letter of 24 March 1683, noting that philosophical discussion of a dogma was not tantamount to rejecting it, and adding: "On many points that I have examined I find that this discussion will be advantageous to the church, rather than harmful; and that Catholic dogmas, explained in a manner that I believe conforms well with the Council of Trent, are the most reasonable doctrines of all. There are only two points of doctrine, namely, that of grace, and that of transubstantiation, that have difficulties, following the explications accepted among the scholastics" (A/1/3/279).[4] Note that the Catholic understanding of grace has joined transubstantiation as a doctrine in need of philosophical elaboration, and that the scholastic explication of transubstantiation has joined that of the Gassendists and Cartesians as one in need of replacement.

Leibniz's philosophical explications relevant to church dogma are not to be found in the correspondence with Ernst. That is to be expected; that role was intended to be filled by the theologian in the triad. With Leibniz's letter of 14 August 1683, authorizing Ernst to send extracts of their correspondence to Arnauld, it is clear that Arnauld, once again, was the triad's theologian of choice. Whereas Ernst may not have been prepared to engage in extended philosophical discussion, he perceived clearly enough how close Leibniz's remarks, such as those just quoted, brought him to Catholicism; and from time to time he pushed the intellectual discussion aside and went for the conversion. Here is an example from Ernst's letter of 2 September 1683: "If you value M. Arnauld so much (as, in fact, you should, as much for his singular piety, as for his great knowledge and capacity), give him then, I beg of you, after God, the honor of your glorious conversion," (A/1/3/327).

Understandably, Leibniz felt obliged to respond to this entreaty, repeated throughout their correspondence. A clear statement of his position occurs in his letter to Ernst of 11 January 1684:

> I say additionally that the visible Catholic church is infallible on all points of belief that are necessary for salvation, by a special assistance of the Holy Spirit that has been promised to it.
>
> After all these declarations his serene highness will ask me, Why then don't you give yourself to it? Here is the reply. It can happen that although the church is infallible concerning the articles of faith that are necessary for salvation, certain other errors or abuses steal into the minds of those in the church. And since it requires the consent of those who would wish to be its members, and who yet believe they have demonstrations to the contrary, they are placed in the impossible position of being in external communion, while they want to be sincere. For example, when the Jansenists were required to sign a proposition of fact whose contrary they believed they knew, it was not in their power to obey, even though they were excluded from the exterior communion of the faithful. . . .

But to return to my case: there are some philosophic opinions of which I believe I have demonstrations, and that it would be impossible for me to change in the current condition of my mind in which I find myself, as long as I do not see a way of satisfying my reasons. Now these opinions, although they are not opposed to anything I know in holy scripture, the tradition, or the definition of any council, may be disapproved and even censured sometimes by the school theologians, who imagine them contrary to the faith. It will be said to me that I could conceal these beliefs in order to avoid censure. But that is not possible. For these propositions are of great importance in philosophy; and when some day I wish to explain some considerable discoveries that I believe I have touching the investigation of truth and the advancement of human knowledge, it will be essential that I put them forward as fundamental. It is true that had I been born in the Roman church I would not have left it. . . . But at present, since I was born and raised outside the communion of Rome, I believe that it is not sincere or safe to present myself for admission to it, when perhaps I would not be accepted, were my heart to be discovered. (A/1/4/320–321)

As one would expect, Ernst immediately sought out the nature of these philosophical opinions to which Leibniz alluded. In a letter of March 1684, Leibniz responded:

I can assure your serene highness that the philosophical doubts of which I spoke in my preceding letter have nothing contrary to the mysteries of Christianity, namely, to the Trinity, the Incarnation, the Eucharist, and the resurrection of the body. I conceive these matters as possible, and, since God has revealed them, I hold them to be truths. One day I want to draw up a paper on some points of controversy between Catholics and Protestants, and if it is approved by judicious and moderate persons, I would receive much joy; but it is not necessary that it be known in some way that the author is not in the Roman communion. (A/1/4/325)

A number of points in these two quotations deserve comment. First, we, like Ernst, would like to know precisely what philosophical opinions it is to which Leibniz alluded. I do not believe that a direct answer to that question is to be found in Leibniz's correspondence with Ernst. But I do not believe that there is much of a mystery here; the philosophical opinions in question are those that found expression in the *Discourse on Metaphysics*, where they are applied specifically to the "questions of grace, the concourse of God and creatures, the cause of sin and the origin of evil" (G/2/11).

However, a minor mystery arises in connection with the second point—namely, Leibniz's suggestion that he draw up a paper dealing with matters of dispute between Catholics and Protestants, written so as to suggest that the author was a Catholic. A close examination of the correspondence with

Ernst indicates that Leibniz came to see reunion as requiring adjudication at three distinct levels. In theoretical to practical order, they are:

1. Analysis, explication, and proof of possibility of a) the basic mysteries of Christianity (the Trinity, the Incarnation, the Eucharist, and the resurrection of the body), and b) the basic relations, postulated by Christianity, between God and man, and problems attendant thereto (for example, those matters of grace, God's concourse, the origin of evil, and so on, just mentioned in connection with the *Discourse*).
2. Less central doctrinal matters in dispute, such as the legitimacy of divorce and the doctrine of the immaculate conception.
3. Practical matters concerning church service, governance, the nature of the ministry, and so on.

The correspondence with Ernst contains numerous statements of the need for discussions of all three, but actual discussion is restricted primarily to the second category, with passing attention given to items in the third category. See, for example, Leibniz's letters of April 1684 (A/1/4/328f.) and March 1688 (A/1/5/75), which are critical of the Catholic view of divorce; his letter on the doctrine of the immaculate conception written early in 1681 (A/1/3/260); his letters of August 1685 (A/1/4/370f.), October 1685 (A/1/4/379f.), and November 1685 (A/1/4/387–388) on the status of the Council of Trent and, in particular, its anathemas—which Protestants, understandably, did not take kindly.

Another work written by Leibniz, covering items in all three categories, is usually cited under the title *Systema theologicum*. Müller and Krönert say that it was "probably written in 1686. Leibniz considered the question of reunion from the standpoint of a Catholic." The *Systema* is a remarkably rich but neglected work, dealing in part with the mystery of the Eucharist.[5] Leibniz's treatment of the Christian mysteries had a long development from the early drafts for the *Catholic Demonstrations* to the mature discussion in the *Theodicy*. But one theme is constant: that a crucial task of the Christian philosopher is to defend the Christian mysteries against the charge of inconsistency or incoherence. In the *Theodicy* Leibniz argued that it suffices to counter such arguments.[6] Earlier he had aimed for something more—a proof of consistency, which does not constitute a proof of truth and thereby eradicate the mystery.

One aspect of Leibniz's treatment of the Eucharist in the *Systema theologicum* is an effort to establish that the dogma is consistent, where the dogma in question is taken to assert the real presence of Christ's body where the bread was at some time during the relevant ceremony. Leibniz began by making his standard criticism of Descartes, namely, that if it is metaphysically necessary "that the essence of body consist in extension, that is, in occupying a determinate space . . . it must be admitted that one body cannot be in several places, not even by divine power" (*Systema* 127). This result, Leibniz argued, would require us to abandon a literal understanding of the

Eucharist. Familiar stuff. But then Leibniz proceeded to offer an alternative account of body, according to which the Eucharist, literally understood— that is, understood as implying real presence—is claimed to be consistent. "The essence of body consists in matter and substantial form, that is, in a principle of action and of passion, for a substance is something that can act and be acted on. Therefore, matter is the first passive power, while substantial form is the initial activity, or initial active power. Although the natural order of things requires that those powers be limited to a place of fixed dimension, no absolute necessity requires it" (*Systema* 127–129).

One concept employed here, that of "the natural order of things," is central to understanding much of what Leibniz has to say about the nature of miracles, the character of faith, and other topics of importance to him. Leibniz thought of the natural order of things as what is true in virtue of the natures of individual substances. He drew a sharp distinction between the *nature* of a substance and its complete individual concept.[7] That distinction, in turn, serves as the basis for Leibniz's account of what a miracle is—an attribute contained in the complete concept of an individual substance, but beyond its nature. I will have more to say on these matters in chapters 4 and 7. The point worth noting here is that in the passage quoted above we see Leibniz employing elements from his emerging metaphysical system in order to provide a consistency proof for a central Christian mystery. After terminating the correspondence with Arnauld, Leibniz engaged in conciliatory correspondence with Paul Pellisson-Fontanier, a converted Huguenot, and also with Jacques-Benigne Bossuet, a French church leader. In these cases Leibniz tended to go light on the metaphysics, emphasizing theological applications. Nonetheless, essentially the same treatment of real presence as noted above from *Systema* is contained in Leibniz's letter to Pellisson of January 1692 (A/1/7/248ff.).

The *Systema theologicum*, then, fits Leibniz's description, of a part of his total reunion package in his letter of March 1684. But there is no evidence in the correspondence with Ernst (at least, none that I can find) indicating that Leibniz ever mentioned to Ernst completing the *Systema*, and no evidence that he sent the document to Ernst. Why? That is the minor mystery. I can only conjecture that the *Discourse on Metaphysics* and the *Systema theologicum*, both written in 1686, constituted Leibniz's "one-two punch" with respect to reunion. In terms of his total project, in particular his aim to contribute to reunion "salvis suis principiis" (each party retaining his own principles), the *Discourse* is the more fundamental document of the two. Its failure to bring Arnauld on board brought the Leibniz-Ernst-Arnauld triad's usefulness to an end. There just was no point in sending the *Systema*, given Arnauld's reaction to the *Discourse*.

The correspondence between Leibniz and Ernst in 1685 makes clear that slowly but surely Arnauld was being involved in the affair: see, for example, Ernst's letter of January 1685, in which he noted that he had sent extracts from some of Leibniz's letters to Arnauld–without identifying the author.

In a letter of 23 December 1685, just a month and a half before sending a summary of the *Discourse* to Ernst, Leibniz noted: "I remember also that formerly your serene highness sent one of my letters to M. Arnauld, with your reflections appended, from which it seemed that you believed that my views went against even the first councils of the Catholic church, to which M. Arnauld replied to you that my words at least witnessed exactly the opposite" (A/1/4/393). At this point Leibniz had some confidence in receiving a fair hearing from Arnauld; their correspondence was about to begin.

Leibniz's correspondence with Ernst did not thereupon degenerate into a mere series of letters for Arnauld with accompanying cover letters; an independent correspondence with Ernst continued until the landgrave's death in 1693. Much of the correspondence with Ernst from late 1685 until 1693 concerned practical aspects of reunion and the development of a plan that came to be Leibniz's platform in subsequent reunion correspondence with Pellison and Bossuet. His slogan for the plan was reunion "salvis principiis partium," without detriment to the principles of the parties to the dispute (A/1/4/380). The basic recommendation was this: that Protestants recognize the authority of the Catholic church and its ecclesiastical hierarchy, while Protestants would be permitted communion in both kinds, marriage of the clergy, and other matters "assez indifférentes," as Leibniz put it (A/1/4/381). Furthermore, since Protestants honestly believed that Trent was not an ecumenical council, and hence that it lacked standing, the Catholic church must not regard Protestants who rejected those doctrines peculiar to Trent as heretics or schismatics. The last component of the plan was to prepare the way for the calling of a genuinely ecumenical council, whose purpose would be to settle outstanding doctrinal matters.

A detailed statement of Leibniz's position may be found in a memorandum on the subject of reunion that he drew up for Ernst while visiting him at Rheinfels in November 1687 (A/1/5/10–21). It is developed, refined, and defended in subsequent correspondence with Pellison and Bossuet. The correspondence with Pellisson and Bossuet also moved through an intermediary, Marie de Brinon, secretary to Louise Hollandine, abbess of Maubuisson, who was herself a convert to Catholicism and the sister of Sophie, duchess of Hannover. In a sense, the pattern of the triads continued. In a letter of July 1692 to Marie de Brinon, Leibniz expressed his frustration with the course of his correspondence with Pellisson and Bossuet:

> I admire everything that I see from the Bishop of Meaux [Bossuet] and Pellisson; the beauty and the force of their expression as well as of their thought charms me to the point of binding my understanding, so to speak, while I am there. But when the force of that charm is dissipated, when I begin to place their reasons in a line of account in my fashion, when I cut out that borrowed brilliance that comes from the author rather than the thing itself, in short, when I begin to play the part of the logician and the calculator, I do not know where I am with respect to it,

and it seems that their reasons, which had struck me so much, vanish between my hands. (A/1/8/125)

It was his ongoing correspondence with Ernst, and not simply the lack of letters from Arnauld, that convinced Leibniz that his correspondence with Arnauld was effectively over in 1688. In a letter to Leibniz of 16 April 1688, Ernst noted: "It is already more than a month, but I forget that M. Arnauld asked me to petition you that, since he is now very busy, he cannot reply to you, especially on a matter so speculative and abstract" (A/1/5/97). Obviously, Leibniz had more at stake in the correspondence than Arnauld; he wanted some sort of closure, as indicated by his response to Ernst of 20 May 1688: "I easily imagine that M. Arnauld has many other things to do than to pass the time disputing with me concerning abstract matters, but I would be pleased if I learned that now, although perhaps he is not yet of my opinion, he no longer finds anything untoward there, as he believed in the beginning, before he understood it thoroughly. And it will be enough if he has the kindness to explain about that, either to your highness or to me" (A/1/5/149). What would have been enough never came to pass.

Chapter 3

❖❖❖❖❖❖❖❖❖

THE GREAT ARNAULD

1. JANSENISM AND LOUIS XIV

On 5 May 1679 Simon Arnauld de Pomponne, the secretary of state for foreign affairs under Louis XIV (but soon to be fired), issued a warning to his uncle, Antoine Arnauld. The King, he said, was increasingly displeased at what Louis took to be Antoine Arnauld's heretical views, as well as his leadership of a group whose interests were contrary to those of the state.[1] Arnauld considered his options carefully, taking into account the character and power of his adversary; on 17 June 1679 he fled France, never to return. On 20 June he arrived at Mons in the Spanish Netherlands (now Belgium), where he stayed for the rest of 1679. He remained in the Netherlands—Spanish and United (now Belgium and the Netherlands)—until his death in 1694.

During his fifteen-year expatriation, Arnauld traveled widely in the Netherlands. He employed an assumed name, Monsieur Davy, for security purposes and had his extensive correspondence sent to various mail drops.[2] Arnauld's friends took measures to preserve his safety. For example, during the summer of 1687, when Arnauld was about to bring the correspondence with Leibniz to closure, Ernst and his two grandsons visited the philosopher in Brussels. Ernst ushered his grandsons into Arnauld's presence without telling them who he was, so that later in life they could be informed that they had indeed met the great Arnauld.[3]

It is not essential for our purposes to explore in detail the circumstances leading to such hostility between Arnauld and Louis XIV. Two items deserve some mention: Arnauld's Jansenism and Louis's *régale*.

In 1640 there was published posthumously a three-volume work by Cornelius Jansen entitled *Augustinus*, purporting to formulate St. Augustine's views on grace and contrasting them with various alternatives. Defense of the views expressed in *Augustinus*—we might as well call the position Jansenism—came to be associated with a monastery located sometimes at Port Royal

26

des Champs outside Paris, sometimes in Paris itself (Port Royal de Paris), and sometimes at both places. We will call it simply Port Royal. The abbess from 1602 until her death in 1661 was Angelique Arnauld, sister of Antoine. Port Royal was more than a nunnery; it also comprised a group of men, both lay and clerical, who engaged in various intellectual projects, including the establishment of schools for children. Arnauld wrote or cowrote three works that grew out of the curriculum of the schools: a *Grammaire générale et raisonnée*, published in 1660; *La logique, ou L'art de penser*, published in 1662; and *Nouveaux éléments*, a presentation of geometry, published in 1667.

Since Jansenism is defined by *Augustinus*, it seems natural to ask what that work says about grace, free will, and related matters. This became a central issue in a struggle that involved, at various times, the faculty of theology at the Sorbonne, numerous Catholic theologians, cardinals, Pascal, Arnauld, and even four popes. The theology faculty and various papal bulls were concerned with five allegedly heretical propositions that opponents of Jansenism claimed were contained in *Augustinus*:

1. Some commandments of God are impossible for righteous men, although they wish to fulfill them and strive to fulfill them in accord with the power they presently possess. They lack the grace that would make it possible.
2. In the state of fallen nature, interior grace is never resisted.
3. In order to deserve merit or demerit in the state of fallen nature, freedom from necessity is not required in men; rather, freedom from constraint is sufficient.
4. The Semi-Pelagians admitted the necessity of prevenient and interior grace for each action, even for the beginning of faith; but they were heretics in that they held that this grace is such that the human will can either resist it or obey it.
5. It is an error of the Semi-Pelagians to say that Christ died or that he shed his blood for everyone without exception.[4]

Perhaps it would be safer to say that these are (translations of) five *sentences* at the heart of the dispute; what *propositions* were to be associated with these sentences was a bone of contention, as was the question of whether the relevant propositions were asserted in *Augustinus*. In 1653 Pope Innocent X issued the bull *Cum occasione*, noting that the French dispute originated in *Augustinus* and asserting that the five propositions were unacceptable to the Catholic church. Arnauld responded in a number of documents, arguing essentially that the propositions the pope had in mind were heretical if he said so, but that they could not be derived from any sentences in *Augustinus*. These and attendant claims were seen as a Jansenist effort to avoid the force of *Cum occasione*. The matter was brought before the faculty of the Sorbonne, which condemned Arnauld's position and removed him from its membership in February 1656.

The entire affair was brought to the attention of the new pope, Alexander VII, who, in October 1656, issued his own bull on the subject. Alexander declared that *Cum occasione* was correct in condemning the five propositions, that each one was asserted in *Augustinus* in a sense that was unacceptable to the Catholic church. Arnauld, under the influence of Pierre Nicole, responded by recognizing the authority of the pope with respect to dogma (in this case, the heretical character of suitably identified propositions) but denying his privileged status with respect to textual exegesis (whether the propositions judged to be heretical were asserted by sentences contained in *Augustinus*). In the latter regard, Arnauld argued, rather boldly, that the pope was simply mistaken. In 1665, at the request of Louis XIV, Alexander VII issued the bull *Regiminis apostolici*, containing a pledge to be signed by all French clerics stating that the five propositions were unacceptable and, moreover, were contained in *Augustinus* in just the senses that the pope had declared unacceptable. With the election of Pope Clement IX in June 1667, the debate took a new turn. The disputants, obeying a royal edict of 23 October 1668 not to write against one another, or even to discuss the controversy publicly, put their theological differences on the back burner. Louis XIV had had enough. Despite one or two contretemps, what came to be called the "Peace of the Church" held for approximately ten years, ending with the affair of the régale.

Régale was a right claimed by the French crown to collect the funds generated in various vacant sees in France until the next bishop was appointed. In 1673 and again in 1675 Louis issued decrees claiming that régale held in all of France, including areas where it had not previously been applied. A number of bishops resisted; ultimately attention focused on François de Caulet, bishop of Pamiers. Caulet was supported by Innocent XI, who had become pope in 1676, and by the Jansenists, with whom he sympathized. Innocent XI had a high regard for Arnauld. All of this was known to Louis XIV. Moreover, many leaders of the Fronde—the unsuccessful revolt of the nobility that nearly deprived Louis of his kingdom—were associated with Port Royal after their defeat. In May 1679 Louis imposed severe restrictions on the monastery, practically putting it into receivership. This, combined with the king's power, explains Arnauld's decision to expatriate.

Since Arnauld did not refer specifically to the two articles of the *Discourse on Metaphysics*, 30 and 31, whose summaries must have made clear to him that Leibniz had something to say on the relation of grace to freedom, we might simply ignore the entire matter. But I think it will prove useful to try to understand what Arnauld deemed to be the essential doctrine, in defense of which he was prepared to take on all comers, popes included.

The fundamental doctrine that Arnauld insisted on was that of efficacious grace. By this he meant a kind of grace such that whenever a human agent S performs a meritorious action A at some time t (provided t is after the Fall), S freely chooses to do A at t. Nonetheless, there is a grace g of the efficacious variety such that g occurred in S at t, and the occurrence of g in S brought it about that S chose to do A. Moreover, S would not (could not) have chosen to do A at t if some grace of the efficacious variety had not brought it about that he so chose, and the occurrence of g in S is not a consequence of any activity on S's part. Arnauld said of this efficacious grace that "although it can always be resisted, because it does not impose necessity on us, and although our freedom always remains in a state of indifference, nevertheless, it never is resisted, because God, who knows better than we ourselves all the motives of our will, and who disposes of them more absolutely than we, brings it about that we will what pleases him, while leaving us always entirely free" ($OA/23/99$–100).

Arnauld accepted the thesis that freedom requires the power to do otherwise—that is, where A is some meritorious act, S did A freely at t only if at the very time that an efficacious grace g brought it about that S chose to do A, even then S had it in his power to choose otherwise. Since he accepted freedom, he attempted to show that a human soul might be subject, at one and the same time, to an efficacious grace bringing about a choice c and the power to choose otherwise.[5]

Arnauld later conceded that the Jansenist scheme could only account for freedom from coercion, not freedom from necessity. Indeed, around 1684 or 1685 Arnauld's views on this topic underwent a fundamental alteration. In a letter of 1692, he recommended a work of his on St. Thomas's theory of grace and freedom, in preference to his earlier writings in defense of Jansen. In the letter Arnauld noted as one of the "great advantages of this [St. Thomas's] explication of freedom" that it explains exactly why "freedom from coercion does not suffice for merit and demerit, but rather freedom from necessity is required"[6] ($OA/3/498$).

In a letter to DuVaucel of August 1691, Arnauld noted his conversion to St. Thomas's position, stating that the true notion of freedom is the power to do otherwise. "Indifference . . . seems to mark an equal propensity to one side and the other, and to be contrary to *determination*, whereas it is easily understood that however determined I would be not to go out into the street stark naked, nevertheless I have the power to do it, and I would do it, if I wished" ($OA/3/364$; emphasis mine).[7] Arnauld expounded his Thomistic views in *De la liberté de l'homme* in 1689.[8] The basic idea is this: Any end that the understanding can conceive only as entirely good—happiness, for example—is such that it is naturally necessitated to desire it. With respect to this one end, the will is not free; otherwise, freedom and determination of the will are entirely consistent.

Arnauld understood the position that St. Thomas expounded in his mature writings as an instance of compatibilism. So did Leibniz. In a letter to Pellisson of August 1692, Leibniz drew attention to his agreement with Arnauld on the thesis of compatibilism. He wrote: "It is true that I am of the opinion of St. Augustine and of St. Thomas and their followers with respect to the consistency of predetermination with freedom and contingency" ($A/1/8/158$). It is worth noting that Leibniz and Arnauld both ascribed compatibilism to St. Thomas and that both accepted compatibilism as well.[9] That is one issue that is not under debate in the correspondence. The reading of St. Thomas shared by Leibniz and Arnauld was not the dominant reading in the seventeenth century, in my opinion. In particular, I understand the theory of those whom Leibniz called "the new Thomists"—the theory of divine premotion of the human will—as an application of a general metaphysical analysis of divine concurrence to the case of the human will, assumed to be in precisely the state of indifference with respect to secondary causes that libertarianism requires.[10]

In this context it is important to distinguish the circumscribed topic of the compatibility of determination with human freedom from the more global theme of which it is a component—God's causation, his providence, his predestination, and justice with respect to human agents, both before and after the Fall. Seventeenth-century debates about the former topic almost always involved differences concerning the more global theme. It is with the more global theme in mind that Arnauld said: "Nothing is more worthy of God and fulfills more the idea we have of the infinitely wise being, who has not only created the universe, but who is also its sovereign administrator, than the manner in which he makes everything done in the world, even by free agents, serve his designs. But also nothing is more difficult to conceive. And it is the difficulty of reconciling that part of Providence with the freedom of intelligent creatures, which causes it to be rejected by the impious, while everyone reasonable recognizes that it must be believed and adored, although it cannot be understood" (*OA*/39/303–304).[11]

Arnauld's intellectual efforts prior to his extended debate with Malebranche, which commenced in 1683, included various theological works in addition to those already cited. Some of these works concerned topics less philosophically charged than that of grace and freedom. *De la fréquente communion*, published by Arnauld in 1643, contains an analysis of the role of the sacraments in the process of absolution, emphasizing the attitude that the penitent must bring to the process if the sacrament is to absolve. No doubt it was more widely read than Arnauld's volumes on grace; its austere recommendations and implied criticisms of Jesuit practice must have done as much to create opposition to Jansenism as any doctrine about grace. Arnauld continued to write on grace and church practice throughout his career.

The period from 1683 through 1685 was one of intense intellectual effort on Arnauld's part, most of it devoted to a criticism of Malebranche's philosophical and theological doctrines, as formulated, respectively, in *De la recherche de la vérité* and *Traité de la Nature et de la Grâce*. Arnauld devoted two complete volumes to a criticism of Malebranche's theory of perception, the theory that we see all things in God: *Des vraies et des fausses idées* (*OA*/38/177–365) and *Défense de M. Arnauld* (*OA*/38/367–671). Nonetheless, Arnauld insisted that his interest in Malebranche's philosophy came about because he saw it as connected with Malebranche's theological doctrines. To the criticism of the *Traité* Arnauld devoted a number of books, the most significant being a three-volume work, *Réflexions philosophiques et théologiques sur le nouveau système de la Nature et de la Grâce*. Book 1 is entitled *Touchant l'ordre de la Nature* (*OA*/39/155–414); book 2, *Touchant l'ordre de la Grâce, par rapport à Dieu* (*OA*/39/415–643); and book 3, *Touchant Jésus Christ* (*OA*/39/645–856). This work was completed just prior to the beginning of the correspondence with Leibniz, although the second and third volumes were not published until 1686.[12]

In February 1686 Arnauld responded to Leibniz's original letter. He wrote two other letters to Leibniz in 1686, followed by two more in 1687. With the letter of 18 August 1687 Arnauld concluded his part in the correspondence. Leibniz responded in October 1687, and again in January 1688; he made an unsuccessful attempt to renew the dialogue in March 1690. Obviously, the correspondence was a central concern for Leibniz during this period; I think the same cannot be said for Arnauld. My guess is that Leibniz was wise to correspond through the good offices of Ernst; I suspect that a direct mail campaign would have gone unanswered. Arnauld had other fish to fry in 1686, 1687, and 1688. During these years he wrote *Fantôme du Jansenisme*, a defense of Jansenism against a published attack, and began his detailed criticism of Nicole's efforts to find an acceptable compromise with respect to the doctrine of grace. In fact, during this period Arnauld was active in the defense of all aspects of Jansenist doctrine and practice.

2. ARNAULD AND DESCARTES

Arnauld was primarily a counterpuncher who raised objections to the philosophical systems of Descartes, Malebranche, and Leibniz. Given his sharp and penetrating criticism of aspects of Descartes's *Meditations*, it may seem surprising that Henri Gouhier would say that "through [Arnauld's] pen, it is Descartes who holds forth against the author of the *Discourse on Metaphysics*, setting up as evident the definition of the essence of matter as extension and not even conceiving the possibility of modernizing substantial forms."[13] Gouhier's central point here is surely correct: Arnauld was partial to the philosophy of Descartes, and Leibniz knew it. Arnauld's mind-body substance dualism served as an impediment to aspects of Leibniz's reunion project —an impediment Leibniz aimed to overcome in the correspondence. But Leibniz knew the odds were long. Writing to Pellisson after the conclusion of the correspondence with Arnauld in 1691, he stated: "Several years ago I exchanged three or four letters with Arnauld on the subject of my views concerning the nature of corporeal substance, which differs from extension. They seemed strange to him at first, but after having seen my explanations, he began to judge them entirely differently. . . . It is true that he did not want to decide anything, having been in all ways for Descartes for a long time" (A/1/7/196).

Still, it is important to understand that Arnauld had his own picture of Descartes's philosophy and took a negative view of Descartes as theologian. Arnauld wrote: "I find it quite strange that this good religious man takes Descartes to be exceedingly enlightened in matters of religion, whereas his letters are full of Pelagianism and, outside of the points of which he was convinced by his philosophy—like the existence of God and the immortality of the soul—all that can be said of him to his greatest advantage is that he always seemed to submit to the Church" (*OA*/1/671).

Recall the key ingredients of Arnauld's criticisms of the *Meditations*, published as the fourth set of objections. Arnauld divided the criticisms into two groups, the philosophical and the theological. The key philosophical items are a brilliant critique of Descartes's arguments, intended to prove that the mind and the body are distinct substances; and a whimsical passage chastizing Descartes for not providing sufficient evidence for the claim that animals lack souls: "For at first glance it seems incredible that it can come about, without the assistance of some soul, that the light reflected from the body of a wolf into the eyes of a sheep should move the minute fibers of the optic nerves, and that on reaching the brain this motion should cause the animal spirits to spread through the nerves in the manner required to precipitate the flight of the sheep" (AT/7/205 [CSM/2/144]). In addition, Arnauld criticized one of Descartes's arguments for the existence of God; expressed a scruple concerning the possibility of avoiding circularity in defending the principle of clear and distinct perception; and criticized Descartes's thesis that nothing occurs in the mind of which it is not conscious.

A crucial item to note here is that most of Arnauld's criticisms are aimed at arguments employed by Descartes, not at the conclusions those arguments were intended to establish. Indeed, even with respect to the arguments it is unusual for Arnauld to claim that some premiss asserted by Descartes is false. Descartes employed the premiss that God is related to himself as an efficient cause is to its effect; Arnauld claimed that that premiss is false.[14] Arnauld claimed that much may be in the mind of which the mind is not conscious, thereby denying one of Descartes's theses.[15] But when it comes to flat-out denial, that is pretty much it. It will be clear, when we turn to subsequent works of Arnauld, that he accepted Descartes's thesis concerning the mind-body distinction without any reservation.

Two key theological points are worth noting in the fourth set of objections. First, Arnauld insisted that the doctrine that we should assent only to what we clearly and distinctly know does not apply to propositions known by faith.[16] Descartes's acceptance of this point was central to Arnauld's enthusiasm for Cartesianism.[17] The second item concerns the doctrine of transubstantiation, that is, the Catholic understanding of the Eucharist. On this point Arnauld, the young theologian, spoke in strong terms. He began his comments thus: "What I foresee will give the greatest offense to theologians is that according to Descartes's doctrines, it seems that what the Church teaches concerning the sacred mysteries of the Eucharist can not remain secure and untouched" (AT/7/216 [CSM/2/152–153]). He ended them thus: "I am sure that the great piety of our famous author will lead him to ponder this matter attentively and diligently and that he will take the view that he is obliged to devote his most strenuous efforts to the problem. For otherwise, although his intention was to defend the cause of God against the impious, he may appear to have endangered that very faith, founded by divine authority, which he hopes will enable him to obtain the eternal life of which he has undertaken to convince mankind" (AT/7/218 [CSM/2/153]).

Two central problems concerning the dogma of transubstantiation vexed thinkers in the seventeenth century. They are formulated by Descartes in a letter of 1646: "There are two principal questions touching this mystery. One is how it can happen that all the accidents of the bread remain in a place where the bread no longer is present and where there is another body in its place; the other is how the body of Jesus Christ can be under the same dimensions where the bread was" (AT/4/374–375). The first problem concerns what to do with the sensible properties of the bread that appear to remain after consecration. Suppose the bread employed was stale. It was agreed that the sensible properties of the bread remained after consecration; it was agreed that the substance then present was that of the body of Jesus Christ. No one wanted to say that his body was stale. One proposed solution was the theory of real accidents: that the sensible properties of the bread remained, but, miraculously, inhered in no substance. Arnauld's point was that Descartes's theory about the relation of mode to substance made that solution a contradiction.

The second major problem had to do with understanding the sense in which Christ's body is present at consecration. Arnauld did not raise the second problem in the fourth set of objections, but he did in a subsequent letter, in which he expressed satisfaction with Descartes's solution to the first problem.[18]

The basic idea of Descartes's solution to the first problem is this: the teaching of the Church in the Council of Trent is that "the whole substance of the bread is changed into the substance of the body of our Lord Christ while the semblance of the bread remains unaltered" (AT/7/251 [CSM/2/175]). Descartes stated that "there is nothing incomprehensible . . . in the supposition that God . . . is able to change one substance into another, or in the supposition that the latter substance remains within the same surface that contained the former substance" (AT/7/255 [CSM/2/177]). But the surface is what we are in contact with, indirectly, of course, in virtue of the intervening air. Hence, whatever semblances we perceive are a direct result of this surface (and the intervening air).[19] But this surface is not part of the bread, nor part of the surrounding air. "It should be taken to be simply the boundary that is conceived to be common to the individual particles [of the bread] and the bodies [air molecules] that surround them; and this boundary has absolutely no reality except a modal one" (AT/7/250–251 [CSM/2/174]). So when the substance of the bread is miraculously changed into that of the substance of the body of Christ, the surface remains unchanged, and, hence, semblances remain unchanged. Descartes concluded his discussion by contrasting his account with the then current theory of real accidents. He expressed the hope that "a time will come when the theory of real accidents will be rejected by theologians as irrational, incomprehensible and hazardous to the faith, while my theory will be accepted in its place as certain and indubitable" (AT/7/255 [CSM/2/177–178]).

Arnauld accepted this solution with enthusiasm, as is clear from a letter he sent to Descartes anonymously in June 1648. That letter contains unequivocal acceptance of Descartes's dualism as well. "What you wrote concerning the distinction between the mind and the body seems to me very clear, evident, and divinely inspired" (AT/5/186). In connection with Descartes's basic dualism, Arnauld recommended a view of the relation of thought to the thinking substance that differed somewhat from Descartes's view that the mind always thinks. "It does not seem necessary that the mind always thinks, although it is the thinking substance; for it is sufficient that the capacity for thinking is in it, just as a corporeal substance is divisible, even if it is not always in fact divided" (AT/5/188).

The same letter also contains two sections bearing on Descartes's thesis that extension is the essence of material substance. In one section Arnauld objected to Descartes's argument that a vacuum is contradictory. Arnauld argued that this conclusion seemed inconsistent with the omnipotence of God. He suggested that God could annihilate the wine in a barrel without replacing it with anything else, thereby creating a vacuum. Arnauld paraphrased Descartes's reasoning, in the form of a reply:

> But, you say, if there were a vacuum, this vacuum would have all the properties of a body, as for example length, width, depth, divisibility, etc.; therefore, it would be a true body.
>
> I respond that no property belongs to that vacuum itself, inasmuch as it is nothing, but only to the concavity of the barrel, whose parts are distant from each other by so many feet, etc. And certainly it seems that the body contained between the sides of the barrel contributes nothing to that; hence, it is no wonder that if that body were destroyed, the same properties belong to that concavity. (AT/5/190–191)

The basic point to make about this section is that although Arnauld's argument *bears* on Descartes's thesis that extension is the essence of material substance, it is not intended to *deny* that thesis. Quite the opposite: the point of Arnauld's subtle remarks is to show a method of describing the imagined situation without predicating properties of any entity that is extended but lacking in matter, that is, without becoming ontologically committed to the existence of vacua. So Arnauld's argument concerning the vacuum is intended to preserve the main thesis concerning the essence of matter by showing that, contrary to what Descartes claimed, that thesis does not imply the impossibility of a vacuum, thus improperly threatening God's omnipotence.

In another section of the same letter Arnauld returned to the question of the compatibility of Descartes's doctrines with the Catholic dogma of transubstantiation, this time concentrating on the second major problem noted above. Arnauld understood Descartes's doctrine—as expounded, for example, in part 2, articles 9, 10, and 11 of the *Principles*—as having the following consequence: For any body *b* and time *t*, there is exactly one place *p* such that at *t* the extension of place *p*, the extension of body *b*, and body *b* itself are all one and the same thing. But the Eucharist might be celebrated simultaneously in Marblehead and Swampscott. Understandably, Arnauld took Catholic doctrine to require that Christ's body be present at consecration on the altar in Marblehead without then being identical with the extension of any place on that altar. He asked Descartes how that was possible, given Descartes's view. Descartes answered: "Since the Council of Trent did not wish to explain this matter and wrote that 'it [the substance of the body of Christ] is there [on the altar] in a manner of existing that we are scarcely able to express in words,' I fear being accused of temerity if I dare to determine something concerning this matter; I prefer to explain my conjectures in person rather than in writing" (AT/5/194).

The "in-person" interview that Descartes preferred never took place. In fact, he had already outlined a more daring solution to the second problem of transubstantiation in letters to Mesland. The contents of those letters spread among French intellectuals; it is unclear to me whether they reached Arnauld. In any case, Arnauld did not associate the more daring solution with Descartes, or, more generally, with those he regarded as Cartesians. In 1680 Arnauld wrote a work with the lengthy title *Examen d'un écrit qui a pour titre: Traité de l'essence du corps, et de l'union de l'âme avec le corps, contre la philosophie de M. Descartes*.[20] Arnauld's work constitutes a defense of the Cartesian thesis that extension is the essence of matter, with particular reference to various alleged theological difficulties, those concerning transubstantiation prominently included. Arnauld summarized his defense of the Cartesians' position on transubstantiation thus: "There are two different difficulties in this mystery, one having to do with the real existence of the body of Jesus Christ in the consecrated host, the other having to do with the appearances of the bread that remain, the bread no longer being there. It is only with respect to the latter that they [the Cartesians] can have said that their manner of explaining seems more satisfactory than that of the Aristotelians. And that is true. . . . But they do not claim the same thing concerning the former, and they agree that it is incomprehensible to them" (*OA*/38/123).

Descartes offered a more daring solution: In one sense, body *a* is numerically identical with body *b* only if every part composing *a* is a part composing *b* and vice versa. In that sense, my body before breakfast is a different body from my body after breakfast. But in another sense, not only do I have the same body before and after breakfast, but I retain the same body, numerically the same body, throughout my entire life. In this latter sense, body *a* is numerically identical with body *b* if there exists some soul *s* such that *a* and *b* are united with *s*. The natural way for bread to become a part of the body of Christ would be for Christ to eat the bread. But that is not what happens at consecration. What happens, according to Descartes, is that, miraculously, at consecration (but not before) the bread is united supernaturally to the soul of Christ, and thereby becomes his body.[21] Descartes's solution has obvious affinities to the solution recommended by Leibniz in the *Systema theologicum*.[22] It has even closer affinities to a solution Leibniz put forward in a letter to Arnauld in 1671.[23]

3. ARNAULD ON SUBSTANTIAL FORMS, OCCASIONALISM, AND TRUTH

In this section I discuss Arnauld's views, as expressed in writings prior to the correspondence, on three central topics of the correspondence: substantial forms, occasionalism, and the concept-containment account of truth.

Substantial forms. As Leibniz realized full well, his thesis that if there are corporeal substances, they must have substantial forms, recalled "postliminio the almost banished substantial forms" (*DM* §11) of the scholastics, and thereby appeared to offer philosophy a giant step backward. In this respect Arnauld was a modern. In many respects, of course, so was Leibniz. Both Leibniz and Arnauld rejected appeal to substantial forms in scientific explanations of phenomena.[24]

A superficial reading of selected passages from *La logique* might suggest that Arnauld, like Leibniz, accepted substantial forms for purposes of metaphysical explanations. Consider these passages:

> "who can doubt that everything is composed of matter and a certain form of that matter? Who can doubt that in order for matter to acquire a new state and a new form, it is necessary that it not already have it, i.e., that it has its privation? Finally, who can doubt concerning these other metaphysical principles that everything depends on form; that matter alone does nothing; that place, motion, and faculties exist? (*La logique* 33 [DJ 26])

> The form is that which makes a thing such and such and distinguishes it from other things, whether it is a being really distinguished from matter, according to the opinion of the Scholastics, or whether it is only the arrangement of its parts. It is by the knowledge of this form that the properties of a thing must be explained. (*La logique* 240 [DJ 244])

The disjunction in the second passage gives the game away. As subsequent chapters of *La logique* make clear, Arnauld was prepared to talk about forms of nonrational creatures only to the extent that those forms were construed as the arrangements of their insensible parts;[25] Arnauld recognized peculiar difficulties in the case of creatures with souls, difficulties concerning the explanation of the substantial union that he assumed must exist between the soul and the body.[26]

Chapter 19, book 3 of *La logique* is a study of sophisms; many of the ex-

amples of sophistical arguments displayed purport to represent scholastic
arguments for the existence of substantial forms in nonrational substances.
One of the arguments analyzed is particularly relevant, since Leibniz came
to employ it in the correspondence. Arnauld wrote:

> Here is another [sophism] of the same sort: If there were no sub-
> stantial forms . . . natural beings would not be wholes of the sort they
> [the Scholastics] call per se, totum per se, but they would be beings by
> accident. Now they are wholes per se. Therefore, there are substantial
> forms.
>
> Again, we must ask those who use this argument to kindly explain
> what they mean by a whole per se, totum per se. For, if they mean, as
> they do, a being composed of matter and form, then it is clear that they
> beg the question, since it is as if they had said: if there were no substan-
> tial forms, then natural beings would not be composed of matter and
> substantial forms. Now they are composed of matter and substantial
> forms. Therefore, there are substantial forms. If they mean something
> else, let them say it, and we will see that it proves nothing. (*La logique*
> 244 [DJ 248])

It is clear that in Leibniz, Arnauld met a friend of the forms who was more
subtle than Arnauld's caricature of the Scholastics.

Occasionalism. Consider the following two theses:

a. For any finite substances x and y, there are no states s and s' such that s
   is a state of x and s' is a state of y and the occurrence of s in x is a real
   cause of s' in y.
b. For any finite substances x and y, if $x \neq y$ then there are no states s and s'
   such that s is a state of x and s' is a state of y and the occurrence of s in x
   is a real cause of s' in y.[27]

Occasionalism consists in a negative thesis about real causation among finite
substances and a positive thesis about the real causality of an infinite substance. Theses (a) and (b) are candidates for the negative thesis; clearly, (a)
is stronger than (b), since (a) excludes intrasubstantial causation for finite
substances, whereas (b) does not. There are numerous passages in various
of Malebranche's works that sound like (a); there are also numerous passages that suggest that in order to preserve human freedom, and thus human
responsibility, Malebranche admitted that finite intelligent natures (humans
and angels) function as real causes with respect to their volitions. Whether
Malebranche accepted (a) or not turns on how "state" is construed therein.
In the sequel, I ascribe (a) to Malebranche. Here is my understanding of
Malebranche on freedom of the will.

Malebranche thought of the will as "the impression or natural impulse
that carries us toward . . . good."[28] Thus, Malebranche pictured the will, or
desire, as a kind of "mental motion." And he thought of a decision to act on a

given desire as a consent to that desire. Malebranche viewed consenting to a desire as removing an inhibition, something like ceasing to resist some force and thereby allowing it to generate action. Hence, he thought of consenting as analogous to rest in the case of motion.[29] Malebranche then argued that consent, like rest in the case of motion, does not require a cause, in virtue of a mental version of the principle of inertia. Malebranche concluded that whereas the human agent is responsible for his consentings, he does not "give himself new modifications that modify or that materially change his substance."[30]

Even if we insist on calling this consenting a state, according to Malebranche it is not a state that requires a cause, since our freedom consists in our ability to consent to, or withhold consent from, our volitions.[31] Thus, he concluded that the exercise of our freedom is perfectly consistent with God's being the only real cause. It is hard to resist the supposition that Malebranche has confused the continuation of a state of rest with its onset. According to the operative analogy, consent looks more like the latter than the former. But while the former may not require a cause, according to a relevant principle of inertia, the latter seems to require one.[32]

Leibniz rejected (a) but affirmed (b); Arnauld rejected both. Consider the following limited version of the negative thesis of occasionalism.

c. For any finite substances x and y, if x is a different kind of substance from y, then there are no states s and s' such that s is a state of x and s' is a state of y and the occurrence of s in x is a real cause of the occurrence of s' in y.

Given that Arnauld recognized two kinds of finite substances, minds and bodies, acceptance of (c) would have committed him to the denial of real causal interaction between minds and bodies. Various of his writings suggest this view: see, for example, *La logique* 74 (DJ 69); *Examen d'un écrit*, part 4 (*OA*/381/146–150); and *Des vraies et des fausses idées*, chapters 7 and 11 (*OA*/38/212 and 234).

In the passages cited from the *Examen*, Arnauld considered three questions: "The first, if it is bodily movements in our [sense] organs that cause the perception of sensible objects in the soul. Another, if it is the soul that forms these perceptions in itself on the occasion of these movements. Last, if it is God who gives them to the soul. The first is very easy to resolve. For movement of one body can at most have a real effect only by moving another body" (*OA*/38/146). Arnauld argued that it cannot be the soul itself that produces perceptions in itself, on the grounds that this would require that the soul have a knowledge of causal mechanisms—in order to produce the right perception at the right time—that it obviously lacks (*OA*/38/147). This line of reasoning, formulated as an attack on Leibniz's doctrine of pre-established harmony, surfaced in the correspondence (see *LA* 65). Arnauld concluded that God causes the relevant perceptions in the soul on the occasion of certain movements in our sense organs, which, in turn, are caused by movements in the objects perceived (*OA*/38/147–148).

All that adds up to some version of occasionalism. It denies that a state of a body can be a real cause of a state of a soul; but that does not yield (c) without the converse claim, that a state of a finite soul cannot be the real cause of the state of a body.

To the best of my knowledge, Arnauld did not reach a conclusion with respect to the converse. But he reached a conclusion about the possibility of the converse in a work published in 1685, just prior to the correspondence with Leibniz, the *Dissertation de M. Arnauld, Docteur de Sorbonne, sur la manière dont Dieu a fait les fréquents miracles d'ancienne loi par le ministère des anges* (*OA*/38/674–741). Arnauld began by claiming that, contrary to many of Malebranche's assertions, Malebranche himself agreed that finite spiritual substances are real causes of their free volitions.[33] But to have a real power with respect to the will is to be able to bring it about that a spiritual substance has a certain modification. But bringing about a modification of a spiritual substance is more noble than bringing about a modification of a corporeal substance. So, since God does give angels a real power to do the former, he certainly can give angels a real power to do the latter. Therefore, Arnauld argued, it is at least possible that angels have the real power to move bodies, since really moving a body is really bringing it about that the body has a new modification. Arnauld then extended the argument to humans: "It is not perhaps so certain as our author [Malebranche] imagines that God has not given a real power to our soul to determine the course of the spirits with respect to the parts of our body that we want to move; it would seem that Descartes believed it and it is perhaps not so easy to prove the contrary" (*OA*/38/690).[34]

Arnauld may have held a limited version of the negative thesis of occasionalism. Leibniz did; unfortunately, their limitations do not match. As it turns out, however, differences with respect to the negative thesis of occasionalism are not the focus of the debate between Leibniz and Arnauld about occasionalism. That debate concerns the correct positive thesis—the correct account of the relation between the real causality of an infinite substance and various finite substances, in those cases where the negative thesis of occasionalism applies. Here Leibniz claimed to have an original thesis—what came to be called the pre-established harmony—which, he claimed, was distinct from any extant form of occasionalism and, of course, preferable. Arnauld denied that what Leibniz offered was preferable on the grounds that what he offered, when carefully analyzed, reduced to humdrum, garden-variety occasionalism. The debate on this and attendant matters is the subject of chapter 7.

The concept-containment account of truth. By the concept-containment account of truth, I mean the thesis that, for any affirmative, categorical proposition *p*, whether universal or singular, *p* is true if and only if the concept of the predicate of *p* is contained in the concept of the subject of *p*. The "if" half of this is innocuous; it is the "only if" half that should raise eyebrows. Consider again Arnauld's famous concession paragraph that concludes the phase of the debate concerning freedom and necessity: "I am satisfied with the way you explain what had at first shocked me, regarding the concept of the individual nature. . . . I was particularly struck with the consideration that in every true affirmative proposition, necessary or contingent, universal or singular, the concept of the attribute is contained in some fashion in that of the subject: the predicate is present in the subject," (*LA* 64).

I find it hard to imagine an impartial, careful reader of the correspondence who would not be taken aback by Arnauld's apparent concession at this point. It follows Leibniz's complex letter on freedom of 14 July 1686, a letter which many would take to indicate how powerful Arnauld's objections really are. But here we find Arnauld speaking favorably of (although not asserting outright) the "hard half" of the concept-containment account of truth, which is a source of those very theses of Leibniz to which Arnauld objected. Our question in this section, then, is this: Is there evidence in Arnauld's work, written prior to the correspondence, that he accepted the concept-containment account of truth?

In his extraordinarily useful introduction to the Mason translation of the correspondence, G. H. R. Parkinson puts the case for an affirmative answer to our question this way: "Leibniz's view about the nature of truth is not questioned by Arnauld. . . . What Arnauld and Nicole say about axioms is close to what Leibniz says about truth in general, and it is not surprising that Arnauld should not have criticized Leibniz's theory of truth."[35] This same point is made in Leroy Loemker's scholarly study "A Note on the Origin and Problem of Leibniz's *Discourse* of 1686."

> One other point Leibniz may have taken from Arnauld. In the *Port Royal Logic* (part IV, chapter VI), Arnauld establishes the rule that in every axiom, the predicate is included in the subject. This rule Leibniz applies, about 1679, to all propositions, and it is not surprising that the argument for the nature of individual substance which he builds upon it is included in the *Discourse*, though it is paradoxical, perhaps, that it is this very argument which Arnauld later chooses to attack.[36]

Louis Couturat made the point first in his seminal article "Sur la metaphysique de Leibniz." Discussing the principle of sufficient reason, Couturat wrote:

> In its exact sense, this principle means that in every true proposition the predicate is contained in the subject, therefore, that every truth can be demonstrated a priori by the simple analysis of terms. In a word, that every truth is analytic. This may seem paradoxical and even shocking to us who have read Kant. But it seemed entirely natural and evident to Leibniz's contemporaries, who, like him, were trained in the Aris-

totelian and scholastic tradition. And the proof of this is that Arnauld, who was extremely averse to admitting certain consequences of this principle (in particular, the major thesis that "the individual notion of each person contains definitively all that will ever happen to him"), never dreamed of expressing any reservation or doubt about it. On the contrary, he accepted it without qualification and without discussion.[37]

More recently, Baruch Brody and Charles Jarrett have demurred.[38]

Let's look at the evidence. To the best of my knowledge, we will not be led astray if we concentrate our attention entirely on *La logique*. The first section from that work that requires our notice is chapter 17 of part 2, which is devoted to a number of topics, including "the nature of affirmation." Arnauld said the following concerning the nature of a proposition: "we cannot express a proposition to others, unless we use two ideas, one for the subject, and another for the attribute, and another word that marks the connection that our mind conceives between them. . . . The nature of affirmation is to connect and to identify the subject with the attribute, since that is what is signified by the word 'is' " (*La logique* 168 [DJ 168]).[39]

In what follows, Arnauld utilized a previously introduced distinction between the comprehension and the extension of an idea. The comprehension of an idea includes all and only those attributes that an entity must have in order for the idea to apply to it; the extension of an idea includes all and only those entities that have all the attributes in its comprehension. (*La logique* 59 [DJ 51]). With the notions of proposition and comprehension in hand, Arnauld was in a position to characterize affirmation. Were he to say that in an affirmation, the comprehension of the idea of the predicate is said to be contained in the comprehension of the idea of the subject, then, for the case of categorical affirmatives, at any rate, Arnauld would be committed to the concept-containment account of truth. And, in fact, this is exactly what the Dickoff-James translation has Arnauld say on page 169: "In a sentence expressing an affirmation the entire comprehension of the idea expressed by the predicate must be contained in the comprehension of the idea expressed by the subject. For example, when we say 'A rectangle is a parallelogram,' we mean that the whole idea of a parallelogram is contained in the idea of a rectangle."

Here is a more literal translation: "An idea is always affirmed according to its comprehension. . . . Consequently, when it is affirmed, it is always according to everything that it comprehends in itself. Thus, when I say that *a rectangle is a parallelogram,* I affirm of the rectangle everything that is contained in the idea of a parallelogram" (*La logique* 169).

In terms of the distinction between sentence and proposition that Dickoff and James employ in their translation, Arnauld's doctrine, strictly interpreted, seems to come to no more than this: in a sentence expressing an affirmative proposition, the entire comprehension of the idea of the predicate is affirmed of the extension of the idea expressed by the subject. That doctrine is innocuous and distinct from the concept-containment account of truth. Arnauld's general conception of a proposition and of affirmation is obscure, but whatever it amounts to, it does not appear to commit him to the concept-containment account of truth.

What about Arnauld's remarks concerning axioms in chapter 6 of part 4 of *La logique*? This is the text cited as confirmation by both Parkinson and Loemker. It is a text whose interpretation is not obvious. Still, it is plausible to suppose that it contains this claim: a proposition p is an axiom only if for some sentence expressing it, the concept of its predicate is contained in the concept of its subject (*La logique* 317 [DJ 320]). Nonetheless, it is natural to respond to Parkinson and Loemker in this fashion. Yes, Arnauld characterized the truth conditions for axioms much in the manner in which Leibniz characterized the truth conditions for all affirmative categorical propositions that are universal or singular. But that is no reason to suppose that Arnauld accepted the stronger claim. To suppose so comes close to arguing that because Arnauld's account of necessary truth was tantamount to Leibniz's account of truth in general, it is not surprising that Arnauld would extend the account to cover contingent truths as well.

Unfortunately, it is not as simple as that. We need to say a word about where axioms fit in Arnauld's general scheme. For Arnauld, axioms are the foundation of all demonstrative knowledge—of all science. In order for a proposition to be an axiom, it must not only pass the concept-containment test, but, in addition, the containment must be evident to a moderately attentive mind without benefit of intermediary ideas. (*La logique* 318 [DJ 321]). Where intermediary ideas are required, we have a demonstrative proposition but no axiom. Furthermore, it appears that Arnauld claimed that a proposition p is demonstrative if and only if there is a series of correct demonstrations terminating in p and commencing with a set of propositions all of whose members are axioms. (*La logique* 319–320 [DJ 321–323]). Arnauld's account of the rules governing demonstration in chapter 8 of part 4 of *La logique* suggests that he took demonstration to be containment-preserving, in the sense that if p is demonstrated from axioms, then the concept of the predicate of p is contained in the concept of the subject of p, even if the containment is not obvious. Perhaps, then, Arnauld was committed to the following: for any proposition p, p is a demonstrative (scientific) truth if and only if the concept of the predicate of p is contained in the concept of the subject of p.

I believe this is the best that can be done for the Couturat-Loemker-Parkinson interpretation on this point. Chapters 12 and 13 of *La logique* make it clear that Arnauld believed that there are contingent truths other than demonstrative (scientific) truths. So what we have in these chapters, even under the liberal interpretation allowed above, does not yield Leibniz's generalized theory of truth. Still, a question remains that deserves further inquiry. Did Arnauld believe that all demonstrative (scientific) propositions are necessary truths? If not, then, given the liberal interpretation above, he did not see concept containment as yielding necessary truth. That result, although puzzling in itself, would relieve *some* of the puzzle of Arnauld's apparent concession. One thing seems clear: we cannot resolve that puzzle by noting Arnauld's antecedent commitment to the concept-containment account of truth; it is just not there.

4. ARNAULD AND MALEBRANCHE

In a broad sense the *Traité de la Nature et de la Grâce* is concerned with the problem of evil; more specifically, it concerns the problem of the distribution of that grace required for faith and meritorious actions, which, in turn, are required for salvation. In Discourse 1, section 38 of the *Traité*, Malebranche set the main problem as follows: "Holy Scripture teaches us on the one hand that God wills that all men be saved and that they come to the knowledge of the truth, and, on the other hand, that he does whatever he wills; and that, nevertheless, faith is not given to everyone, and the number of those who perish is very much greater than the number of the predestined. How is that to be reconciled with his power?" The addition to section 38 provides a short version of Malebranche's answer: "It is because God's wisdom renders him impotent, so to speak. Since his wisdom obliges him to act by the simplest means, it is not possible that all men be saved, because of the simplicity of the means he employs."

We need to understand what this solution amounts to and what led Malebranche to it. His starting point was a consideration of the attributes of God; in particular he focused attention on the omnipotence, wisdom, and immutability of God. It is a commonplace among theologians to hold that there cannot be two distinct omnipotent beings. Malebranche went the theologians one better; he held that no being other than God has any power at all, in the sense of acting by its own force, a thesis he formulated in the claim that only God is a true cause.[40] All other substances are, or involve, at best occasional causes.

Malebranche argued that God's creation of anything outside himself is an entirely free act.[41] But given that God did freely decide to create a world, God must act in the manner that best expressed his attributes.[42] This is where Malebranche's analysis of God's wisdom and immutability comes in. It includes the following claims: God's immutability requires that he act in a uniform and regular manner; God's wisdom requires that he act in a simple manner.[43] These two requirements, in turn, require that God create a world governed by general laws that are few in number, simple, and uniform. With these principles as a basis, Malebranche thought he had in hand the tools for a general solution to the problem of natural evil: "An excellent workman must proportion his action to his work. He must not make by exceedingly complicated means what he can bring about by simpler ones. . . . It is necessary to conclude from that, that God, having discovered in the infinite treasures of his wisdom an infinity of possible worlds, as the necessary consequences of the laws of motion that he could establish, decided to create that which he could produce by the simplest laws, or what must be the most perfect, in relation to the simplicity of the means necessary for its production, or its conservation."[44]

In an addition to section 13, Malebranche stated his position this way: "God wants the means to be the wisest, as well as the designs. He does not want the designs to honor him and the means to dishonor him. He compares the wisdom of the design with the wisdom of the means, and he chooses the design and the means that, taken together, most bear the character of his attributes. That is my principle by which I will justify the wisdom and goodness of God in spite of the disorders of Nature, the monsters, the sin, the miseries to which we are subject." And in section 14 he drew his conclusion: "Without doubt God could have created a world more perfect than that in which we live. . . . But in order to create this more perfect world, it would have been necessary that he change the simplicity of his means and that he multiply the laws of the communication of motion, by which our world subsists, and then there would no longer be this proportion between God and his work, which is necessary in order to determine an infinitely wise being to act."

A number of features of this scheme are to be found in Leibniz's *Discourse*. First, there is the supposition that some reason, other than brute appeal to God's will, must be found to explain why God decided to create a world, and why he decided to create just this world. Second, there is the appeal to the notion of an infinity of possible worlds which God knew through and through at the time of selection. Third, there is the appeal to the idea that God's choice is in some way constrained by his nature, his attributes. Fourth, there is the idea that the result of that constraint is the selection of a possible world that is at a maximum with respect to some measure or measures. Fifth, there is the idea that the measures are, roughly speaking, (a) simplicity of means and (b) value of the outcomes. Sixth, there is the idea that simplicity of means amounts to choice of a world governed by uniform laws that are few in number—the fewer the simpler, other things being equal.

Leaving aside differences between Malebranche and Leibniz concerning what entities, if any, other than God are real causes, and attendant differences between occasionalism and the pre-established harmony, and concentrating entirely on the six items noted above, do the two schemes—that of the *Traité* and that of the *Discourse*—come to the same thing? Leibniz's remarks in the *Theodicy* might lead one to believe that Leibniz thought so. After noting various differences between himself and Malebranche in the areas we are leaving aside, Leibniz concluded his summary of Malebranche's system based on the six features noted above: "The ways of God are the simplest and the most uniform. . . . They are also the most productive in relation to the simplicity of these ways. . . . Indeed, these two conditions, simplicity and productivity, may be reduced to a single advantage, which is to produce the greatest amount of perfection possible; and by this means, the system of Malebranche is reduced to mine on this point" (*Theodicy* §208).

Perhaps Leibniz would have been right had he claimed that *if* the two conditions mentioned reduce to a single advantage—that of producing the greatest amount of perfection possible—*then* his system and Malebranche's join on the point at issue. But in a letter to Leibniz in 1711, Malebranche, after praising the *Theodicy* and noting its similarity to his own system, resisted the relevant reduction: "God's work is the most perfect possible, nevertheless not absolutely, but compared to the means that carry it out. For God does not honor himself only by the excellence of his work, but also by the simplicity and productivity—the wisdom—of his ways" (G/I/359). In his response, Leibniz acknowledged that he and Malebranche differed on this item: "When I consider the work of God, I consider his ways as a part of the work, and the simplicity joined to the productivity of his ways constitute a part of the excellence of the work" (G/I/360).

The fact is that Malebranche at first was unsettled on the relation of the two relevant measures, simplicity of means and value of the outcomes (or designs—*desseins* in the French). Some of our quotations above display that tentativeness. But later additions make clear that Leibniz's reduction was not part of Malebranche's scheme, and that in interesting cases of conflict the winner is simplicity, not the value of the world chosen. The addition to section 39 of Discourse 1 is clear on this point: "God has more love for his wisdom than for his work, because . . . his wisdom prescribes to him means which most bear the character of his attributes."

We have been concentrating on items 4 through 6, where Leibniz and Malebranche appear to differ on details, albeit details of substance. Let us now concentrate on Arnauld's major criticisms of Malebranche's system as they concern the first three items, where Malebranche and Leibniz agree. Consider item 3—the idea that God's choice of one among infinitely many possible worlds is in some way constrained by his nature. In chapter 26, book 2 of *Réflexions*, Arnauld commented on Malebranche's articulation of item 3 as follows:

God must produce the most perfect [possible world]. And the design being formed, he is no longer free to choose the means to execute it. For he chooses *necessarily* ways that are general, which are the ones most worthy of his wisdom, his grandeur, and his goodness. Now, the design being taken and the means fixed, he [Malebranche] often calls what follows from that, *the necessary consequences of the general laws*. Thus, God is only free with respect to having willed to create something; but all the rest has been the result of a more than stoical necessity, with the exception of the miracles that God has brought about by particular volitions. And I do not even know if miracles should be excepted, since, according to what our author says, God brings them about only when *order requires it*. Now, according to him, this *order* is the most *indispensable* rule of the volitions of God. (*OA*/39/599)

This "more than stoical necessity" was, of course, totally unacceptable to Arnauld. Arnauld wrote this passage just before receiving the outline of the *Discourse* from Leibniz. Compare it with his very first criticism of the *Discourse*, a criticism that begins with a quotation from Leibniz's summary of section 13: " 'That the individual concept of each person contains once for all everything that will ever happen to him,' etc. If that is so, God was free to create or not create Adam; but supposing that he wished to create him, everything that has happened since and will ever happen to the human race was and is obliged to happen through a more than fatal necessity" (LA 15). The necessity has gone from stoical to fatal, its source is different, but from Arnauld's point of view the same unacceptable consequence is involved in Leibniz's scheme as in Malebranche's.

In the case of Malebranche, but not of Leibniz, Arnauld actually went further in his criticism:

I have said that according to our author [Malebranche] God is free and indifferent only with respect to creating his design. . . . But I doubt that that can agree with the manner in which he conceives that God acts. . . .

Even while following him in the manner in which he conceives God, I do not see that God could be indifferent with respect to creating or not creating something outside himself, if he was not indifferent with respect to choosing among several works and among several methods of producing them. For, according to our author, what brings it about that God has not been indifferent in the latter case, is that, having consulted his wisdom, he is necessarily determined to produce the work that his wisdom has shown him to be the most perfect and to choose the methods that his wisdom has also shown him to be the most worthy of him. Now, there is the same reason for supposing that before deciding to create the world or not to create it, he consulted his wisdom. Hence, there is the same ground for believing that, his wisdom having replied to him that it was better to create it, he was determined necessarily to create it. In all of this I argue only from the principles of our author, and from the manner in which he depicts for us everywhere that God is determined to act. For I am very much persuaded that it is to conceive of God entirely humanly and that one cannot have these thoughts, if one only consults the idea of an infinitely perfect being. (*OA*/39/599–600)

I have no doubt that had Arnauld grasped the full scope of the principle of sufficient reason in Leibniz's philosophy, in particular, its application to God's will in every single act of that will, even creation, Arnauld would have been convinced that Leibniz's scheme fared no better than Malebranche's with respect to a proper account of God's freedom in creation. The fact is that Arnauld saw item one—the idea that there must be some reason for

God's decision to create, other than simple appeal to his will—as the real culprit. Arnauld referred approvingly to St. Thomas's thesis that with the exception of his own goodness, God does not will other things necessarily, and that in cases outside of God himself the divine will is determined solely by itself.[45] Arnauld added: "Notice that he [Aquinas] did not say that it is the wisdom of God that determines his will by proposing to it what it is most fitting for the will to do; but that it is the divine will that determines itself, freely and indifferently, toward all those things to which it does not have a necessary relation, i.e., toward everything that is not God" (*OA*/39/599).

What Arnauld took to be Descartes's main virtue with respect to theology —his reluctance to construct philosophical hypotheses in order to resolve theological problems—he found lacking in Malebranche and Leibniz. In them he saw the boldness of reason which would, in time, spark the Englightenment.

Chapter 4

❖❖❖❖❖❖❖❖❖

FREEDOM AND CONTINGENCY

In the *Discourse* and the correspondence, Leibniz employed a structure of possible worlds, composed of complete individual concepts, in order to discuss important theological and philosophical problems. Leibniz was enamored of this scheme. Some aspects of his thinking about this structure are philosophically and theologically more innocent than others. By isolating the relatively innocent components, we may subsequently focus attention on the less innocent components, or at any rate on those components so regarded by Arnauld.

1. CONCEPTS AND WORLDS

Clearly concepts, and in particular complete individual concepts, have an important role in Leibniz's thinking about possible worlds. It is important to see that there is a certain innocent interpretation of concepts, especially complete individual concepts, that Leibniz put at center stage on various occasions during the correspondence. It cannot be the whole story. The innocent interpretation is exhibited in Leibniz's first response to Arnauld (letter of 12 April 1686 [LA 17]) and in two letters of 14 July, when the debate on freedom and contingency came to a close (see LA 53 and 131). Assume that the actual world is composed of various individual substances, their properties and relations. Assume, furthermore, that there is a viable distinction between the primitive properties of the world's individual substances and other nonprimitive properties, grounded in them. Leibniz thought that there were no serious impediments to the claim that God has knowledge of all the primitive properties of all the world's individual substances, based on his knowledge of his own ideas and his own will. So with each individual substance we may associate a concept including all and only those primitive properties that God knows that substance to have. We might identify this concept with an idea God has of the substance in question. Given the character of God's knowledge, we have associated a complete individual concept with each actual individual substance. At LA 53 Leibniz referred to the line of reasoning just outlined as a deduction of the existence of a complete concept for each individual substance from the character of God's knowledge.[1]

It may seem that the deduction described employs God's omniscience in an inessential way. Leibniz suggested as much: "One could therefore prove it in like manner without mentioning God" (LA 53). Thus, consider any actual individual substance x; there will be some set C whose members are all and only the primitive properties of x. Now C, being a set, is perhaps not exactly what Leibniz and Arnauld had in mind when they talked about concepts. God's role in the deduction is simply to insure that corresponding to any such set C there is a concept including exactly the membership of C —an idea in God's mind of x. For those who feel no need for a guarantee, or have another one in hand, God's role is inessential.

One might naturally suppose that God could organize his knowledge of nonindividuals in the actual world into concepts that were complete in an analogous sense; and so Leibniz said in the following rhetorical question: "Can one deny that everything (whether genus, species, or individual) has a complete concept, according to which God, who conceives everything perfectly, conceives of it . . . ?" (LA 131)[2] But this puts in jeopardy Leibniz's important claim that *only* individual substances have complete concepts. However, that thesis is not our present concern.[3]

The innocent interpretation is the simple assertion of the existence of a complete concept for each actual individual substance; it is not in dispute between Leibniz and Arnauld. Innocence is lost, and meaningful debate ensues, only when principles affirming a connection between the concept assigned to an individual and various truths about that individual are adopted. There is a real chance for philosophers to argue at cross purposes, if their principles fail to match. Problems of this variety arise in understanding the debate between Leibniz and Arnauld. On occasion, Leibniz unfairly retreated to the innocent interpretation, as if that was all there was to the matter. Thus, in the letter of 12 April, after reciting Arnauld's objection to the thesis that "the individual concept of each person includes everything that will ever happen to that person"—the objection being that it leads to "a necessity more than fatal"—Leibniz noted derisively: "As if concepts or previsions made things necessary, and as if a free action could not be contained in the concept or perfect view that God has of the person to whom it will belong" (LA 17).

Arnauld was not objecting to the claim that for each individual substance there exists a complete concept under which it falls. He had in mind some principle stating a connection between the concept assigned to an individual, as *the* individual concept of that individual and various truths about that individual. He thought the principle in question, when combined with the assignment of its complete concept as *the* individual concept of that individual, led to a necessity more than fatal. And Leibniz knew that. Whereas the summary of *DM* §13, received by Arnauld, simply asserts that the complete-concept theory is consistent with freedom and contingency, the article itself, which Arnauld never received, contains a convoluted effort to answer objections quite similar to Arnauld's—to show that the theory does not have the consequence that, as Leibniz put it, "an absolute fate will reign" (*DM* §13).

We have considered an innocent interpretation of complete individual concepts. Leibniz aimed for a similarly innocent treatment of possible worlds. In both the *Discourse* and the correspondence, he freely referred to possible individuals inhabiting possible worlds.[4] Arnauld reacted adversely to Leibniz's picture of God choosing among possible worlds, composed of possible individuals, much as he had reacted to Malebranche. He wrote: "I confess in good faith that I have no conception of these purely possible substances, that is to say, the ones that God will never create" (LA 31–32). Leibniz's response, contained both in the draft and in the long letter of 14 July 1686, is important: "In order to call something possible, it is enough for me that one can form a concept of it even though it should only exist in the divine understanding, which is, so to speak, the domain of possible realities" (LA 55 [RL 42] and LA 45).[5] Based on this, we may suppose that Leibniz was prepared to parse his talk about possible individuals in possible worlds in terms of collections of complete individual concepts. No doubt the intended parsings are complex. It is unlikely to cause harm if we talk of possible worlds as if they were the very collections with respect to which talk of them is to be parsed.

Something will be said about Leibniz's distinction between primitive and nonprimitive properties in the fifth section of this chapter. For now, we may assume an enumeration of primitive properties, with concepts formed by selecting, for each primitive property in the enumeration, either it or its complement. Concepts so constructed, under which some individual could fall, are complete individual concepts.

What conditions must a collection of complete individual concepts satisfy, according to Leibniz, in order to represent a possible world? Obviously, the complete individual concepts in the collection must be compossible, that is, it must be possible that they be jointly satisfied. The texts are clear on this requirement. The texts also suggest another requirement, namely, maximality. A collection of complete individual concepts X is maximal just in case, for any complete individual concept C not in X, $X \cup \{C\}$ is not compossible. For present purposes I include maximality, so we take a possible world to be represented by a collection of complete individual concepts that is compossible and maximal.[6]

We are assuming that the nonprimitive properties of individual substances are, in some sense, grounded in their primitive properties, so that the complete individual concept of an individual substance contains full information about that substance, relative to some world. Since no two worlds are exactly the same, it is natural to assume that each substance in a world will have some properties reflecting that particular world. Given these assumptions,

no complete individual concept is a member of distinct collections constituting possible worlds as characterized above; in other words, each complete
individual concept is in exactly one world. This is a totally innocent claim.
For example, it is independent of the thesis that no possible object exists in
more than one possible world. Thus, consider the concept that contains all
and only the primitive properties that Arnauld has in the actual world. Suppose that this concept is in the actual world and no other. This is consistent
with the supposition that Arnauld exists in other worlds. For each such world
there will be a distinct complete concept containing all and only the primitive
properties Arnauld has in that world. Clearly, if we think that Arnauld exists
in worlds other than the actual world, we will regard the expression "the
complete individual concept of Arnauld" as elliptical—short for "the complete individual concept of Arnauld in the actual world" or, more generally,
"the complete individual concept of Arnauld in possible world W."

There are a number of ways in which innocence might be lost relative
to this construction of possible worlds, based on maximal collections of
compossible complete individual concepts. For example, failure to relativize
the assignment of complete concept to individual to a world in the manner
noted above, taken together with a particular modal semantics based on this
construction of possible worlds, could produce striking results. By a modal
semantics based on this construction, I mean a set of rules assigning truth
values to sentences, particularly modal sentences, based on an interpretation
of those sentences relative to our construction of possible worlds in terms
of maximally compossible collections of complete individual concepts. For
example, suppose we say that an individual x has a property f essentially just
in case x has f in every possible world in which x exists; suppose further that
we say that x exists in a world W just in case there is a complete individual
concept of x in the collection representing W.[7] Failure to relativize appropriately will then have the striking result that x has all its properties essentially,
since only one concept will be the complete individual concept of x, and it
will exist in exactly one world.

The doctrine that each individual substance has all its properties essentially may be called superessentialism. Many have ascribed it to Leibniz.
But if Leibniz accepted superessentialism, he did not reach it via the route
outlined above—not in our time period, at any rate. True, he did not relativize the assignment of concept to individual to a world. So he took the
first step, but not the second. His primary characterization of modality—
necessity, impossibility, possibility, and contingency—was not based on a
structure of possible worlds. The basic definition of absolute necessity that
Leibniz employed is clearly stated in the important paper *Necessary and Contingent Truths*, where he defined an absolutely necessary proposition as one
whose opposite implies a contradiction.[8]

Still, it seems clear to me that Leibniz accepted the thesis that if a proposition is true in every possible world, then it is necessarily true.[9] But what
matters for us, when the question concerns superessentialism and the like,

is Leibniz's treatment of *de re* modalities, where the issue is the modality of the connection between a substance and one of its properties. In our time period, Leibniz did not use the structure of possible worlds to account for de re modalities. He used it primarily as a vehicle to discuss creation and attendant theological matters, which explains why, on Leibniz's scheme, God is not in any possible world.[10] So it would be a mistake to look for an explanation of Leibniz's metaphysical commitments in his de re modal semantics based on possible worlds, since he did not have such a de re modal semantics. It would be more profitable to speculate about what his de re modal semantics would have been like, based on an understanding of his metaphysical commitments.

The details of Leibniz's use of the structure of possible worlds in connection with creation and other theological matters has been criticized by writers from Arnauld to Plantinga (but by few in between).[11] Some of the details of Leibniz's thinking about possible worlds from the point of view of creation may be found in sections 1 through 7 of the *Discourse*, and in the draft and long letter of 14 July 1686.[12] In the long letter Leibniz wrote: "I conceive that there was an infinite number of possible ways of creating the world according to the different plans that God could form, and that each possible world depends upon certain principal plans or ends of God, which are peculiar to it, i.e., upon certain primitive free decrees (conceived *sub ratione possibilitatis*) or laws of general order of that possible universe, to which they are suited and whose concept they determine, as well as the concepts of all the individual substances that must enter into this same universe" (LA 51).

In Leibniz's framework, each possible world seems to correspond to the following items: (a) a goal or plan that that world would uniquely bring to fruition were it actual; (b) a law (or set of laws) of the general order that that world uniquely satisfies; (c) a concept of that world, which is unique to that world and determined by the relevant laws of general order; and (d) a unique set of concepts, one for each individual substance, that would be actual were that world the chosen one. The elements of this set are also determined by the relevant law (or laws) of general order. The key item here is (b), the laws of general order, since, with the exception of (a), those laws determine the other items—that is, a world concept (about which Leibniz said little) and the set of complete concepts whose instantiation would constitute a world.[13]

The laws of general order (also termed free, primitive decrees of God) must not be confused with laws of nature, which are also regarded by Leibniz as free decrees of God. According to Leibniz, a law of general order is analogous to an algebraic equation determining a line; it yields the sequence of events for the world to which it applies (*DM* §6). By definition it has no exceptions. We may think of it as a function assigning total states of its world to instants of time. Given that every possible world is fully characterized in terms of the properties and relations of its individual substances, the law of order for a world may also be thought of as determining a set of laws of order—one for each substance in its world.[14] We might call laws of this sort, whether applying to the whole world or to individual substances within a world, "developmental laws," since they specify—given some initial state—the development of that world, or substance, from that initial state to termination, if such there be. The mere existential claim that, for each possible world, there is a unique developmental law specifying total states of that world as a function of time, is innocent; and the same is true of the claim that for each individual substance in each possible world there exists a developmental law specifying its states as a function of time.

By definition, developmental laws have no exceptions. By contrast, laws of nature, which Leibniz also called "subordinate maxims" (*DM* §7), are in conformity with the nature of things, but are sometimes superseded by miracles (*DM* §§7 and 16). The notion of an individual nature will loom large in what follows. It will suffice for our present purposes to note that what Leibniz regarded as laws of nature governing the natural behavior of bodies, in the actual world have a hierarchical structure. First, the most general conservation principle: the effect must be equivalent to the full cause. Second, subordinate conservation principles: the conservation of motive force, the conservation of the quantity of motion in a given direction. Third, yet more subordinate principles governing the outcomes of collisions, under varying circumstances.[15]

2. THE THEORY OF MEANING

So much for innocence. Two types of principles are relevant to Leibniz's loss of innocence: those concerning the internal structure of concepts, that is, what they include; and those concerning the role concepts are taken to occupy in relevant theory—in the case in hand, theories of cognition and meaning. Any concept under which an individual falls is *a* concept of that entity; so any concept that includes only properties of a given individual is *a* concept of that individual. Consider the infinite set of concepts under which Alexander the Great falls—that is, consider the infinite set of concepts of Alexander the Great. Neither Leibniz nor Arnauld had the least compunction about identifying a single element of this set as the referent of the definite description "the individual concept of Alexander the Great," although, as it turned out, they picked different concepts.

The introduction to the first chapter of the first part of *La logique* begins with Arnauld's formulation of a basic premiss of what Thomas Reid came to call the "ideal theory": "Since we can have no knowledge of what is outside us except through the mediation of ideas that are in us, the reflections that can be made about ideas are perhaps what is most important in logic, because it is the foundation of all the rest."[16] Leibniz shared this assumption. For both Leibniz and Arnauld, a mind's utilization of ideas is what permits that mind to have thoughts about various types of entities outside itself. For both men, utilization of a language amounts to expressing thought by means of various conventional artifacts; hence, meaning is to be explained in terms of ideas. We have already seen some of these assumptions at work in the case of Arnauld's distinction between the comprehension of an idea and its extension. Part 2 of *La logique* employs these ideas to formulate a rudimentary theory of meaning. By contrast, Leibniz created a sophisticated theory, centered around the idea of a rational language—something on the order of a logically perfect language.[17]

It is important to bear in mind that Leibniz's reasoning sometimes presupposed the existence of a rational language. Here is an example that is relevant to our concerns: In chapter 1 we noted that the claim that the complete-concept theory of substance is a consequence of the concept-containment account of truth appears to be mistaken. But attention to aspects of the rational language, as Leibniz understood it, is relevant. Given Leibniz's commitment to the Aristotelian conception of substance, substances occur as referents of the subject term in subject-predicate sentences. So, given the concept-containment account of truth, we must assign a complete concept to a substance, and also to subject terms referring to it. That is the easy half of what the complete-concept theory requires; the hard half is that only substances must be assigned complete concepts. But then, how are we to handle a sentence like "Modesty is a virtue?" It is categorical and singular; its subject term *modesty* refers to a nonsubstance—the abstraction "modesty." But does not the concept-containment account of truth require that we assign a complete concept to modesty and, derivatively, to the word *modesty*? It would, were the sentence "Modesty is a virtue" a sentence in the language to which the truth definition is applied, that is, the rational language. But it is not, because the rational language does not contain singular designations for abstractions. In the *Verbal Characteristic* (usually dated around 1680), Leibniz wrote: "Abstractions may be dispensed with in the philosophical language, and once this is established many things are blocked. . . . However, it must be recalled that in dealing with proportions and numbers it is not easy to dispense with abstractions. Hence, it suffices to adopt the principle that they must be avoided as far as possible. I hold it as certain that they can be avoided completely when the characteristic has been correctly constituted" (C 435).[18]

We may explain apparent anomalies in Leibniz's remarks about the assignment of concept to object if we bear in mind that, for Leibniz, assignments are mediated by salient features of the envisaged rational language. Consider the following anomaly: in the draft for the long letter of 14 July 1686, in order to convince Arnauld that "it is necessary to philosophize one way about the concept of an individual substance and another way about the species concept of a sphere," Leibniz contrasted the incomplete concept of the abstract sphere—including only essential properties of spheres —with the concept of the spherical physical object that Archimedes directed to be placed on his tomb. Leibniz claimed: "The concept of the sphere that Archimedes had placed on his tomb is complete and must contain all that belongs to the subject of that form" (LA 38–39). Here we find Leibniz carefully distinguishing between a certain spherical individual and a particular abstract entity—the sphere—claiming that the one has a complete concept and that the other does not, just as his theory requires. Hence, the one—the sphere on Archimedes' tomb—is an individual substance according to Leibniz's theory, while the other is not. So where is the anomaly? Commentators have plausibly attributed a wide variety of theories of substance to Leibniz on the basis of the *Discourse* and the correspondence. Not one of them has as a consequence that the sphere on Archimedes' tomb is a substance. In fact, every one of them, when conjoined with some obvious truths—that the sphere on the tomb is not an animal, for example—implies that the sphere in question is not an individual substance.

I suggest that the most felicitous way to solve this small problem is this: we suppose that Leibniz's projected assignment of concepts to objects is mediated by an initial assignment of concepts to appropriate linguistic items in some fixed language and derivatively to objects, in virtue of their association (via reference, for example) with linguistic items. Thus, we may take Leibniz to have said: *If* ordinary French were the language of choice—relative to which assignments of concepts to linguistic items are to be made—then the sphere on Archimedes' tomb, as the referent of "la sphère qu'Archimède a fait mettre sur son tombeau," would be assigned a complete concept. But that definite singular term does not occur in the rational language. It refers to what Leibniz called an aggregate, and, in the rational language, sentences about aggregates are replaced by sentences about the individual substances aggregated. Of course, it would be an egregious error to infer from this that Leibniz's metaphysics is somehow founded on his philosophy of language; obviously, the rational language is shaped to fit the metaphysics, not vice versa.[19]

Many of Leibniz's remarks that seem to involve error are rendered harmless when it is realized that they are made relative to a presupposed rational language from which ambiguity, vagueness, and other untidy features of natural languages have been eliminated. Consider the proper name "Julius Caesar." Linguistic expressions of this type signify concepts, according to Leibniz.[20] He was well aware that different people have different ideas of Julius Caesar, yet, relative to the rational language, he insisted on a single assignment of concept to the proper name and to its referent Julius Caesar. He viewed this concept as *the* meaning of "Julius Caesar" and, hence, *the* individual concept of Julius Caesar.[21] It is true that the concept chosen may be *derived* from the nature of God's knowledge of Julius Caesar and, hence, that the concept chosen may be *identified* with God's concept of Julius Caesar. Part of the aim of this book is to emphasize the theological setting of the *Discourse* and correspondence, and the light that setting sheds on the meaning and justification of various of Leibniz's doctrines propounded therein. But in the present case, Leibniz's motivation was not primarily theological. For anyone who accepts the basic features of the ideal theory—that what we mean by what we say is to be explained with reference to ideas—there is a problem about the objectivity and agreement in meaning within a community, given the obvious divergence in the contents of our ideas of the same thing. We talk about *the* meaning of a given linguistic item, although we know that various users of that linguistic item have ideas of its referent with diverse contents. Leibniz's assignment of a unique concept to each individual, and to proper names of that individual, is part of an effort to formulate a theory adequate to account for presupposed agreement and objectivity of meaning, given the commitments of the ideal theory.

The details of Leibniz's efforts to secure objectivity are not our concern. In an obvious way they motivate the requirement that whatever concept we pick to be *the* meaning of a proper name—*the* concept of the individual to which that proper name refers—must have content sufficient to distinguish that individual from all other individuals; hence the following principle:

1. For any individual x, C is the individual concept of x only if, for any y, if $y \neq x$ then y does not have every property included in C.

In fact, Leibniz insisted on something substantially stronger, namely:

2. For any individual x, C is the individual concept of x only if, for any *possible y*, if $y \neq x$ then y does not have every property in C.[22]

Leibniz's exact justification for (2) need not concern us. It is a postulate derived from the role concepts are to play in an account of meaning and cognition that leads to the following account:

3. Where x is an individual, C is the individual concept of x if and only if x has every property included in C and it is not possible that there is some individual y ($y \neq x$) such that y has every property included in C.[23]

It may seem that in failing to plumb the depths of Leibniz's justification for (2) and, hence, (3), we have allowed an enemy to slip through the gates. But I do not think so. It is true that from (3) Leibniz purported to derive a major segment of the complete-concept theory of substance; namely:

4. Where x is an individual substance, C is the individual concept of x if and only if C includes all and only the properties of x.[24]

It is the arguments by which Leibniz purported to derive (4) from (3) wherein interest lies, not in (3).[25]

The other segment of the complete-concept theory of substance—that concepts of abstractions (accidents, attributes, properties, species, genera, and so on) are not complete—is sustainable because Leibniz's assignment of concepts to entities was mediated by the rational language, whose features presuppose considerable metaphysics. Let S be some abstraction, a species, for example. Then, on Leibniz's account, *the* concept of S does not contain properties of that species, but rather properties of individuals that are members of that species. Thus:

5. Where S is an abstraction, C is the concept of S if and only if C includes all and only those properties exemplified by everything that exemplifies S.[26]

Leibniz commenced with intuitions about the role that the concept of an individual is to play in picking out its bearer and then purported to derive results about specific content, first, with respect to concepts of individuals, and then, almost as an afterthought, with respect to concepts of abstractions. By contrast, Arnauld commenced with intuitions about content, based on his distinction between comprehension and extension. Such intuitions are, perhaps, clearer in the case of predicate expressions; hence, it is not surprising that he first characterized the concept of an abstraction, and then extended it by analogy to the case of the concept of an individual. Thus, Arnauld held,

6. Where S is an abstraction, C is the concept of S if and only if C includes all and only those properties such that, were a thing to lack one of them, it would not be (an) S.
7. Where x is an individual, C is the individual concept of x if and only if C includes all and only those properties such that, for any y, were y to lack one of them, y would not be x. (LA 32–33, 30–31)

The differences between (5) and (6) are not relevant to our concerns. We may assume that Leibniz and Arnauld agreed on the concept of an abstraction. The first proposition, which we attributed to Leibniz, is based on the intuition that the concept of an individual must, at a minimum, distinguish that individual from all other actual individuals. It is natural to expect Arnauld to share that intuition. I know of no texts that unambiguously indicate that he did. But I take it that the natural interpretation of the following passage from Arnauld would commit him to (1): "My self is necessarily a particular individual nature, which is the same as having a particular individual concept" (LA 30). Consider an individual x and a property f that x has; if f is such that, for any y, were y to lack f then y would not be x, then let us say that x has f *intrinsically*. In asserting (7), then, Arnauld was claiming that the concept of an individual includes all and only the properties it has intrinsically. What is not so clear is whether he thought that the properties an individual has intrinsically suffice to distinguish that individual from all other actual individuals. Unclarity about Arnauld's attitude toward (1) applies as well to (2) and (3). Fortunately, from our point of view, what matters is his attitude toward (4). And there matters are crystal-clear; he thought it was a disaster. Why so? Because, in conjunction with (7), it has what he took to be the disastrous consequence that every individual has all its properties intrinsically—a doctrine we might call "superintrinsicalness."

Let us say that an individual x has a property f *essentially* (necessarily) just in case it has f, and that it is metaphysically impossible that x exists and yet lacks f.[27] Now consider:

8. For any individual *x* and property *f*, *x* has *f* intrinsically if and only if *x* has *f* essentially.

Given (8), which I believe Arnauld simply took for granted, if Leibniz was committed to superintrinsicalness, then he was equally well committed to superessentialism—a view that Arnauld thought incompatible with God's freedom.

Two questions remain in our inventory of attitudes. What was Leibniz's reaction to (7)? In a word, he accepted it, because he accepted superintrinsicalness.[28] And what about (8)? There's the rub. My view is that Leibniz rejected (8) and, hence, superessentialism. The relevant issues are discussed in the remainder of this chapter.

Arnauld intended his characterization of the concept of an individual substance (7) to yield different assignments of concepts to objects from that produced by Leibniz's characterization (4). At least initially, Arnauld was unsure about Leibniz's attitude concerning the relation of (4) and (7). Prior to Leibniz's last letter on this topic (the long letter of 14 July 1686), Arnauld had no evidence suggesting that Leibniz was prepared, even eager, to affirm superintrinsicalness, that is, that every substance has all its properties intrinsically. Had he known that, he could have produced a very simple argument for his main thesis—that Leibniz's views are inconsistent with God's freedom. The argument is this: consider any individual substance that actually exists (for example, Adam) and any property that substance actually has (for example, that of having posterity). In virtue of superintrinsicalness, Adam has the property of having posterity intrinsically; in virtue of (8), Adam has the property of having posterity essentially. Hence, God could not have brought it about that Adam existed and yet lacked posterity—a claim that is flatly inconsistent with God's freedom. Of course, this only increases our puzzle about Arnauld's apparent concession. Once Arnauld was in possession of the material for this simple argument, Arnauld did not produce it; he conceded—or, so it seems.

In the next section we will concentrate our attention on the major argument Arnauld *did* produce for the thesis of the simple argument above, namely, that Leibniz's characterization of the concept of an individual is inconsistent with God's freedom. Then we will consider Leibniz's response.

3. ARNAULD'S ARGUMENT

The Leibniz-Arnauld correspondence started inauspiciously, not only because Leibniz was offended by Arnauld's initial remarks, but also because the process of using an intermediary, with attendant copying and recopying of letters, led to misrepresentation. Consider, again, Arnauld's reaction to Leibniz's summary of *DM* §13: " 'That the individual concept of each person includes once for all everything that will ever happen to him,' etc. If that is so, God was free to create [or not create Adam; but supposing he wished to create him,] everything that has happened since and will ever happen to the human race was and is obliged to happen through a more than fatal necessity" (LA 15).

Read the above, including the words enclosed in brackets, and you have what Arnauld wrote; read it without the words enclosed in brackets and you have what Leibniz received. Leibniz recognized a copy error, guessed at what Arnauld intended, and guessed wrong. In Leibniz's reconstruction, the passage after "if that is so" proceeds thus: "God was not free to create everything that has happened since to the human race, and whatever will ever happen to it was and is obliged to happen through a more than fatal necessity" (RL 29).[29] The reconstruction misses the mark; the result is that the real debate concerning freedom between Arnauld and Leibniz is restricted to two letters—Arnauld's letter of 13 May and Leibniz's long letter of 14 July. Although Leibniz's April letters are off the mark, they are instructive. Leibniz then thought that Arnauld's objection could be met by a simple distinction between absolute necessity and hypothetical necessity. What he then said about hypothetical necessity quite naturally suggests a commitment to superessentialism. It is instructive to trace the development of Leibniz's attitude toward certain relevant conditionals in the correspondence.

The main outline of Arnauld's central argument is clear enough. Consider the following:

1. Necessarily, if Adam exists, then Adam has posterity.
2. Necessarily, if God decides to create Adam, then Adam has posterity.
3. If God decides to create Adam, then God is not free with respect to whether Adam has posterity.

Arnauld's argument is this: Leibniz's views about individual concepts—when conjoined with certain facts about Adam—imply (1), which in turn implies (2), which in turn implies (3), which is heretical.[30] So far, so easy. The difficult part is to grasp Arnauld's argument for the claim that Leibniz's views about individual concepts imply (1).

The argument in question occurs at LA 28–29. It is a strange brew of premises about possible objects and concepts. Fortunately, the argument can be recast in a coherent form, if we formulate it as an argument about concepts rather than possible objects. We know already (see section 1 of this chapter) that Leibniz was prepared to formulate premises about possible objects in terms of individual concepts. We may safely assume that Leibniz would have construed Arnauld's complicated argument in the following form: Concepts exist and include their components (that is, the properties they include) independent of the free decrees of God (that is, the will of God). In other words, for any concept C and property f included in C, there is no free decree d of God such that had God not willed d then C would not have included f. But what is independent of God's free decrees is either necessary or impossible. Therefore, for any concept C and property f included in C, it is necessary that f is included in C. Now consider the complete individual concept of Adam—C_{Adam} for short—such that C_{Adam} includes all and only the properties of Adam. Let f be some such property, for example, the property of having posterity. C_{Adam} includes f; hence, C_{Adam} includes f necessarily. Let's record the result:

4. Necessarily, C_{Adam} includes the property of having posterity.

Now we need a premiss about concepts, corresponding to Arnauld's claim that it is "the same Adam considered now as possible and now as created" (LA 29). Given Leibniz's commitment to the complete-concept theory, and the fact that Arnauld's argument is a reductio, we might try:

5. C_{Adam} is the individual concept of Adam.

It is too weak for Arnauld's purposes. Consider:

6. For any individual x and concept C, if C is the individual concept of x, then, necessarily, C is the individual concept of x.

Propositions (5) and (6) yield what Arnauld's argument requires:

7. Necessarily, C_{Adam} is the individual concept of Adam.

Propositions (7) and (4) yield (1). The route from (1) to heresy—that is, (3) —has been noted. That, I believe, is the heart of Arnauld's major argument against the thesis that the concept of an individual must be complete.

We turn to an analysis of Leibniz's response to Arnauld's major argument. There is at least one interpretation of Leibniz's doctrines on divine freedom according to which all the freedom that Leibniz wished to attribute to God in connection with Adam is consistent with the truth of (1) and (2). Consider:

8. Adam has posterity.

Leibniz regarded (8) as contingent, because it entails that Adam exists and existence is a property not included in the complete concept of any creature, according to Leibniz.[31] Proponents of this line of reasoning claim to extract all the freedom Leibniz wished to attribute to God in connection with Adam from the contingency of (8). Perhaps Leibniz attributed some variety of freedom to God in virtue of the contingency of (8). But this is not the main thrust of the major documents we must consider—*DM* §13 and the letters and drafts of 14 July. Proponents of this line of reasoning insist, however, that Leibniz's views on hypothetical necessity leave no room for attributing more freedom to God than what can be eked out from the contingency of (8). I disagree. We prepare the way for a consideration of Leibniz's actual defense by considering what he said concerning hypothetical necessity.

Like every other topic considered in this book, Leibniz's treatment of hypothetical necessity is more complicated than it at first appears. Even a superficial examination of his various remarks on the subject suggests that Leibniz took sentences of the form "p is hypothetically necessary" as elliptical for "p is hypothetically necessary relative to q." In many contexts where

Leibniz claimed that a proposition p is hypothetically necessary, he did not clearly specify the proposition q relative to which p is hypothetically necessary. Sometimes the context makes it clear, but not always. Where we find Leibniz saying that, for example, "Adam has posterity" is hypothetically necessary, it is important to carefully investigate just what proposition it is relative to which Leibniz was claiming hypothetical necessity. Often it will turn out to be something like "God knows that Adam will have posterity," or "God decided that Adam was to have posterity"—a perfectly innocent claim (see, for example, Grua 362).

Various texts (see, for example, Grua 270–271 and *Theodicy* §37) suggest the following definitions:

Definition 1. Proposition p is absolutely (metaphysically, logically, geometrically) necessary = *df*. The negation of p entails a contradiction.

Definition 2. Proposition q is hypothetically necessary relative to proposition p = *df*. The conditional proposition ⌐if p then q⌐ is absolutely necessary.[32]

My thesis is this: all things considered, the most plausible interpretation of the position Leibniz developed in *DM* §13 and in the letters from 12 April through 14 July 1686 is that he *denied* that the proposition that Adam has posterity is hypothetically necessary relative to either of the propositions—that Adam exists, or that God decides to create Adam.[33] But it is a matter of "all things considered"; let's look at some of the detail.

In a letter of 12 April, written under the impression that Arnauld's problem concerned only absolute necessity, Leibniz made a point that he repeated throughout the correspondence: God does not decide on creation piecemeal; he does not decide that he would like Adam in a garden, perhaps at Eden, and then cogitate on supplementary details. God selects an entire world, with every single detail determinate, for creation.[34] Having made this point, Leibniz concluded: "It has pleased God to choose precisely this particular order of the universe; and all that follows from his decision is necessary only by a hypothetical necessity" (LA 20). The same line of reasoning occurs at LA 23 and in the letter of 14 July at LA 48 and 51. But this is not quite the same as asserting (1) or (2). True, if God decides to create Adam, then God, then and there (so to speak), makes a decision—"This world shall be" —relative to which the proposition that Adam has posterity is hypothetically necessary. But the proposition relative to which "Adam has posterity" is hypothetically necessary, is not simply that God decides to create Adam. It is necessarily true that if God decides to create Adam, then God has decided whether Adam will have posterity. But the proposition that God decides to create Adam does not entail what decision God has made about Adam's posterity. The relevant distinctions are to be found in texts from our time period. Consider the following passage from Leibniz's *De libertate, fato, gratia dei,* dated 1685–1687 in the *Vorausedition:* "You will insist the denial of Peter . . . follows from the divine essence, for God foresees by virtue of his own essence all future things. . . . I respond that it is certainly essential to God that he foresee any truth whatsoever, that is, that he can resolve every question; but it is not essential in itself that he resolve it affirmatively or negatively" (Grua 309).

We turn next to the draft for the long letter of 14 July, at which time Leibniz knew that claiming that (8) was contingent, while (1) and (2) were true, would not satisfy Arnauld. Leibniz's difficulties in formulating a coherent response are best illustrated by the following passage with which the draft initially commenced, but which was subsequently struck, and, hence, has not been published: "There are degrees among the consequences of a metaphysical necessity, such as the one of which M. Arnauld gives an example; there are others of them, where the connection itself is founded on a free decree of God, such as all the consequences that depend on the rules of mechanics or on the nature of the will inclined to choose what appears best" (LBr 59).[35]

This is an extraordinary passage; it goes against the interpretation I am recommending, since I claim that Leibniz, in the end, did not see consequences of the second type as having metaphysical necessity. In the sequel we hear no more about various degrees of metaphysical necessity.[36] This passage is followed by another, equally interesting and also struck, that starts by favoring the interpretation I reject and concludes by favoring the one I accept:

> I understand better now the view of M. Arnauld. The use of the term *necessary* had misled me and had convinced me that he imputed an absolute necessity to me. Now that he declares that he is only talking about a hypothetical necessity, the dispute has changed its face, for perhaps it would not be so absurd to say that from the single supposition that God decided to create Adam, all the rest follows necessarily, at least according to me, who believes that each individual substance expresses the entire universe according to a certain relation. Nevertheless, I call this consequence certain rather than necessary, unless one supposes furthermore the free decrees on which it is founded. For this supposition, joined to the first supposition, then hypothetical necessity is achieved. (LBr 59)

In the part of the draft that replaced the passage quoted above, Leibniz made exactly the same point—the implication relation between the antecedent of (2) and its consequent is characterized as certain, not as metaphysically necessary (see LA 38). There Leibniz characterized the connection between the antecedent of (2) and its consequent as *physical,* as opposed to one that is metaphysically necessary. He said that when a proposition asserting that the relevant free decrees obtain is conjoined with the antecedent, "the consequence is achieved." It is an indication of Leibniz's churning on this point that the surviving line—"It is true, I say, that then the consequence is achieved"—had the following predecessors, all subsequently struck: "Then hypothetical necessity is achieved; it is true, I say, that then hypothetical necessity is achieved; it is true, I say, that then certitude is achieved." He began the replacement passage thus: "M. Arnauld still finds strange what *it seems that I maintain*, 'that all human events occur by hypothetical necessity from the single supposition that God wished to create Adam'" (LA 37; emphasis mine). The italicized words are Leibniz's cue that he did not then maintain the thesis expressed by the quoted passage.

In the draft for the long letter of 14 July, Leibniz proceeded to introduce machinery, the intent of which was to explicate and ground a distinction between an implication relation characterized as certain, and one characterized as metaphysically necessary, in order to rationalize his denial of (1) and (2). After introducing the same machinery, for the same purpose, in the letter itself of 14 July, Leibniz concluded: "Thus, all human events could not fail to occur as in fact they did occur, once the choice of Adam is assumed; but not so much because of the individual concept of Adam, although this concept includes them, but because of God's plans, which also enter into the individual concept of Adam" (LA 51).

I suggest that Leibniz was making the familiar point here: when God decided to create Adam, he made decisions concerning the entire created world, relative to which any proposition asserting the occurrence of an event that will, in fact, occur is hypothetically necessary. What is not so easily finessed is the import of the phrase "although this concept includes them." There is a problem that we must now face, which is exemplified in each of the passages that I have cited as favoring ascription of the denial of (1) and (2) to Leibniz, based on a distinction between certain or physical consequences and metaphysical consequences. Let R be the conjunction of those free decrees, such that, when conjoined with the proposition "Adam exists" (or the proposition "God decides to create Adam") to form the antecedent of a conditional whose consequent is the proposition "Adam has posterity," then, according to Leibniz, "hypothetical necessity is achieved." Now consider the following conditional:

9.   If Adam exists, then R.

Our texts are as one in claiming that the state of affairs to which R refers is included in the concept of Adam.[37] So, can't we ascribe the following to Leibniz:

10.   Necessarily, if Adam exists, then R.

From LBr 59, and LA 38, we know that Leibniz accepted:

11.   Necessarily, if Adam exists and R, then Adam has posterity.

But from (10) and (11), we may infer (1).

This reasoning about Leibniz's reasoning is wrong; Leibniz would reject the claim that whatever is included in an individual concept is included necessarily. Our analysis of Leibniz's convoluted remarks about hypothetical necessity has a bonus; we have located the step in Arnauld's major argument that Leibniz rejected, namely, (4). Corresponding to the distinction between physical (certain) and metaphysical implication relations, Leibniz postulated two types of inclusion relations and, correspondingly, two types of connection between a substance and its properties. The distinction is phrased in terms of intrinsic as opposed to necessary connections.[38] The change in terminology, and the fact that this particular terminology is not predominant in texts other than the correspondence with Arnauld, are easily explained. The terminology was introduced by Arnauld in his letter of 13 May.[39] In the correspondence the distinction is utilized primarily with respect to the connection between a substance and a property of that substance. In writings from the same time period (notably *General Inquiries*), the distinction turns up in connection with two types of inclusion relation between a concept and some property (or concept) included in it, a distinction characterized in terms of finite as opposed to infinite analysis.

By way of housekeeping, we should note that Leibniz appeared ready to accept the claim that whatever individual concept a substance had, it had of necessity, which is the claim backing (7)—the premiss in my reconstruction of Arnauld's argument that is least Arnauldic. It is, in fact, thoroughly Leibnizian. It is the point of the following passage from *DM* §13. Discussing Julius Caesar and the property of becoming dictator, Leibniz wrote: "It might be said that it is not by virtue of his concept or idea that he must commit this action, since it is only appropriate to him because God knows all. But it will be replied that his nature or form corresponds to this concept, and since God has imposed on him this person, it is henceforth necessary for him to satisfy it."

The culprit in Arnauld's argument, from Leibniz's point of view, is (4). Leibniz claimed that some components of a complete individual concept are included in it necessarily, some contingently. Correspondingly, he claimed that whereas a substance has each of its properties intrinsically, it has only some of them essentially. Furthermore, in texts from our time period he set out to establish the relevant distinction in two quite different ways—what we might call the *sub ratione generalitatis* strategy and the possible free decree strategy. The basic idea of the sub ratione generalitatis strategy occurs in *De libertate, fato, gratia Dei*. Leibniz put the following words in the mouth of a critic: "God has in his intellect a perfect concept or idea of possible Peter containing all truths concerning Peter, the objective reality of which constitutes the entire nature or essence of Peter, and accordingly that he would deny is essential to Peter." To which Leibniz responded thus: "In this complete concept of possible Peter, which I concede is observed by God, are contained not only essential or necessary items, namely, those that flow from an incomplete or species concept, and are demonstrated from terms so that the contrary implies a contradiction, but also existential things, so to speak, or contingent items are included there, because it is of the nature of an individual substance that its concept is perfect or complete" (Grua 311).

Similar points are made in other texts from our period, such as *De libertate creaturae et electione divina* (Grua 383), and, of course, *DM* §13, LA 39, and LA 52, where Leibniz wrote: "I agree . . . that I am free to take this journey or not, for although it is included in my concept that I shall take it, it is also included therein that I shall take it freely. And there is nothing in me of all that can be conceived in general terms—i.e., in terms of essence, or a species concept, or an incomplete concept—from which one can infer that I shall take it, whereas from the fact that I am a man, one can conclude that I am capable of thought."[40] Leibniz was not consistent in his use of some of the key terms utilized to state the doctrine involved; in particular, the term *essence*, which here refers to a component concept of a complete concept, is sometimes used by Leibniz to refer to a complete concept itself, even in the same texts. But this terminological instability must not obscure the central point, namely, that Leibniz set out to explain in conceptual terms a dichotomy between essential and contingent properties of an individual. What we have here is the very antithesis of superessentialism.[41]

Without straining for more detail than Leibniz's exposition provides, we may outline his basic points as follows, beginning with a presupposition. The presupposition is that for each individual substance there is a unique species such that that substance is of that species. We make use of this presupposition in the following formulation:

12. For any individual substance x, property f, and concept D, if D is the concept of the species to which x belongs, then x has f essentially if and only if D entails f.[42]

The possible free decree strategy takes two quite different forms in our main texts. In one form, it is intended to issue in a thesis that complements (12)—that is, an account, entirely in terms of concept inclusion, of the circumstances under which an individual substance x has some property f contingently. We examine that form first. Recall Leibniz's statement of a difficulty and its resolution in *DM* §13: "But (it will be said) if a conclusion can be deduced infallibly from a definition or concept, it will be necessary. Now we are maintaining that all that is to happen to any person is already contained virtually in his nature or concept, as are the properties in the definition of the circle; thus the difficulty subsists." Here are key passages from Leibniz's effort at resolution: "To meet it soundly, I say that connection . . . is of two sorts: the one is absolutely necessary, of which the contrary implies a contradiction . . . , the other is only necessary ex hypothesi . . . , but in itself is contingent, the contrary implying no contradiction."[43]

Leibniz then turned to an example. He asked us to consider the individual, Julius Caesar, and a contingent property of Caesar, for example, the property of crossing the Rubicon. In applying his remarks about a distinction between connections, Leibniz wrote: "For it would be found that this demonstration [that Caesar has the property of crossing the Rubicon] is not as absolute as those of numbers." He went on to say that this demonstration presupposes various free decrees of God and concluded: "Every truth that is founded on these sorts of decrees is contingent." The idea seems to be this: let x be an individual substance and C its complete individual concept. We identify some concept D such that D is a subconcept of C—that is, every property included in D is included in C, but not vice versa. Then we say that x has property f contingently if the information contained in D, when and only when conjoined with certain free decrees of God (laws $L_1 \ldots L_n$), entails that x has f. This strategy is not very promising. The specification of D is crucial; to obtain the results Leibniz wanted, D must include contingent properties of x. There is little hope that this strategy would yield a noncircular necessary and sufficient condition of a contingent property of an individual.

We took the sub ratione generalitatis strategy to be intended to yield a necessary and sufficient condition of an essential property; perhaps Leibniz hoped that the possible free decree strategy, in the form just considered, would yield a necessary and sufficient condition of a contingent property. To what end? Either, if successful, would show that Leibniz could provide a method of dividing the properties of an individual into two mutually exclusive and jointly exhaustive classes, corresponding to the division between the essential and the contingent properties of an individual, that Arnauld wished to draw. But what do these distinctions, however aptly drawn, have to do with Arnauld's argument in favor of (4)? Surely Arnauld would have been entitled to say to Leibniz: "Your division of the properties of an individual into those that are contingent and those that are essential is on target. We share the same intuitions with respect to this distinction. Your problem is that you are not entitled to it. You concede (7); you have not touched my argument for (4). Propositions (4) and (7) yield that Adam has posterity essentially. Based on your own (12), having posterity is not essential to Adam. So your position is incoherent." Of course, Arnauld did not say any of this. Fortunately, Leibniz offered another form of the free decree strategy in the correspondence; it is aimed at Arnauld's argument for (4). It is a genuine defense, and so I call it the possible free decree defense.

The possible free decree defense is stated in the draft for the long letter of 14 July (LA 40), and in the actual letter of 14 July (LA 51). Like Arnauld's formulation of the argument to which it is a reply, Leibniz's response moved easily between talk of concepts and talk of possible individuals. In the draft, Leibniz first summarized what he took to be Arnauld's central point: "I consider the individual concept of Adam as possible, maintaining that among an infinity of possible concepts God chose that of a particular Adam; now, *possible concepts in themselves do not depend on the free decrees of God*" (LA 41; emphasis mine). His response is curt: "As for the objection, that the possibles are independent of the decrees of God, I grant it of actual decrees (although the Cartesians do not agree), but I maintain that possible individual concepts include some possible free decrees" (LA 41). Leibniz, then, denied a basic premiss in Arnauld's argument for (4); namely, that a proposition p is contingent just in case there is some *actual* free decree d of God such that the truth value of p depends on d. Thus, Leibniz denied that the contingent may be identified with what depends on the actual will of God.

Suppose that at the last minute (so to speak) God had decided not to create any possible world. Still, by Leibniz's lights, the following would have been true and contingent:

13. C_{Adam} includes the property of having posterity.

In the envisaged circumstance, (13) would have been true and contingent, but independent of all God's actual decrees relative to creation, because there would have been none. The radical nature of Leibniz's philosophical theology here can be obscured by the fact that he held that a proposition is contingent just in case there is some free decree of God (actual or possible) such that the truth value of p depends on d. And so he could say that the contingent may be identified with what depends on the will of God, intending, of course, to include God's possible will, as well as his actual will.

Leibniz made little use of the possible free decree defense outside the correspondence with Arnauld. And, unfortunately, in an area where we might have expected help from Arnauld, we receive none. In my opinion, Leibniz continued to reject (4) and its ilk. But he found what he took to be a better, deeper way, based on the distinction between finite and infinite analysis, which I will discuss in section 8 of this chapter. The possible free decree defense rests contingency ultimately in God's will, actual and possible. But, of course, in God's free will, which presupposes contingency. Leibniz saw the circle; in reading notes on *Scientia media* by De Twisse, Leibniz noted: "The root of contingency according to Scotus is the will of God insofar as it is free." To which he added, "But this is circular." [44] I am not suggesting that the doctrine of infinite analysis replaced the free decree defense in the sense that Leibniz affirmed the former and rejected the latter. I believe that Leibniz saw the doctrine of infinite analysis as putting the free decree defense on firm, noncircular footing.

4. SUPERESSENTIALISM AND SUPERINTRINSICALNESS

Whether Leibniz wished to accept superessentialism in our texts and time period is a vexed question. By contrast, the question of whether he wished to accept superintrinsicalness is easily answered: he did.[45] Perhaps the most dramatic affirmation of the doctrine occurs in the draft for the long letter of 14 July. Leibniz, paraphrasing Arnauld, wrote: "I am not sure whether I shall take the journey, but I am sure that whether I do or not, I shall always be myself.[46] To which Leibniz replied: "We are concerned here with a prejudice that is not to be confused with a distinct concept or item of knowledge" (LA 45). The doctrine is stated forthrightly in the actual letter to Arnauld at LA 53. It is put to a theological use in *DM* §30, and is implied by the summary of that section, sent to Arnauld. In the summary Leibniz said: "We must not ask why Judas sins, since this free action is contained in his concept, but only why Judas the sinner is admitted to existence in preference to some other possible persons."[47] In the text of *DM* §30, Leibniz, once again considering an imaginary critic, wrote: "But another will say, whence comes it that this man will sin? The reply is easy; it is that otherwise it would not be this man."

The theodicean strategy involved here appears in numerous texts from our time period.[48]

Surely the temptation is to argue that Leibniz's point in these passages is this: don't ask why God did not bring it about that Judas exists but does not sin, because the envisaged state of affairs is impossible, since sinning is included in the concept of Judas and whatever property is included in the concept of an individual is such that it is metaphysically necessary that if that individual exists, then the individual has that property. But even God cannot do what is metaphysically impossible. Therefore, even God cannot do what you ask. In other words, the best explanation of Leibniz's theodicean maneuver here is to admit his commitment to superessentialism. So why do I continue to resist ascribing that commitment to him? Because the explanation just stated, based on superessentialism, is so simple, so obvious, so compelling for one who accepts its premises, that I can not bring myself to believe that Leibniz would have accepted it but never stated it. But there is nothing remotely like it in the texts from our period, nor from any thereafter, so far as I know.

Some with whom I have discussed these matters are not persuaded on the ground that Leibniz rarely stated his arguments in full detail; hence, they suggest that not much should be made of the lack of detail in this case. Lack of detail is one thing; I grant that it was Leibniz's usual course. But there is no modal terminology deployed in any of the texts noted in the previous note, or in any Leibnizian text utilizing the relevant theodicean strategy, to the best of my knowledge. The argument, based on superessentialism, just is not there at all. In fact, contrary to what appears to be nearly uncontested opinion, there is no basic theodicean strategy employed by Leibniz that relies essentially on the doctrine of superintrinsicalness. Without question, numerous illustrations of the strategy employed by Leibniz utilize superintrinsicalness. The point of the strategy therein illustrated is to bring about a certain economy of vulnerability with respect to God's decisions. The basic strategy is evident in those passages where Leibniz maximized the benefits. Consider the following, from *Extraits des Arminiens* (dated by Grua 1691–1695?):

Therefore, it must not be held that God decides specifically concerning aids [to grace] given to Peter or to Judas, but he decides whether he wishes to admit to existence the possibles—this Peter, this Judas— with the total series of aids and circumstances already included in the complete concept of each of them. *In fact, he does not even decide that in itself,* but rather whether he wishes to admit to existence this universal series of possibles in which Peter and Judas, endowed with the qualities stated, are contained among infinitely many others. (Grua 343; emphasis mine)

In the same piece Leibniz drew the moral: "Therefore, the object of the divine decree is not the man, but rather the total series of possibles making up this universe taken together with all its states, past, present, and future" (Grua 345). Thus, when the question concerns the value of the outcomes of God's choices concerning creatures, God is ultimately responsible for exactly one choice, namely, that of an entire world.[49] The object of God's choice—an entire possible world—has all its states intrinsically.[50] But the viability of the recommended theodicean strategy is entirely independent of whether the elements of a possible world—that is, possible substances —have their properties intrinsically. Hence, the doctrine of superintrinsicalness—that individual substances have all their properties intrinsically— is not an essential component of the basic theodicean strategy deployed by Leibniz in the texts cited.

Even if superintrinsicalness is not an essential component of any basic theodicean strategy deployed by Leibniz, it is a thesis that he accepted without reservation. Attributing it to him, while not attributing superessentialism to him, generates problems of interpretation. Special, irrelevant considerations are involved in the matter of God's freedom, so we will concentrate on human freedom. Consider, then, the case of Leibniz's journey to Paris, an example Leibniz employed when discussing human freedom in the draft for the long letter of 14 July, and in the letter itself. I take what Leibniz said at LA 52 to commit him to the following:

1. Leibniz journeyed to Paris in 1672.
2. Leibniz was free not to journey to Paris in 1672.
3. It is not metaphysically necessary that if Leibniz exists, then Leibniz journeyed to Paris in 1672.

Furthermore, I take it that what he said at LA 53 committed him to:

4. For any y, had y not journeyed to Paris in 1672 then y would not have been Leibniz.[51]

In summarizing his position on freedom and necessity at the close of the long letter of 14 July, Leibniz said: "I have demonstrated that the connection depends on [God's free] decrees, in my opinion, and that it is not necessary, although it is intrinsic. You have insisted upon the objection there would be to saying that if I do not take the journey that I am to take, I shall not be me, and I have explained how one can say it or not" (LA 56). I have assumed that when Leibniz said that you could *not* say it, he meant that, while you must say (4), you can also say (3), that is, deny that the connection is necessary. This is confirmed by an examination of the original version of the draft. There, at LA 46, just after his criticism of Arnauld's "I remain me whether I take the journey or not" remark, Leibniz wrote: "In fact, when I consider the concept that I have of every true proposition, I find that every predicate . . . is contained in the concept of the subject, and I ask no more [although I agree that the connection, although intrinsic, is not always necessary. And it is in this sense that I could grant what Arnauld says . . .]" (LBr 6ov). The material in brackets was subsequently struck.

It is natural to reason as follows. Surely it is unacceptable to assert both (3) and (4). Hence, good scholarly methodology requires that we investigate the possibility that the propositions Leibniz associated with (3) or (4) are distinct from those normally associated. Those who reason in this manner view the sub ratione generalitatis strategy, the possible free decree strategy, and even the doctrine of infinite analysis as efforts by Leibniz to explicate an idea of having a property contingently, not involving *de re* metaphysical modality, yielding a special nonmodal notion consistent with superintrinsicalness and yet sufficient, when joined with other requirements, to yield freedom.[52] I reject this approach. Perhaps we have reached the level where it is a matter of comparing intuitions. Here is my intuition. In the first chapter of *The Nature of Necessity*, Alvin Plantinga set out to focus the reader's mind on what he called "broadly logical necessity." I believe that Leibniz would identify what he called "metaphysical, logical, geometrical necessity" with Plantinga's broadly logical necessity. He would accept Plantinga's distinction between *de dicto* and *de re* modality. Moreover, Leibniz and Arnauld would agree with each other and with Plantinga, on the whole, in the way they divided up the properties of individual substances into those that are contingent as opposed to those that are necessary, provided Plantinga steered clear of his more esoteric examples of properties. I believe Leibniz had his mind clearly focused on broadly logical necessity and the associated notion of contingency when he formulated the doctrine of infinite analysis. His claim was to provide a deep analysis of just those notions, not some surrogates.

The problem is that the intuitions just noted generate a serious problem of interpretation, whose dimensions we now consider. Consider the following formulas:

5. $Fa \land \Box((\exists y)(y = a) \rightarrow Fa)$
6. $Fa \land (\sim Fa > \sim(\exists y)(y = a))$
7. $Fa \land (y)(\sim Fy > y \neq a)$
8. $Fa \land (\sim Fa > a \neq a)$[53]

Formula (5) is relatively straightforward; it is our rendering of the sentence "*a* has F essentially." Formulas (6) and (7) are formalizations of alternative ways in which Leibniz seems to have construed "*a* has F intrinsically." As a rendering of "*a* has F intrinsically," (6) is suggested by Leibniz's remarks in the *Confessio* (see A/6/3/148). Formula (7) is suggested by numerous texts in our time period (for example, Grua 314 and *DM* §30), as well as in the correspondence (for example, at LA 42, 45, and 53). Grua 327 suggests that Leibniz took (6) and (7) to come to the same thing. There Leibniz considered why God did not give you more strength (to resist temptation): "If he had done this, you would not exist, for he would have produced not you but another creature." Formula (8) seems to capture one of Arnauld's ways of putting the matter (see LA 30 and 31). Contemporary treatments of subjunctive conditionals offer insight into various propositions that we might associate with sentences in our texts that (6), (7), and (8) are intended to render. But we must be wary of forcing the systems of Stalnaker or Lewis, for example, on Leibniz and Arnauld.

One possible program is this: We might utilize contemporary treatments of modality and subjunctive conditionals in order to forge a distinction between (5) and (6) (or [7]) sufficient to sustain the claim that while (5) implies (6) (or [7]), the converse fails. The distinction forged must be sufficient to sustain the claim that superintrinsicalness does not imply superessentialism. The second step in this program would involve using the distinction forged in its first part in order to motivate Leibniz's acceptance of superintrinsicalness. Section 3 of chapter 6 contains speculation about Leibniz's criteria for identity of substances over time. The basic idea is that according to Leibniz, created substance y at t' is identical with created substance x at t (t' later than t) just in case some state of x at t is a real causal ancestor of some state of y at t'. The plausibility of this analysis depends upon various Leibnizian theses concerning causality, including commitment to a strong notion of causal determination. Section 3 of chapter 6 includes the outline of a derivation of superintrinsicalness from the criterion of substantial persistence and related theses concerning causality. There is textual support for linking Leibniz's view about persistence and causality with his commitment to superintrinsicalness. The ". . . we are concerned here with a prejudice . . ." passage (LA 45), in which Leibniz clearly committed himself to superintrinsicalness, continues: "These things appear to us to be *undetermined* only because the advance signs or indications of them in our substance are not recognizable to us" (LA 45; emphasis mine).

This program leans heavily on its first step-forging a distinction between (5) and (6) (or [7]), sufficient to bear the weight of the remainder of the program. Suppose that the resources of contemporary treatments of modality and subjunctive conditionals will not bear that weight. I am so convinced that we are on the right track that, in that case, I would recommend that we construe Leibniz's understanding of what it is to have a property intrinsically (and, hence, his understanding of [6] and [7]) in terms of his reasoning in support of superintrinsicalness, utilizing some of his theses about causality and persistence. So, if we finally conclude that understanding Leibniz requires attributing to him either an off-beat notion of what it is to have a property essentially or an off-beat notion of what it is to have a property intrinsically, better the latter than the former.

The details of these projects of rational reconstruction go well beyond any Leibnizian texts known to me. Hence, their elucubration is left to others.[54]

5. THE CONTENT OF CONCEPTS: INTRINSIC DENOMINATIONS

The claim that an incomplete concept will not distinguish an individual substance from all other possible individual substances was important to Leibniz. In conjunction with the principle that the concept of an individual must distinguish that individual from all other possible individuals, it yields his thesis that an incomplete concept cannot be the concept of an individual substance. Leibniz wanted more than this negative thesis. He also wanted the thesis that only one individual falls under a given complete concept. In order to obtain his positive thesis, we need to add that no two possible individual substances have the same complete individual concept—what we might call the identity of indiscernibles. Given Leibniz's views about the content of concepts, the identity of indiscernibles is no mere triviality. Part of the point of this section is to confirm the nontriviality of the identity of indiscernibles, by providing a brief account of Leibniz's thinking about the content of individual concepts in our time period.

Here are some of the ways in which Leibniz characterized the contents of a complete individual concept in our two primary texts: where x is an individual substance, Leibniz claimed that the concept of x includes everything that pertains to x (LA 53); what is sufficient to account for all the phenomena that occur to x (LA 53); once and for all everything that will ever happen to x (*DM* §13); enough so that everything that can be attributed to x can be deduced from it (LA 42, 46). Here is a somewhat more austere way in which Leibniz characterized the contents of a complete individual concept: "All the predicates of Adam either depend upon other predicates of this same Adam, or they do not so depend. Putting aside, then, those that do depend on others, we have only to take together the primitive predicates in order to form the complete concept of Adam, which is sufficient to make it possible to deduce from it everything that must happen to him" (LA 44).

The plethora of nonequivalent characterizations of the content of a concept creates no serious problem of interpretation. True, for any individual substance x, there may be more than one concept that Leibniz viewed as denotation of "the individual concept of x," but the passage from LA 44 surely steers us toward the candidate Leibniz would have presented, had he been questioned on his lax use of the definite article. We might call it the strict complete concept of x; by contrast, the others are various flabby complete concepts of x. In order to understand the strict concept, we need to look at its innards, that is, at the primitive properties mentioned at LA 44. The passages from LA 42, 46, and 53 suggest that various flabby concepts result from applying some operation to the information strictly supplied by the strict concept. Thus, fastening on *DM* §13, LA 42, or LA 46, we might hold that a flabby concept of *x* is simply the deductive closure of its strict concept. In any case, our texts make clear that Leibniz held that a complete individual concept, flabby or strict, includes, in some fashion, complete information about the properties of its bearer.

But there is more. In the draft for the long letter of 14 July, Leibniz wrote: "It is the nature of an individual substance to have such a complete concept from which one can deduce everything one can attribute to it, *and even the entire universe* [because of the connections among things] (LA 41; emphasis mine).[55] And this is no aberration. A similar expansion—from the properties of an individual to those of every individual in the universe, via "the connection of things"—occurs at *DM* §8, *Specimen* (G/7/311 [MP 77]), *Primary Truths* 520–521 (MP 89–90), as well as in the correspondence at LBr 69. A similar expansion of the contents of an individual concept has been attributed to Leibniz with respect to laws of nature. Thus, the discussion of the derivation of some of Caesar's properties from others in *DM* §13 might suggest that Leibniz then took laws of nature not to be included in individual concepts.

By contrast, we find the following in the draft for the long letter of 14 July: "Each possible individual of any one world includes in its concept the laws of its world" (LA 40).[56] This has led some to suppose that Leibniz engaged in "concept packing." The idea is this: In its prepacked form the complete concept of an individual includes all and only its primitive properties. From the information about its own primitive properties contained in its prepacked concept, plus information supplied by "the connection of things" (that is, true relational propositions in which *x* occurs as a term), information about the properties of all other individuals in the universe may be derived. Perhaps Leibniz held that only one set of natural laws is compatible with the information so far gathered.[57] According to the "concept packing" picture, Leibniz simply packed the required information into each complete concept.[58]

I do not believe that Leibniz engaged in premeditated concept packing, or that he packed concepts inadvertently. I believe that he was committed to doctrines that he took to have the consequence that any strict individual concept supplied complete information about the world to which it belongs. My view is at best partially supported by the textual evidence in my ken; the same is true of its interesting competitors. We consider, in turn, the provenance of the primitive properties contained in strict concepts, their logical form, and their relation to more mundane properties. In the matter of the provenance of properties contained in strict concepts, the right place to begin is with Leibniz's conception of creation.

Consider this passage from *Specimen*: "And since the full reason for a thing is the aggregate of all its primitive requisites (those that do not require other requisites) it is evident that the causes of all things can be reduced to the attributes of God" (G/7/310 [MP 77]). Here Leibniz utilized the idea that creation consists in God's instantiating various limited versions of properties that constitute God's perfections.[59] With the passage of time Leibniz came to put the point in somewhat florid language. Here is a sample:

> Since all minds are unities, it can be said that God is the primary unity, expressed by all the others according to their points of view. His goodness moves him to act, and there are in him three primordial attributes —power, knowledge, and will. It is from these that operation or the created thing results, which is varied according to the different combinations of unity with zero, or rather, the positive with privation, for privation is nothing other than limits, and there are limits everywhere in creatures. Nevertheless, creatures are something more than limits, for they have received some perfection or virtue from God. (Grua 126)[60]

Since creation consists in God's instantiating various properties that are limited versions of God's perfections, substances may be completely characterized and, hence, individuated in terms of those properties. Consider the following from a paper entitled *Definitionen* (for which the editors of the *Vorausedition* suggest a probable date of 1681–1686): "There can be as many individual substances as there are diverse combinations of all compatible attributes. And from this the principle of individuation is evident" (*LH* IV 7C Bl. 107–108). The idea that created individual substances result from God's instantiating various limited versions of his own attributes played an important role in Leibniz's thought about the nature of created substances. It is what is behind Leibniz's idea, expressed in *DM* §9, that created individual substances imitate, in some limited way, God's omniscience and omnipotence. There Leibniz claimed that each created substance perceives every other, although in a confused way, and all other substances accommodate in some degree to the desires of any given substance. In a passage from a work entitled *Mira de Natura substantiae corporeae* (*Wonders Concerning the Nature of Corporeal Substance*), tentatively dated 1683 in the *Vorausedition*, Leibniz said: "In every creature there is both limitation and infinity. It is limited with respect to distinct knowledge and irresistible power; unlimited with respect to confused knowledge and impaired power. For there is nothing in the whole world that it does not perceive, and nothing that it attempts that does not extend to infinity" (*LH* IV 1, 14 Bl. 11). The *Discourse* doctrine seems to promise that whatever you want, everything else will give a little. The *Wonders* doctrine seems to promise that whatever you attempt, your efforts are bound to have an effect on everything else. They are obviously connected.

Consideration of Leibniz's views concerning creation tells us something about the nature of the primitive properties that are contained in strict individual concepts, but not much about their logical form. For help on that topic we need to take heed of some of Leibniz's remarks concerning "the alphabet of human thought," whose elements are primitive properties or concepts.

Leibniz wrote in *De characteristica* (preliminarily dated in the *Vorausedition* 1678–1682): "The alphabet of human thoughts is a catalogue of primitive concepts, i.e., those of which we are unable to provide a clearer definition" (*LH* IV 7C Bl. 160–161).[61] Leibniz's project here was twofold; first, to draw up the catalogue, or relevant parts thereof, and, second, to outline how we could explain nonprimitive concepts as arising from the primitive by way of some operations—usually concept conjunction and complementation.[62] A fundamental thesis about the primitive properties forming the subject matter of the alphabet of human thoughts is formulated in *Meditatio de principio individui* (A/6/3/490–491, 1 April 1676), in which Leibniz argued that individuals cannot differ solely with respect to extrinsic features, but that they must differ with respect to intrinsic properties as well.[63] The doctrine involved—a potent form of the identity of indiscernibles—is one that Leibniz accepted throughout his career. A later expression of it is in *New Essays*: "Every substantial thing . . . must always differ from every other in respect of intrinsic denominations" (p. 110).[64] The primitive properties, then, that constitute the contents of strict concepts are all intrinsic denominations. Without aiming for more detail than Leibniz's remarks provide, we may say that an intrinsic denomination is a nonrelational property that, to follow Robert Adams, "could be expressed in a language sufficiently rich, without the aid of such referential devices as proper names, proper adjectives and verbs (such as 'Leibnizian' and 'pegasizes'), indexical expressions, and referential uses of definitive descriptions."[65]

The notion of an intrinsic denomination is central to the potent form of the identity of indiscernibles to which Leibniz was committed. It is also involved in another doctrine of significance to Leibniz, what I call "the weak thesis of intrinsic foundations." The basic idea is that when you have said what there is to say about the distribution of intrinsic denominations among individual substances in a given world, you have said it all; that is, any other contingent truths about that world (except truths about God's relation to it) must supervene on what has already been said.[66]

This thesis provides support for Leibniz's well-known doctrine that there are no purely extrinsic denominations.[67] A property *f* would be a *purely* extrinsic denomination of substance *x* if *x* had *f*, but *f* were not grounded in intrinsic denominations in the way the weak thesis of intrinsic foundations requires. Thus, Leibniz said of position and quantity (properties he took to be extrinsic denominations): "when I considered the matter more accurately, I saw that they are nothing but mere results [*meras resultationes*], which do not constitute any intrinsic denomination per se, and so they are only relations that require a foundation [*fundamento*] derived from the category of quality, i.e., from an intrinsic accidental denomination" (C 9 [MP 134]).

It seems reasonably clear that Leibniz used the relevant locutions in such fashion that if *a* is a "mere result" of *b*, *c*, and *d*, then the latter are the "foundations" of the former. So, if we grasped one of these technical terms (such as "mere result"), we would have the other ("foundation"). I do not claim to have a proper account of what Leibniz meant by these terms. The notions crop up in crucial segments of Leibniz's philosophy—for example, in his theory of relations and in his mature phenomenalism. Leibniz wrote to De Volder about the monads: "Accurately speaking, however, matter is not composed of these constitutive unities, but *results* from them, since matter or extended mass is nothing but a phenomenon *founded* in things" (G/2/268 [L 536]; emphasis mine). Consider his account of relations. In *On Terms, Predicates, and Relations* (tentatively dated 1690–1691 in the *Vorausedition*), Leibniz considered the proposition "A is similar to B." He wrote: "This is resolved in the end to two [propositions], one concerning only A, the other concerning only B, e.g., A is red and B is red, and therefore A is similar (in this respect) to B" (*LH* IV 7C Bl. 17). The *result* in this case, A's being similar to B, is entailed by its *foundations*, A's being red and B's being red. Leibniz was well aware that the converse does not hold—that the proposition formulating the result does not entail the propositions formulating the foundations. Still, it seems clear that he saw a reduction here; that is, he held that there is really no more to the result than what is contained in its foundations.[68]

The general idea involved seems to be this: where *a* and *b* are individual substances and R some binary relation, if the proposition "*aRb*" is true, then there are sets of primitive intrinsic denominations F and G such that *a* has every member of F and *b* has every member of G; and the proposition "*a* has every member of F and *b* has every member of G" entails the proposition "*aRb*." Moreover, although the converse entailment does not hold, there really is no more to *a*'s bearing R to *b* than *a*'s having every member of F and *b*'s having every member of G.

Generalizing the (admittedly vague) notion of reduction involved here, we may reformulate the weak thesis of intrinsic foundations as follows. Let us associate with each individual substance in some world W its strict complete individual concept, including all and only its primitive intrinsic denominations. Think of a world description as providing total information about the contents of these strict concepts, with the added piece of information that the concepts given include strict concepts of all substances in W. Then, according to Leibniz, any truth entirely about W not strictly contained in the information so far supplied must supervene on it, that is, be reducible to W's world description.[69] This is a strong doctrine. Even so, it is not enough to blunt the charge of concept packing. The information yielded by a world description, according to the doctrine just formulated, appears to be exactly the same information that Leibniz claimed is derivable in some fashion from the strict complete concept of *each* individual substance in a world. How can that be? The doctrine of universal expression is the answer—if Leibniz offered one in our period.

The doctrine of universal expression is discussed in section 5 of chapter 7. It will be clear that Leibniz sometimes ascribed considerably more content to universal expression than his arguments appear to warrant. So

I distinguish a weak thesis of universal expression, warranted by the arguments offered, from a strong thesis of universal expression. The weak thesis amounts to this: let x and y be individual substances in some world W; let p be some truth about y; then there is some property f such that x has f and p is derivable from the proposition that x has f. Treating weak universal expression as a triviality, we might think of f as the property of being such that p. When expression is treated in this fashion as a mere triviality, the charge of concept packing may be avoided only by ascribing a strong thesis about intrinsic foundations to Leibniz.

The strong thesis of intrinsic foundations is this:

> For any individual substance x and property f, if x has f, then there is a set of properties A such that: (a) x has every property in A, and (b) every property in A is a primitive intrinsic denomination, and (c) x's having f is reducible to x's having every property in A.

The contrast between the weak and strong theses of intrinsic foundations may be illustrated by an example. Suppose some substance a bears relation R to another substance b. According to the weak thesis there are sets of intrinsic denominations F and G such that a has every member of F, b has every member of G, and the proposition that aRb is reducible to the proposition that a has every member of F and b has every member of G—in the sense of reducibility previously described. Let f be the relational property of bearing R to b. Under our present supposition, a has it. According to the strong thesis of intrinsic foundations (but not the weak thesis), there must be a set of intrinsic denominations A such that the proposition that a has f is reducible to the proposition that a has every member of A. The weak version of expression ensures that full information about all the created substances in a world is encoded into the relational properties of every substance in that world. The strong thesis of intrinsic foundations then guarantees that the information contained in a world description is contained in the strict complete individual concept of each created substance of the world described.

Should we ascribe the strong thesis to Leibniz? The passages previously quoted concerning his denial of purely extrinsic denominations might be read as supporting the strong thesis. A fundamental question would concern whether Leibniz held that each open sentence in one free variable x satisfied by a given object, but *not* expressing an intrinsic denomination of it, expressed an extrinsic denomination of that object. I do not believe that texts from our time period settle that question. On the other hand, Leibniz's actual practice, exhibited in various proposed analyses of relational propositions, suggests otherwise. As noted previously, the idea of the proposed analyses is to reduce a proposition of the form aRb to the conjunction of a proposition attributing intrinsic denominations to a and a similar proposition about b. There is simply no hint that Leibniz then envisaged a yet deeper analysis to a proposition attributing intrinsic denominations to a alone.

All things considered, it seems to me that the weak thesis of intrinsic foundations is Leibniz's doctrine of choice in this area. I believe that at times he combined it with a strong form of the doctrine of universal expression— one attributing at least low-level cognition of its world to each substance in a world—thereby providing materials for a response to the charge of concept packing. A problem remains, of course, concerning his warrant for the strong form of universal expression. These issues will be taken up again in section 5 of chapter 7.

6. THE STRUCTURE OF CONCEPTS: ESSENCE, NATURE, AND ACCIDENT

In section 5 we concentrated on the contents of strict complete concept. In this section we consider the structure of complete concepts, strict or flabby. Around 1711, Leibniz gave an extremely useful account of his differences with Malebranche's conception of substance. In one of his few successful ventures into the dialogue form, *Conversation of Philarete and Ariste, following a Conversation of Ariste and Theodore*, Leibniz wrote: "One can distinguish three degrees among predicates: the essential, the natural, and what is simply accidental" (G/6/584 [L 621]). The same tripartite distinction may be found in *Theodicy* §§383–390. Although the terminology is used in an unstable way, the same distinctions occur in our time period. We have already noted the distinction between the necessary (essential) and the contingent (accidental) in *De libertate, fato, gratia Dei.*[70] Hence, we need to say something about the distinction between the complete concept of a substance and its nature, as the distinction is drawn in *DM* §16, in order to account for the third "degree" of predicates, the natural.

The doctrine of superintrinsicalness ensures that every property of a substance is included in some sense in its concept. But, according to the *Discourse on Metaphysics*, not every property of a substance need be in its nature, where the nature of a substance is characterized in terms of what it brings about through its own limited force. "What is limited in us could be called our nature or our power, and in this regard what surpasses the natures of all created substances is supernatural" (*DM* §16). If we put this passage together with earlier remarks in the *Discourse* concerning miracles and subordinate maxims, we could come away with the wrong result. In *DM* §16 Leibniz noted that miracles are "above subordinate maxims"; and, in *DM* §7, Leibniz contrasted miracles with "natural operations, so-called because they are in conformity with certain subordinate maxims that we call the nature of things." These quotations, particularly the last, suggest that the nature of a thing is simply the sum of its natural operations, which, in turn, are simply whatever operations of the thing are in accordance with what we independently determine to be the correct natural laws, that is, the correct subordinate maxims. In this sense, even Malebranche was prepared to admit natural operations, and so, natures.[71]

Leibniz meant something entirely different and metaphysically potent—

natures which are primitive forces, hence real causes, in created substances. Natural operations are then construed as the results of the activity of the primitive forces in created substances; and natural laws are construed as generalizations that are true of created substances in virtue of their natural operations. This is the doctrine of *DM* §16. The concept of the miraculous, as what exceeds the powers of created entities, occurs in Leibniz's letter of 30 April (LA 93), and is therein presented as a definition. It is similarly presented in *Theodicy* §207 and *New Essays* 65–66. However, Leibniz's characterization of the natural, as a type or "degree" of predicate, does not include every property of a substance that depends upon its nature; the latter would include every contingent property of a substance, except those whose exemplification by the substance in question is miraculous. Leibniz's notion of the natural—as a type of property—is more circumscribed than that. Roughly speaking, on Leibniz's characterization, a property *f* is natural to a given substance *x* just in case it would be miraculous (that is, contrary to its nature) were a member of the species to which *x* belongs to lack *f*.

The distinctions involved here are basic to Leibniz's scheme. I believe he held fast to these distinctions even though he subsequently rode roughshod over the terminology in which they are formulated here. Even in the texts within our time period, Leibniz employed the relevant terminology in a loose way. After the careful distinction between a substance's concept and its nature in *DM* §16, matters degenerate even in the correspondence with Arnauld. Surely the low watermark is contained in a draft for the letter of 8 December 1686, where Leibniz asserted: "The soul being an individual substance, it is necessary that its *concept, idea, essence* or *nature* envelope everything that is to happen to it" (LA 68–69; emphasis mine).

In summary, I see Leibniz drawing a traditional distinction between the essential (necessary) properties of an individual substance and its contingent (broadly construed, accidental) properties. Within the latter class and relative to individual substances of a given species, there is a further distinction between properties that are natural to substances of that species and properties that are not.

Those who believe that Leibniz accepted superessentialism view matters differently, of course. They are likely to point to numerous passages in which Leibniz connected essential properties with perpetual properties. As noted previously, I agree that Leibniz held that only perpetual properties are essential properties. He may have held that all perpetual properties of a substance are essential to a substance, although that seems less clear.[72] On occasion he may even have used "essential property" as synonymous with "perpetual property." But it seems quite clear to me that in *De contingentia* (see especially Grua 303), *De libertate, fato, gratia Dei*, and *De libertate creaturae et electione divina*, and in the correspondence with Arnauld, where a problem generating much of the steam concerns freedom, divine and human, Leibniz had a modal distinction in mind. Whether he was entitled to the distinctions he sought is another matter.

In "Leibniz and the Doctrine of Inter-World Identity," Fabrizio Mondadori notes that in some cases Leibniz's distinction between essential and accidental properties may be given a temporal interpretation. But he agrees that the temporal interpretation is not a plausible rendering of many of the passages from the *Discourse* and the correspondence, among others. With respect to these, Mondadori takes a "reductionist" reading.[73] Thus, he suggests that at LA 52—where Leibniz offered the sub ratione generalitatis account—what we have is a distinction between accidental and essential properties that just amounts to a distinction between what does and what does not depend on a species in certain ways, and hence, in and by itself, has no modal significance whatever. He concludes his penetrating discussion thus: "The fact that there are passages in Leibniz's writings where the distinction between essential (i.e., relating to a species) and accidental properties is mentioned and used, is no evidence against my claim that the theory of complete concepts entails that all of a given individual's properties are essential to him; nor is it evidence that Leibniz thought otherwise."[74]

Certainly it is not evidence against the first-mentioned claim; perhaps, in and by itself, it is not conclusive evidence for the claim "that Leibniz thought otherwise." But when we examine the contexts in which formulation of the distinction occurs, at least those provided by texts from our period, it is abundantly clear that establishing that there are connections that are "intrinsic but not necessary," in order to preserve freedom of action, is the main point of the distinction developed therein between accidental and essential connections.

7. THE POSSIBLE-IN-ITS-OWN-NATURE DEFENSE

In the next two sections we consider two strategies that Leibniz employed to account for freedom and contingency. Neither occurs prominently in the *Discourse* or the correspondence, although reference to each may be read into what is said there. They are the possible-in-its-own-nature defense and the doctrine of infinite analysis.

The possible-in-its-own-nature defense is a centerpiece of Leibniz's efforts to preserve contingency and divine freedom in the *Confessio*. We consider it briefly. In *Theodicy* §288 Leibniz presented his classic, mature analysis of freedom. According to that analysis, freedom "consists in intelligence, which involves a clear knowledge of the object of deliberation, in spontaneity, whereby we determine, and in contingency, that is, in the exclusion of logical or metaphysical necessity." We might, then, characterize Leibniz's mature conception of freedom in the following way:

1. Agent A freely brings it about that state of affairs *e* obtains, just in case agent A brings it about that *e* obtains, and
   (i) A understands *e* and its alternatives; and

(ii) the source of the action whereby A brings it about that *e* obtains is internal to A; and

(iii) it is metaphysically possible that *e* not obtain.

The "possible-in-its-own-nature defense" involves an alteration in this conception of a free action; for clause (iii) in the definition, it substitutes the following:

(iii') It is possible in its own nature that *e* not obtain.

Without aiming for more precision than the subject permits, we might characterize the notion of "possible in its own nature" thus:

2. State of affairs *e* is possible in its own nature just in case there is no set of sentences S (in a sufficiently rich language) such that:
   (i) every sentence in S expresses a proposition that is metaphysically necessary; and
   (ii) no sentence in S contains a device of singular reference referring to some individual not referred to by the devices of singular reference in sentences expressing the proposition that *e* obtains; and
   (iii) the conjunction of the sentences in S with a sentence expressing the proposition that *e* obtains formally implies a formal contradiction.

By contrast, we might characterize garden-variety metaphysical possibility with respect to the obtaining of a state of affairs by simply deleting condition (ii) from our characterization of possibility in its own nature. Although our primary concern is the relation of these modal notions to freedom of action (hence, our concern with states of affairs), there is an obvious and direct extension to a distinction between metaphysical possibility and possibility in its own nature as applied to propositions. Note that whereas metaphysical possibility implies possibility in its own nature, the converse fails. Necessity in its own nature implies metaphysical necessity, but the converse fails. We should note the following: the inference from ⌜it is metaphysically necessary that if p then q⌝ conjoined with ⌜it is metaphysically necessary that p⌝ to ⌜it is metaphysically necessary that q⌝ is a good inference; it gives a case in which necessity of the consequence yields necessity of the consequent. But the inference from ⌜it is metaphysically necessary that if p then q⌝ conjoined with ⌜it is necessary in its own nature that p⌝ to ⌜it is necessary in its own nature that q⌝ is not a valid inference. That it is not a valid inference played a crucial role in Leibniz's first effort to satisfy Arnauld on the matter of freedom and contingency, the *Confessio philosophi*, first drafted in 1673.

In the *Confessio* Leibniz had his opponent say: "What will you respond to the argument . . . that the existence of God is necessary; these sins contained in the series of things follow from this existence; what follows from the necessary, is necessary? Therefore, sins are necessary" (A/6/3/127). Consider Leibniz's reply (the material in corners was added subsequent to 1673 and prior to 1683): "I reply that it is false that whatever follows from what is necessary ⟨through itself⟩ is necessary ⟨through itself⟩. Indeed it is evident that from truths nothing follows except what is true. Since nevertheless a particular can follow from purely universal propositions, as in Darapti and Felapton, why could not something contingent ⟨i.e., something necessary on the hypothesis of something else⟩ follow from what is necessary ⟨through itself⟩?" (A/6/3/127–128). The same strategy appears to be at work in *De libertate*, an important work from our time period.[75] Leibniz there considered this objection: God chooses the best of necessity. The world that is the best, is so of necessity. Therefore, it is necessary that if God chooses any world, he chooses this world. Hence, God's choice is not free. He responded that a world not chosen "remains possible in its own nature, even if it is not possible with respect to the divine will, because we define as possible in its own nature what in itself does not imply a contradiction, even if its coexistence with God can be said in some way to imply a contradiction."[76] Utilizing clause (iii′) rather than (iii) in the account of a free action, Leibniz argued that God's choice is free because he chooses among worlds possible in their own nature.

Once one is onto this strategy, it may seem to appear throughout Leibniz's writings. Consider, for example, the following from *DM* §13, where, considering Caesar's crossing the Rubicon, Leibniz wrote: "It was reasonable and consequently assured that this would happen, but . . . it is not necessary *in itself*, nor does the contrary imply a contradiction. In almost the same way as it is reasonable and assured that God always does the best, although that which is less perfect does not imply a contradiction [*in itself*]" (emphasis mine).[77]

In his marvelous study of the possible-in-its-own-nature defense, Robert Adams says that it constitutes "the innermost and surest bastion of Leibniz's defenses against the denial of contingency."[78] Adams sees Leibniz as holding onto this defense throughout his career. I have some minor reservations. No doubt the defense is a leading strategy in the *Confessio*; perhaps, it is central in other theological works in the period 1673–1683, such as *De libertate*. But once Leibniz convinced himself of the benefits of the doctrine of infinite analysis, it is not clear to me that he continued to subscribe to the possible in-its-own-nature defense. True, the linguistic items associated with the defense persist, such as "in its own nature" and "through itself." But in most such cases it strikes me as plausible to suppose that Leibniz was eschewing the possible-in-its-own-nature defense—hence, utilizing clause (iii) rather (iii′) in the account of free action. In the passages where Leibniz used the expressions "in its own nature," "through itself," and so on, he was simply warning us that when we consider whether it is metaphysically possible (in the garden-variety sense) that a state of affairs *e* does not obtain, we must not import any contingent considerations into our inquiry. The warning would be: when we consider whether the proposition "state of affairs *e* does not obtain" is possible, by seeing whether, when conjoined with elements of some set S, it yields a contradiction, we must take care that the elements of S are all metaphysically necessary. That is, we must take care that no contingent propositions have been imported into the deliberations; that we are considering *e*, and not some more complicated state of affairs— just *e* "in its own nature," in an utterly nontechnical sense of those words.

This warning would be particularly relevant to the kinds of cases under study, if one holds that the proposition "God chooses what is best" is contingent. Consider the following from *Theodicy* §235:

> When one speaks of the possibility of a thing, it is not a question of causes that are capable of bringing about or preventing its actual existence: otherwise one would change the nature of the terms, and one would render useless the distinction between the possible and the actual. . . . That is why, when one asks if a thing is possible or necessary, and one brings in there the consideration of what God wills or chooses, one changes the question. For God chooses among the possibles, and it is for that reason that he chooses freely and that he is not necessitated. There would be neither choice nor liberty, if there were only a single course possible.

The context here is one in which we have been explicitly told that the proposition that God chooses the best is morally necessary, but not metaphysically necessary (§234). Hence, it seems to me that §235 (and many similar passages in *Theodicy*) may consist in a quite humdrum (but correct) warning: when considering whether state of affairs *e* is possible, consider just that state of affairs; do not shift to an enlarged state of affairs by importing contingent considerations into the inquiry. In fairness, it should be noted that some of the paragraphs in the vicinity of *Theodicy* §234 make it sound as if the possible-in-its-own-nature strategy were being employed to justify Leibniz's claim that God's choice of the best is only morally necessary. Were Leibniz to have no other strategy available, then the possible-in-its-own-nature strategy would be more central to his mature thought than I am suggesting. But Leibniz had an alternative available.

The defense with which Leibniz was most enamored in our period is not the possible-in-its-own-nature defense, nor the free decree defense of the correspondence, but rather the defense implicit in the doctrine of infinite analysis. It is the subject of the next section.

8. INFINITE ANALYSIS

Leibniz's best-known effort to bring about Protestant-Catholic reunion commenced after the correspondence with Arnauld ended. The effort is exhibited in two sets of correspondence, one with Pellisson, the other with Bossuet. On 6 August 1692, Leibniz wrote to Pellisson: "For a long time I had doubts whether there was a way to preserve contingency, and to avoid the necessity of events, since in fact every event is determined by a priori reasons. But finally I . . . saw how these reasons incline without necessitating and that contingency is something in metaphysics that corresponds to incommensurables in geometry" (A/1/8/158). Reference to the alleged analogy between contingency in metaphysics and incommensurables in geometry is the cue that the doctrine Leibniz had in mind, the doctrine that seemed to him "to lead to the source of things," is the doctrine of infinite analysis.[79] Indeed, Leibniz wrote a paper in which the analogy between contingency and incommensurable proportions is displayed in parallel columns. Its title is *The Origin of Contingent Truths from an Infinite Process, Compared with the Example of Proportions between Incommensurable Quantities.*[80] The basic idea in the case of proportions is clear. Leibniz had in mind Euclid's well-known algorithm for determining the greatest common divisor of two numbers, where there is such, that is, where the numbers are commensurable.[81]

The strategy is outlined in *Specimen*, where equally strong claims for it are made:

> There is an essential difference between necessary or eternal truths, and truths of fact or contingent truths, and they differ from one another much in the way that rational numbers and surds differ. For necessary truths can be resolved into identical truths, just as commensurable quantities can be resolved into a common measure; but in the case of contingent truths, as in the case of surds, the resolution proceeds to infinity and is never terminated. Therefore, the certitude and perfect reason of contingent truths is known only to God, who grasps the infinite in a single intuition. When this secret is known, the difficulty concerning the absolute necessity of all things is removed and the difference between the infallible and the necessary is clear. (G/7/309 [MP 75])

This passage is typical of the vast majority of passages in which Leibniz expressed the doctrine of infinite analysis. The distinction between necessary and contingent truths is said to be this: necessary truths can be reduced to identicals by a process of concept-analysis; contingent truths can not. In the case of contingent truths, every concept-analysis "proceeds to infinity and is never terminated." But, of course, that applies to contingent falsehoods as well as contingent truths. So one problem such passages leave unresolved is Leibniz's characterization of the distinction between contingent truth and contingent falsehood. Leibniz framed that distinction in terms of an analogy with the behavior of the Euclidean algorithm, when applied to numbers whose greatest common divisor is irrational, such as the square root of 2. In that case the Euclidean algorithm yields a sequence of numbers that approaches the square root of 2 as its limit. The analogy is drawn in most detail in the working draft, *General Inquires about the Analysis of Concepts and Truths*, where Leibniz wrote:

> A true necessary proposition can be proved by reduction to identicals. . . .

A true contingent proposition cannot be reduced to identicals; nevertheless, it is proved by showing that an analysis continued further and further approaches identicals, yet never reaches them. Therefore, it is God alone, who grasps the entire infinite in his mind, who knows the certainty of all contingent truths.

So the distinction between necessary and contingent truths is the same as that between lines which meet and asmyptotes, or commensurable and incommensurable numbers. (C 388 [P 77])[82]

In trying to come to grips with Leibniz's thought, it is useful to distinguish three different entities to which he referred, more or less indifferently, as "proofs," namely, reductions to identicals, nonterminating proof-sequences, and meta-proofs.[83] Let us concentrate our attention (as Leibniz so often did) on propositions that are categorical, affirmative, and either universal or singular. Think of a proposition p (of this variety) as an ordered pair whose first term is the subject concept of p and whose second term is the predicate concept of p; we may think of the concepts involved as sets of properties. On this construal, an identical proposition is an ordered pair whose terms are sets of properties, where the second term is a subset of the first. Leibniz thought of complex concepts as arising from simple concepts by property conjunction; thus, analysis of a concept may be construed as a step-by-step decomposition of that concept into simpler components. An analysis of a proposition p is a sequence of ordered pairs, the first term of which is p, with each subsequent pair just like its predecessor except that one concept is replaced by a set that constitutes a one-step analysis of it. Finally, we may say that such a sequence constitutes a reduction of p to an identity, provided that it commences with p and terminates with an identical proposition. The sequence just described may be thought of as existing as a set-theoretical entity, independent of whether any created mind ever thinks of it. In *Primary Truths* 518 (MP 87), such a reduction to identicals is identified with an a priori proof. In numerous pre-infinite analysis texts, Leibniz held that a proposition is true just in case it has an a priori proof in this sense, that is, is reducible (in a finite number of steps) to identicals.[84]

Once the doctrine of infinite analysis was in hand, Leibniz viewed reduction to identicals as the defining characteristic of necessary truths.[85] Thereafter, when Leibniz heeded his terminology carefully, reduction to identicals was called a *demonstration*, and Leibniz was careful to note that only necessary truths have demonstrations.[86]

Using the same machinery as we associated with a reduction to identicals, we may formulate Leibniz's main claim about contingent truth thus: If p is contingent and true, then there is no sequence S constituting a reduction of p to some identical, but there is some sequence S', commencing with p, such that items in S' successively approach some identical proposition as a limit.

Obviously, "approach some identical proposition as a limit" is metaphorical. Unfortunately, Leibniz offered little by way of explanation. It seems to me that the idea involved must be something like this: we assume that with each concept C we may associate its ultimate decomposition set, UC, containing all and only the primitive properties conjoined to form C. Suppose, further, that some ultimate decomposition sets are infinite. Consider some true contingent proposition p, with subject concept C_s and predicate concept C_p, that is, $p = \langle C_s, C_p \rangle$. Now consider $q = \langle UC_s, UC_p \rangle$. I take it that Leibniz's idea was that q is an identical proposition which the items in the proof-sequence for p continuously approach, as the relevant concepts, C_s and C_p, are analyzed.[87] Call such a sequence a nonterminating proof-sequence for p. As in the case of reduction to identicals, the proof-sequence associated with some contingent truth should be thought of as existing independently of created minds.

In *On Freedom*, Leibniz displayed his high regard for the doctrine of infinite analysis: "I saw that it is common to all true affirmative propositions—universal or singular, necessary or contingent—that the predicate is in the subject, i.e., that the concept of the predicate is in some manner involved in the concept of the subject. . . . But this seemed to increase the difficulty. . . . A new and unexpected light arose finally in a quarter from which I least hoped for it, namely, out of mathematical considerations of the nature of the infinite" (FC 179–180 [MP 107]). The light led Leibniz to claim that a proposition p (of the relevant variety) is true just in case the concept of its predicate is included in the concept of its subject; that is, just in case there is some identical proposition q such that either p is reducible to q or there is a nonterminating sequence commencing with p, whose limit is q. In the first case, p is a necessary truth; in the latter case, a contingent truth.

We would like more information about the notion of analysis involved, and about the notion of a nonterminating proof-sequence approaching a proposition as a limit. Leibniz was concerned with a different problem, whose elucidation is facilitated by the notion of a meta-proof. By a meta-proof of p, I mean a proof, in the usual informal sense, either that some sequence is a reduction of p to an identity, or that some sequence is a nonterminating proof-sequence for p, with some identity as its limit. The only proviso I want to add is that the information utilized in a meta-proof of p be restricted to a priori, conceptual information pertaining to the concepts that are subject and predicate concepts of p. The intention here is that a meta-proof of p yield a priori knowledge of p to anyone in possession of the proof.[88] In the case of a reduction to an identity, the notion of a meta-proof is of little significance, since the meta-proof can be a sequence of words exactly reflecting the sequence of sets of properties making up the reduction. But a meta-proof, being a proof in the usual informal sense, must be of finite length; hence, it cannot bear this one-to-one relationship to a nonterminating proof sequence.

Now we are in position to formulate Leibniz's problem in this area. In *General Inquiries*, after noting that necessary truths are related to contingent truths in the way commensurable numbers are related to incommensurable numbers, Leibniz wrote: "But a difficulty stands before us. We are able to demonstrate that some line, namely an asymptote, constantly approaches some other line . . . by showing what will be the case if the progression is continued as far as one pleases. Therefore, human beings will be able to comprehend contingent truths with certainty. But it must be replied that there is indeed a likeness, but there is not complete agreement" (C 388–389 [P 77–78]). The difficulty that stands before us, then, is that there are meta-proofs in mathematics that certain nonterminating sequences are convergent. The analogy, on which Leibniz based his doctrine, suggests that there will be meta-proofs of contingent truths. So what is the problem? Consider three basic theses to which Leibniz was committed:

1. Truth may be characterized in terms of concept containment.
2. The distinction between necessary truths and contingent truths is metaphysical and absolute, not epistemological or relative.
3. For any finite mind S, S knows a proposition to be true a priori only if that proposition is a necessary truth.[89]

The doctrine of infinite analysis allowed Leibniz to hold (1) and (2) jointly. The analogy on which the doctrine is based threatens the joint consistency of (1), (2), and (3). If there were meta-proofs of contingent propositions, then finite minds might thereby gain a priori knowledge of contingent truths. Leibniz wrestled with this problem in the *General Inquiries*. His conclusion seems to be that just here the analogy with incommensurables breaks down—that there are no meta-proofs of contingent truths. In subsequent texts in which Leibniz discussed the question, his opinion seems firm—no meta-proofs of contingent truths.[90]

We have seen that the doctrine of infinite analysis provided Leibniz with a mechanism for denying proposition (4) of section (3) above—"Necessarily, C_{Adam} includes the property of having posterity"—and, more generally, for denying that whatever properties are included in any concept are included necessarily. It thereby provided him a mechanism for countering Arnauld's major argument against his position. Leibniz also employed infinite analysis to meet another threat to freedom and contingency, noted in chapter 1. The argument in question is this: it is necessary that if God chooses to create a world, then he chooses the best, but whatever world is the best, is so of necessity. Let that world be A. Then it is necessary that if God chooses to create a world, then God chooses to create A. So God has no choice among worlds; at most, he has the choice not to create at all. In *De contingentia* (Grua 305–306) and in his reading notes on Denis Petau's *Theologica dogmata*, Leibniz rejected this argument, asserting that "this proposition—"A is the best"—is certain, but it is not necessary, because it cannot be demonstrated" (Grua 336). The context in *De contingentia* makes it clear that the doctrine of infinite analysis is the key here as well.

The doctrine of infinite analysis provided Leibniz with a mechanism for countering Arnauld's major argument, but it is not the mechanism employed in the correspondence. Indeed, on the basis of the correspondence through 14 July 1686 when debate closed on the topic of freedom and contingency, I doubt that Leibniz was then in possession of the doctrine. Since apparently he was in possession of it sometime in 1686, a good conjecture would be that it came to him as a result of ruminating on the debate with Arnauld after July 1686. The unpublished draft for the short letter of 14 July 1686 is particularly revealing. At LBr 68–68v, Leibniz asserted that every true proposition has an a priori proof—that is, every true proposition can be reduced to identicals via conceptual analysis. Nonetheless, he claimed, "Contingent truths do not have demonstrations, properly speaking, but they must have their a priori proofs" (LBr 68v).

The text suggests that what distinguishes a demonstration from an a priori proof is that a demonstration makes no appeal to free decrees of any mind, divine or created. The text also suggests that a priori proofs of contingent truths elude created minds because of their complexity, thus seeming to make the distinction between necessary and contingent truths epistemological and relative. By Leibniz's lights, the doctrine of infinite analysis puts these matters right. Apparently, Leibniz was in possession of the doctrine prior to the termination of the correspondence with Arnauld. Why, then, did he not expound it to Arnauld? My conjecture is that by the time Leibniz had confidence in the doctrine of infinite analysis, he already had what he took to be Arnauld's concession on the matter of freedom and contingency. If we carefully distinguish what is strictly asserted in the *Discourse* and correspondence concerning freedom and contingency from what is only suggested, then nothing that is strictly asserted in the *Discourse* or the letters sent to Arnauld is inconsistent with the doctrine of infinite analysis.[91] So Leibniz had nothing to take back. And, perhaps, at this point diplomatic considerations set in. The doctrine expounded in the *Discourse* and correspondence rests contingency ultimately in God's will; the doctrine of infinite analysis purports to go deeper, providing a metaphysical basis for contingency, thereby allowing a noncircular account of the sense in which God's will is free. My guess is that Leibniz knew that Arnauld would not be attracted to these features of Leibniz's new doctrine. So at this point he decided to leave well enough alone.

The doctrine of infinite analysis has its problems. It is difficult to locate the substance behind the metaphors employed to express it. Moreover, it is difficult to grasp how Leibniz could have seen it as providing a deep account of the distinction between necessary and contingent truths. These difficulties, coupled with the apparent paucity of references to the doctrine in texts from later in Leibniz's career, have suggested to some that his reliance on the doctrine was fleeting. Wishful thinking, in my opinion. Note that the quotation from the letter to Pellisson at the beginning of this section is dated 1692. It contains a clear reference to the doctrine of infinite analysis. So does a passage from an appendix to the *Theodicy*: "If, when analyzing a truth, one sees that it depends on truths whose contrary implies a contradiction, it can be said that it is absolutely necessary. But when, carrying out the analysis as far as you please, you would never arrive at such elements of the given truth, it must be said that it is contingent" (G/6/414; Huggard's translation of the *Theodicy*, p. 419). Leibniz expressed essentially the same point in a letter to Louis Bourguet in August 1715, during the last year of his life.[92] The evidence is that Leibniz's commitment to the doctrine of infinite analysis was long-term.

9. ARNAULD'S CONCESSION

The point of this section is twofold: first, to investigate some of the considerations in favor of superintrinsicalness that may be found in our primary texts; second, to ponder Arnauld's apparent conversion to the concept-containment account of truth, as expressed in his letter of 28 September 1686 (LA 63–64).

Leibniz, although a genius at devising logical systems and locating subtle logical errors in the arguments of his fellow philosophers, was not given to clear formulations of arguments for his own metaphysical conclusions. Superintrinsicalness—the doctrine that each substance has all its basic properties intrinsically—fits the pattern. Various items, or lines of reasoning, scattered about our texts point in its direction. In this section we will review some of these items, leaving the most enigmatic, but perhaps the most fecund, to section 3 of chapter 6.[93]

It may seem that the natural place to look for an argument for the ubiquity of intrinsic connections is the argument based on the concept-containment account of truth. Leibniz said as much in our primary texts: *DM* §8, the draft for the long letter of 14 July (LA 46), the long letter itself (LA 56 and 57), and the draft for the short letter of 14 July (LBr 68v). But here we must take care. We are assuming that assignments of concepts to entities are mediated by initial assignments of concepts to linguistic entities in the rational language—a language devoid of singular terms referring to nonsubstances. In the rational language, then, all sentences expressing categorical affirmative singular propositions, predicate some property of a substance. The claim that such a proposition is true, according to the concept-containment account of truth, just *is* the claim that the relevant substance has the relevant property intrinsically. There is no room for one to explain the other, unless we can provide independent motivation for superintrinsicalness or for the concept-containment account of truth.

We might, then, look for motivations that led Leibniz to a general account of truth, based on concept containment, which, when applied to singular propositions, yields the result that each substance has all its properties intrinsically. Surely, Leibniz's own statements suggest that this was his course. As a general theory of truth, the concept-containment account of truth clearly is in need of motivation. Powerful motivation certainly would have been required to convince Arnauld. I argued in section (3) of chapter 3 that Arnauld had no commitment to the concept-containment account of truth prior to the correspondence with Leibniz. Many of the most astute interpreters of Leibniz have recommended that commitment to the principle of sufficient reason is the ultimate source of Leibniz's theory of truth. For example, Fabrizio Mondadori has argued that "on the one hand, the definition of truth as containment 'vindicates' the principle of sufficient reason (for the latter . . . follows from the former in an obvious way), on the other hand Leibniz's definition of truth as containment is ultimately motivated by Leibniz's adherence to the principle of sufficient reason."[94] Mondadori's recommendation is an improvement on Couturat's effort to motivate Leibniz's commitment to the concept-containment account of truth in terms of the principle of sufficient reason.[95] My basic problem with the Couturat-Mondadori approach is that unless we concoct a version of the principle of sufficient reason specifically designed to fit the concept-containment account of truth, there will be a variety of theories of truth that yield the principle of sufficient reason. That principle, in its intuitive form, is inadequate to motivate a specific theory of truth.[96] It should also be noted that an argument based on the principle of sufficient reason would probably not have moved Arnauld.[97]

I think we are moving in the wrong direction. It seems to me more plausible to suppose that commitment to superintrinsicalness motivated Leibniz's acceptance of the concept-containment account of truth than vice versa. We would then view Leibniz as engaging in a deep metaphysical analysis of the nature of a continuant—a substance that endures through time—and its relation to its properties, an analysis that demonstrates that each substance has all its properties intrinsically. Given the then standard account of what it is for a given concept to be the concept of a given entity (abstraction or individual), superintrinsicalness and the concept-containment account of truth, when applied to singular propositions, come to the same thing.[98] Leibniz then set out to generalize the notion of truth to categorical propositions other than singulars. The generalization did not come easily. We may take for granted various simplifying devices associated with the rational language. Still, the slogan "An affirmative categorical proposition is true just in case the concept of its subject includes the concept of its predicate" fits in only a narrow range of cases without qualification. Consider:

1. Peter denies Christ.
2. All humans are animals.

These cases work out satisfactorily. That is, the concept-containment account yields the right truth value. Now consider:

3. Pegasus is a winged horse.
4. All humans are mortal.

Utilizing our slogan version of the concept-containment account of truth, and assignments of concepts to entities of which Leibniz would approve, (3) turns out true and (4) false. In *General Inquiries* Leibniz noted a distinction between essential and existential interpretations of sentences.[99] Consider:

3'. Pegasus exists and Pegasus is a winged horse.
3". If Pegasus exists, then Pegasus is a winged horse.

Proposition (3") is the essential reading of (3); (3') is the existential reading. Clearly, the concept containment account of truth, at least in its slogan form, is made to order for the essential, not the existential, reading of singulars. The essential reading is restricted to the *connection* of the substance (possible or actual) and some alleged property thereof. It simply says that the connection is intrinsic. Similarly with respect to the universals, (2) and (4), the slogan version interprets them essentially as referring to all possible humans, thereby making (4), so read, false. But suppose we want it to come out true, when read existentially—that is, read as a claim about all existent humans, rather than about all possible humans. That requires some manipulation.[100] I do not claim that appropriate adjustments cannot be made. My point is that the guiding intuition provided by the concept-containment account of truth seems to peter out when we move beyond the supposed intrinsic connection between property and substance; thereafter, we are making required adjustments. And bear in mind that we have concentrated on the most straightforward cases.

Consider next:

5. Some humans are saved.

There is the usual matter of a distinction between existential and essential readings. On neither does it come out true, when the slogan is applied.[101] Considerable manipulation is required in this case to state an acceptable truth definition, formulated with respect to concept containment. I do not claim that it cannot be done; my point is the same as above: the guiding intuition is not a general account of truth, but rather a metaphysical analysis of substances and their relations to their properties. Some of the writings from the *Catholic Demonstrations* clearly indicate Leibniz's enduring concern with the relation of a substance to its attributes, for example, *De transsubtantione* (1668), *Confessio naturae contra atheistas* (1668), and *De incarnatione Dei seu de unione hypostatica* (1669–1670). These same writings employ principles of the sort that I ascribe to Leibniz in section 3 of chapter 6, in order to account for his commitment to superintrinsicalness.[102]

Leaving aside the enigmatic passage at LA 53, three lines of reasoning favoring superintrinsicalness surface in the correspondence, each of which appears initially to lack plausibility. I will review them before considering Arnauld's concession.

1. Leibniz carefully considered the question whether the world might have

been different. In notes on a discussion with Gabriel Wagner, Leibniz said that he preferred to put this in terms of a different world being actual.[103] Leibniz made the point explicitly in *Theodicy* §9: "Nothing can be changed in the world (no more than in a number) except its essence, or, if you will, except its numerical individuality. Thus, if the least evil that occurs in the world were lacking, it would no longer be this world." In other words, Leibniz held that each internal feature of a possible world is intrinsic to that world. There are numerous passages where Leibniz seemed to assume casually that, in the matter of alternatives, what holds for worlds, holds for individuals in worlds. Consider the following from the long letter of 14 July: "Moreover, if in the life of some person, and even in this entire universe, something were to go otherwise than the way it went, nothing would prevent us from saying that it would be another person or another possible universe that God would have chosen. It would therefore truly be another [individual]" (LA 53 [RL 40]).[104]

On the other hand, the passage just quoted is the lead-in to the enigmatic line of reasoning, mentioned at the beginning of this section, which will be probed in chapter 6. Perhaps, then, Leibniz would insist that the similarity in his treatment of worlds and individuals in worlds, in the respect noted, is anything but casual; he earned it.

2. Leibniz accepted Arnauld's postulate that whatever properties are included in the concept of an individual are intrinsic to that individual. As we have seen, Leibniz insisted on a further postulate—that the properties included in the concept of an individual must suffice to distinguish that individual from every other possible individual.

Let us call a set of properties sufficient to distinguish their exemplifier from all other possible individuals, a haecceity set for that individual.[105] As noted in section 2 above, Leibniz held that for any individual substance x, only the complete concept of x is a haecceity set for x. The problem is to locate Leibniz's reasoning in support of the thesis that *only* the complete concept of an individual will serve as its haecceity set. Generally, what we find is no more than affirmation of the very thesis requiring justification.[106] Perhaps the most detailed statement hinting at an argument may be found in *De liberate, fato, gratia Dei*: "It is of the nature of an individual substance that its concept be perfect and complete and that it contain every individual circumstance, even those that are contingent, even to the least significant. Otherwise it would not be ultimate nor would it be distinguished from all others, for those things that differ, even in the least, will be diverse individuals, and a concept in the least indeterminate will not be ultimate, but can be common to two distinct individuals" (Grua 311).

Doesn't it look as if Leibniz reasoned as follows: Suppose C is a consistent concept, including only primitive properties of individuals. Suppose that for some primitive property f, C entails neither f nor its complement, non-f. Consider, then, $C' = C \cup \{f\}$ and $C'' = C \cup \{\text{non-}f\}$. Both C' and C'' are consistent and composed of primitive properties of individuals. Therefore, there are possible individuals x and y such that x has every property in C′ and y has every property in C″. Now, no object can have both f and non-f. Therefore, $x \neq y$. But both x and y satisfy C, by construction. Hence, no incomplete concept can individuate one individual from all other possible individuals. There is an obvious response to this argument. Perhaps possible objects x and y satisfy both C′ and C″, and yet $x = y$. Of course, if x (that is, y) satisfies both C′ and C″, it must do so in distinct worlds. The argument outlined simply presupposes that this is not a viable alternative. Consider the following non-Leibnizian claim: for each individual substance x, there exists an incomplete concept C such that the set whose members are exactly the properties included in C is a haecceity set for x. That thesis survives.

3. At LA 52, in the long letter of 14 July, Leibniz summarized his position that a substance has all its properties intrinsically, adding the following strident passage: "Since it is certain that I shall take it [a journey to Paris], there must indeed be some connection between me and . . . the journey. . . . A falsity would therefore exist if I did not take it, which would destroy the individual or complete concept of me." Leibniz then wrote the following paragraph, which appeared in Arnauld's copy, but was subsequently struck from Leibniz's.[107] "But without going so far, if it is certain that A is B, whoever is not B, is not A. Therefore, if A signifies me and B signifies whoever will take this journey, it can be concluded that whoever will not take this journey is not me. And this conclusion can be drawn from the single certainty of my future journey, without it being necessary to ascribe it to my proposition" (RL 39).

The reasoning here is impeccable. But surely it crosses the mind (and must have crossed Arnauld's mind) that Leibniz may (however briefly) have confused this impeccable reasoning with the following peccant reasoning: "Suppose A is B, then whoever is not B, is not A. Therefore, if A signifies me, and B signifies whoever will take this journey, then, for any y whatever, were y not B, then y would not be A. Hence, were I not to take this journey, then I would not be me. Therefore, I have the property of taking this journey intrinsically."

We are now in a position to examine Arnauld's apparent concession. My hypothesis is that Arnauld was not in the least persuaded to change his mind in any significant way in virtue of Leibniz's long letter of 14 July— the letter prompting the apparent concession. My hypothesis (undoubtedly unverifiable) is that Arnauld saw what we have seen—that Leibniz wished to uncouple superessentialism from superintrinsicalness. With respect to the relevant de re modal distinctions—that is, between the contingent and the necessary properties of individuals—Arnauld saw that his own intuitions matched those of Leibniz. Furthermore, from the letters he received, Arnauld would have concluded that Leibniz wished to insist on God's freedom just where he too insisted on it.

But Arnauld believed that superintrinsicalness implies superessentialism, which, in turn, is inconsistent with aspects of God's freedom. Surely argumentative, abrasive Arnauld would not have let it go at that, if he thought a substantive issue remained. But perhaps he thought that Leibniz's convolutions in the letter of 14 July effectively removed all the substance from his pronouncements on the issues at hand. Consider:

6. For any individual x and property f, if x has f, then, for any y, were y to lack f, then y would not be x.
7. For any individual x and property f, if x has f, then, for any y, if y lacks f, then y is not x.

The passage at RL 39, which was contained in Arnauld's copy of Leibniz's long letter of 14 July, but struck from Leibniz's copy, would have tempted Arnauld to suppose that Leibniz read no more into unacceptable (6) then was in innocent (7)—that Leibniz had squeezed all the juice out of the idea of an intrinsic connection. Hence, when Arnauld applauded Leibniz's truth definition, noting that "the concept of the attribute is in a sense included in that of the subject: the predicate is present in the subject," he took the clause preceding the colon to have no content other than the content of the clause following the colon, and that interpreted in an utterly innocent way.

Both Leibniz and Arnauld were aware that theses about the content of concepts might be construed so as to have implications concerning modality, specifically, possibility, and, hence, possible worlds. Arnauld feared that Leibniz's doctrine might yet lead to heresy, as applied by Leibniz to "this way of conceiving of God as having chosen the universe . . . amongst an infinite number of other possible universes" (LA 64). And so at that point he demurred. At any rate, that is my hypothesis.

Chapter 5

❖❖❖❖❖❖❖❖❖

SUBSTANCE

At the close of the draft for the long letter of 14 July 1686, as well as at the close of the letter itself, Leibniz set out to change the subject—to draw Arnauld's attention to aspects of the *Discourse* other than those bearing on freedom and contingency. In the draft Leibniz focused attention almost exclusively on the hypothesis of concomitance; in the letter itself the hypothesis of concomitance shares the spotlight with Leibniz's theory of corporeal substance, including his commitment to substantial forms. Most of the remainder of the correspondence concerns these two topics. Substance and substantial forms are the topics of chapters 5 and 6; the hypothesis of concomitance is the subject of chapter 7.

There is no doubt that Leibniz thought that the notion of an individual substance is a basic notion in philosophy. Toward the close of his letter of 30 April 1687, the last of his letters to which Arnauld responded, Leibniz wrote: "As long as one will not distinguish what is truly a complete entity or a substance, one will have nothing on which to settle, and that is the only way to establish real, solid principles" (LA 102). Leibniz claimed that the notion of an individual substance had a pivotal place in his own system. Toward the close of the letter of 9 October 1687, to which Arnauld did not respond, Leibniz wrote, with what is surely a hint of impatience: "If you could find the time to look again one day at what we had finally established about the concept of an individual substance, you would find that in conceding me these beginnings, one is obliged subsequently to grant me all the rest" (LA 127).

The *Discourse* and the correspondence with Arnauld are seminal for understanding Leibniz's mature metaphysics, in part because in them Leibniz first worked out in detail his conception of an individual substance and what he took to be its philosophical consequences. In the *Discourse* and the correspondence Leibniz articulated the intension of the term *individual substance* in terms of his various metaphysical theses about the nature of complete entities.[1] These theses remained fixed in his thinking. It is in this sense that our texts provide the basis for his mature philosophy. I believe that the conception of an individual substance brought to fruition in our texts is essentially that of the *Monadology*. Still, there is a marked difference between our texts and the *Monadology*, bearing on the notion of substance. There is a confidence about what things are substances, about the extension of the term *individual substance*, in the *Monadology* that is surely lacking in our texts. In section 1 below, I will outline various accounts of the nature of an individual substance, each consistent with the metaphysical theses mentioned in note 1, and each suggested by some texts taken from the *Discourse*, correspondence, or other texts from our time period. In section 2, I will trace the development in Leibniz's thinking about the nature of an individual substance from the early autograph version of the *Discourse* through the final fair copy version and the correspondence. It will become clear that the correct characterization of Leibniz's final theory of substance in the correspondence turns, in part, on his attitude toward the nature and reality of extension and its principal modes, which is the subject of section 3.

1. THEORIES OF SUBSTANCE

In this section I outline four accounts of substance, consideration of which will prove useful in our examination of Leibniz's views on substance in our time period. The four accounts are: the spiritual theory, the corporeal substance theory, the modified corporeal substance theory, and the monadological theory.[2] I begin with some significant background distinctions.

In the letter of 9 October 1687, in a passage in the margin (which was not sent to Arnauld), Leibniz distinguished between primary and secondary matter: "If one were to understand by the term 'matter' something that is always essential to the same substance, one might in the sense of certain Scholastics understand thereby the primitive passive power of a substance, and in this sense matter would not be extended or divisible, although it would be the principle of divisibility or that which amounts to it in a substance." Just preceding this remark Leibniz had written (in the margin as well): "If one considers as matter of bodily substances . . . a second matter that is the multitude of substances whose mass is that of the total body, it may be said that these substances are parts of this matter" (LA 119–120).[3] These passages occur in a context where Leibniz appeared to take an animal as a good example of a substance, for example, Arnauld. Leibniz regarded Arnauld's body as an aggregate of (other) animals, that is, corporeal substances. Furthermore, Leibniz regarded that aggregate as itself an individual, although not an individual substance. In the case of Arnauld, this aggregate is his secondary matter. On the other hand, Arnauld's primitive passive power—his primary matter—is not an individual at all; it is what Leibniz called an abstraction.

It is crucial, I believe, to see that there is an analogous distinction to be drawn between two ways in which Leibniz used the term *substantial form* (and related terms, such as *soul*). Sometimes these terms were used by Leibniz to refer to an individual, and, indeed, an individual substance. At other times, Leibniz used the same terms to refer to aspects or principles in substances, that is, to abstractions. Under this latter conception, a substantial form (or soul) is construed as an abstract component of a substance, but not itself an individual.[4]

In the *Discourse* and the correspondence, Leibniz struggled to gain clarity on these matters. It is useful to bear in mind a clear statement of the view at which he eventually arrived. Consider this from Leibniz's letter of 20 June 1703 to De Volder: "Therefore, I distinguish (1) the primitive entelechy or soul, (2) primary matter, i.e., primitive passive power, (3) monads completed from these two, (4) mass, i.e., second matter, or the organic machine, in which innumerable subordinate monads come together, (5) the animal, i.e., corporeal substance, which a dominating monad makes into one machine" (G/2/252 [L 530–531]).[5] Here (4) and (2) are, respectively, matter construed as an individual, and matter construed as an abstraction; (3) and (1) are, respectively, the soul (substantial form) construed first as an individual, and then as an abstraction. In his later writings Leibniz often employed separate terms, utilizing *monad* to refer to an individual and *entelechy* to refer to an abstraction.[6] Similarly, in the correspondence the expression *individual substance* is used to refer to a basic individual—a complete being, the ultimate subject of predication. By contrast, the expression *the substance of*———is used to refer to an abstract component of a complete being.[7]

The most careful statement of the relevant distinction in my ken in texts in the vicinity of our time period is contained in a letter of 18 January 1692 to Paul Pellisson, in which Leibniz set out to explain the virtues of his system, as opposed to Descartes's, with respect to the Eucharist.

> The word *substance* is taken in two ways—for the subject itself, and for the essence of the subject. For the subject itself, when it is said that the body or the bread is a substance; for the essence of the subject when one says "the substance of the body," or "the substance of the bread," and then it is something abstract. Hence, when it is said that the primitive force constitutes the substance of bodies, their nature or essence is meant; so Aristotle said that nature is the principle of motion and rest; and primitive force is nothing other than this principle in each body, from which all actions and passions arise. I consider matter as the first internal principle of passion and resistance, and it is by this that bodies are naturally impenetrable; the substantial form is nothing other than the first internal principle of action. . . . Thus, no one could object if the substance *in abstracto* is taken to be the primitive force which always remains the same in the same body and brings about, successively, accidental forces, and particular actions, which are all nothing but the nature or primitive subsisting force applied to other things. . . .

Nevertheless, it is true that the substance *in concreto* is something other than force, for it is the subject taken with this force. (A/1/7/248–249)

Theories about substance in abstracto are theories about the internal structure of substances in concreto. In the seventeenth century, a theory telling us what were the substances in concreto was a theory about the ultimate furniture of the universe. Substances in concreto, with their properties, were taken to constitute the base on which every other fact about the universe supervened. The spiritual theory, the corporeal substance theory, and the monadological theory are alternative accounts of substance in concreto, that is, alternative accounts of the ultimate furniture of the universe.

The spiritual theory. A fundamental, though often unheeded, distinction in Leibniz's philosophy is that between spirits (*esprits* in the French) and souls that are not spirits. At *DM* §34, Leibniz, contrasting nonspiritual souls with genuine spirits, wrote: "The principal difference is that they [the nonspiritual souls] do not know what they are or what they do, and consequently, not being able to reflect, they are not able to discover necessary and universal truths."[8] According to Leibniz, we have knowledge of three levels of spirits: the infinite spirit (that is, God), angelic souls, and human souls.

The spiritual theory posits that there are no substances (in concreto) except spirits. Hence, although it may be legitimate to talk about extended entities in virtue of the mutual correspondence of the perceptions of various spirits, still, in metaphysical rigor, there is nothing to bodies over and above well-regulated, mutually corresponding perceptions. The spiritual theory can accommodate a distinction between bodies organized in the way living things are and bodies that are not, and thus distinguish between corporeal substances and aggregates thereof. But, of course, the so-called corporeal substances will not really be substances at all—not in metaphysical rigor. The spiritual theory, along with a phenomenalistic account of extended items, is in the background, although not outright asserted at *DM* §§14 and 34. The theory is particularly evident in the initial autograph version of the *Discourse.* I believe a careful reading of this version indicates that no thesis asserted therein entails that there are nonspiritual substances.

The corporeal substance theory. The remaining theories that we need to note differ from the first in this fundamental respect: according to each, there are created substances whose existence is metaphysically independent of the existence of all created spiritual substances. The corporeal substance theory maintains that there are infinitely many created soul-like entities—some spiritual, some not—each of which is the form of some corporeal substance. It maintains that each corporeal substance is a complete entity, consisting of an aggregate of (other) corporeal substances (that is, its organic body), all of which are combined into a single individual with true, substantial unity by a soul-like entity—the substantial form of that corporeal substance. So each corporeal substance involves an infinite descent, in the sense that each corporeal substance is composed of other corporeal substances, each of which is similarly composed—without end.[9] Furthermore, the entire created world may be decomposed into created corporeal substances. Nonetheless, there are infinitely many extended items that are not corporeal substances, but rather mere aggregates of corporeal substance. On this theory, each such aggregate is phenomenal in the somewhat attentuated sense that what leads us to regard it as a single thing involves something subjective and relative to our perceptions. Moreover, on this theory, corporeal substances are the only created substances (in concreto) in the universe. Each such substance has a soul-like entity—its substantial form—which is a substance in abstracto. Hence, corporeal substances are the ultimate subjects of predication. Furthermore, extension, motion, and shape—the chief properties of bodies—are not analyzable into properties of soul-like entities.[10]

We should also bear in mind a variant of this theory—what we will call the "modified corporeal substance theory." In article 11 of the *Discourse*, Leibniz claimed to "rehabilitate in some way the ancient philosophy and to recall postlimino the almost banished substantial forms." In the ensuing discussion in that article, only St. Thomas is mentioned by name. In St. Thomas's theory (see, for example, *De unitate intellectus contra Averroistas* §§83–85), the human soul occupies a unique position; it is the sole form of matter (*forma materiae*) that is not a material form (*forma materialis*). A material form is said to exist through the act of existing of the composite of which it is the form; by contrast, the human soul, being an immaterial form, is said to exist by its own act of existing. Thus, before death, and again after the resurrection of the body, a human soul acts in the manner of a form of matter to form an individual substance. But between death and resurrection the human soul exists in its own right, independent of matter, as a quasi-individual substance. So, on St. Thomas's theory, the human soul behaves in some ways like a substance in abstracto—as a form of matter—and in some ways like a substance in concreto—as an immaterial form. This possibility is the subject of the first three questions in St. Thomas's *Quaestiones de anima*. The first question is "whether the human soul can be both a form and a *hoc aliquid* (an individual entity)?" St. Thomas argued that it can be both and, indeed, is both, although "the human soul is not an individual entity in the sense of being a complete substance which possesses its specific nature." [11]

On the modified corporeal substance theory, all substantial forms—not just human spirits—are viewed as occupying this dual position, that is, as behaving in some respects like substances in abstracto, and in other respects like substances in concreto. Except for this treatment of substantial forms, the modified corporeal substance theory is like the corporeal substance theory. It holds the following three key theses:

a. Some substances in concreto are composite entities, with components some of which are also substances in concreto.
b. All substances in concreto—including those that are composite—meet the most stringent and exacting standards of substantial unity.

c. The basic properties characterizing the corporeal—that is, extension and its modes—are not analyzable in terms of yet more basic properties of soul-like entities.

The monadological theory. On this theory, the only substances in concreto are soul-like entities—the monads. Created monads, although simple in the sense of lacking parts, are composed of primary matter and substantial form —that is, entelechies—which are substances in abstracto. This is the theory at which Leibniz ultimately arrived. It accomodates the notion of a corporeal substance as a body of a distinguished sort, whose unity is on a firmer footing than that of extended entities that are mere aggregates. But on the monadological theory all bodies, corporeal substances included, are phenomenal in the ontologically weighty sense that truths about them must supervene on facts concerning the properties of the monads. Hence, extension, motion, and shape—the chief properties of bodies—must be analyzable into properties of soul-like entities. So, on the monadological theory, corporeal substances are substances by courtesy. In the end, they must yield to phenomenalistic analysis of some sort. In this respect the monadological theory is closer to the spiritual theory than to the corporeal substance theory. But the monadological theory has a much wider base available, since it postulates infinitely many nonspiritual monads, as well as the spiritual monads.

It is natural to see a progression in Leibniz's thinking during the period of the *Discourse* and correspondence from an initial attraction to the spiritual theory, to its replacement by a commitment to the modified corporeal substance theory, followed in 1690 (or thereabouts) by acceptance of the unmodified corporeal substance theory, followed later still by rejection of the corporeal substance theory in favor of the monadological theory.[12] The purported shift from the modified to the unmodified corporeal substance theory deserves comment. In reading notes dated 1690, constituting a response to criticisms of Fardella, Leibniz wrote: "I do not say that bodies are composed of souls, nor that an aggregate of souls constitutes a body, but rather an aggregate of substances. Moreover, properly and accurately speaking, a soul is not a substance, but rather a substantial form, i.e., the primitive form existing in a substance—the first act, first active faculty."[13] The theory presented to Fardella is similar to that of the letter of 9 October 1687 to Arnauld, except that in the letter to Fardella we have an explicit assertion of that which primarily distinguishes the unmodified version of the corporeal substance theory from the modified version.

Our survey of the texts in the next section surely suggests that during the correspondence Leibniz moved away from the spiritual theory, toward some other theory. But what theory? That is the hard question. It is not clear to me that Leibniz had reached a stable, set theory by the time he wrote the letter of 9 October 1687. There is much talk in the correspondence about corporeal substances. But, as we have seen, a distinction between extended items that are called corporeal substances and mere aggregates thereof is common to the corporeal substance theory, modified or unmodified, and the monado-logical theory. And, in fact, there is no special problem about incorporating such a distinction into the spiritual theory. Part of the problem of interpreta-tion concerns Leibniz's attitude toward the exact ontological status of souls; and there the distinction between the modified and unmodified versions of the corporeal substance theory is useful.

Part of the problem of interpretation concerns Leibniz's attitude in the correspondence toward key features of the corporeal substance theory, modi-fied or unmodified, noted above. Our examination of the correspondence will exhibit Leibniz's commitment to the infinite descent aspect of the cor-poreal substance theory. We will also note Leibniz's acceptance of the thesis that some composite entities whose components are substances in concreto meet the most stringent and exacting standards of substantial unity. So the central question is Leibniz's attitude concerning the metaphysical status of extension and its chief modes. That is the subject of section 3. I will argue that, all things considered, the account of extension offered in the *Discourse* and correspondence is closer to the monadological theory than any version of the corporeal substance theory.

2. SUBSTANCE IN THE DISCOURSE AND THE CORRESPONDENCE

A useful way to begin our inquiry is by considering various respects, bear-ing on the notion of substance, in which the early autograph copy of the *Discourse* differs from the later amended fair copy. As noted in chapter 1, our main source of information here is Lestienne's edition of the *Discourse*. Fortunately, all the significant variations between the autograph and the fair copy, discovered by Lestienne, are provided in the Lucas and Grint trans-lation of the *Discourse*. The first significant alteration occurs in the crucial article 8, where the fair copy lists two examples of substances—Alexander the Great, and Alexander's soul.[14] The autograph version employed a totally different and rather bizarre example in place of Alexander, namely, the ring of Gyges. Leibniz drew a contrast between the circular figure of the ring and the ring itself, analogous to the distinction in the fair copy between the property of being a king and Alexander the Great. Leibniz concluded his discussion of the ring of Gyges with this remark: "I speak here as if it were assured that this ring had a consciousness." Subsequently, he replaced "had a consciousness" by "is a substance." I take it that at least prior to this last replacement Leibniz was assuming that whatever lacks consciousness is no substance; that is, that the only substances are spirits.

A related alteration occurs at *DM* §9, the article in which Leibniz derived the "notable paradoxes" from the complete-concept theory of *DM* §8. The following "paradox," contained in the autograph version, was deleted from the fair copy: "If bodies are substances, it is not possible that their nature

consists solely in size, shape, and motion, but something else is required."
Notice that the consequent of the deleted conditional is asserted in the fair
copy at *DM* §12, with a slight elaboration: "The whole nature of body does
not consist solely in extension, i.e., size, shape, and motion; there must necessarily be recognized there something which is related to souls and which is
commonly called substantial form." Not surprisingly, the autograph version
of *DM* §12 contains something different. The passage just quoted is preceded by the following (with the part contained in the autograph version, but
deleted in the fair copy, in brackets): "I believe that anyone who meditates
on the nature of substance, which I have explained above, will find [either
that bodies are not substances in metaphysical rigor (which was in fact the
view of the Platonics) or . . .] that the whole nature of body . . . ."[15]

Other significant variations occur at *DM* §§10, 11, 34, and 35. Consider
the heading for *DM* §10 displayed below. (The passage in brackets occurs
in Leibniz's copy, where it is struck, but not in Arnauld's copy). "That the
opinion that there are substantial forms has something solid to it [if there
are bodies that are substances], but that these forms change nothing in phenomena, and must not be employed in order to explain particular effects"
(LBr 46). At *DM* §11 of the fair copy, Leibniz defended his recalling "postlimino the almost banished substantial forms." In a passage in the autograph
copy, not retained in the fair copy, he added that he did so "ex hypothesi,
insofar as one can say that bodies are substances."

In *DM* §34 in the fair copy, Leibniz made the point that if we suppose
that bodies that constitute a *unum per se*, in the way that humans do, are
substances with substantial forms, then those substantial forms cannot perish, although they may alter radically. The autograph copy began thus: "It is
something that I do not yet undertake to determine whether bodies are substances, speaking in metaphysical rigor, or whether they are only true phenomena, like the rainbow, nor consequently whether there are substances,
souls, or substantial forms that are not intelligent." A similar deletion occurs
at *DM* §35. The following passage from the autograph copy also occurs in
the original of the fair copy, later to be struck by Leibniz: "Spirits are either
the only substances that exist in the world, in which case bodies are only
true phenomena, or they are at least the most perfect."

We noted at the close of section (1) that the autograph version of the
Discourse asserts the existence of spiritual substances and, moreover, is consistent with the thesis that there are no nonspiritual substances. Furthermore, Leibniz set out in *DM* §14 to provide the outline of a phenomenalistic
account of bodies, as well as a phenomenalistic account of the interaction
among substances. The latter account, phrased in terms of the notion of
degree of confusion in perception, is contained in *DM* §15; there is a particularly detailed account of the matter in a long passage at the close of
DM §14, which was struck by Leibniz before copies were made. Still, much
of the phenomenalistic material of *DM* §§14 and 15 remains in the fair copy.
Nonetheless, any plausible reading of the fair copy version of *DM* §§11 and

12 must see them as denying that all substances are spiritual, and as affirming that there are corporeal substances—although that terminology is not employed.[16]

Leibniz began his summation in the draft for the long letter of 14 July, as well as in the letter itself, by noting some alleged consequences of his complete-concept theory of substance. In the draft, the consequences are alleged to hold of souls; in the letter itself, of individual substances.[17] In the letter itself, individual substances are not explicitly identified with corporeal substances, but the term *corporeal substance* has its initial occurrence in the correspondence there.[18] Moreover, the human soul is there identified as the form of its body. In the penultimate paragraph of the letter itself, Leibniz set out to raise the relevant issues: "If the body is a substance and not a simple phenomenon like the rainbow, nor an entity united by accident or by aggregation like a heap of stones, it cannot consist of extension, and one must necessarily conceive there something that one calls substantial form, and that corresponds in some way to the soul."[19]

This passage deserves comment. Note that the conditional sheds light on the meaning of its antecedent. Whenever, in our time period, Leibniz cogitated on the possibility that the sentence "The body is a substance' expresses a true proposition, the proposition under cogitation is that there are corporeal substances, that is, extended items organized into a single individual with substantial unity by a substantial form. Thus, when Leibniz pondered "whether bodies are substances . . . or only true phenomena, like the rainbow" at *DM* §34 of the autograph version, he was not entertaining the proposition that either all bodies are substances or all bodies are true phenomena. The disjunction pondered is this: either there are some bodies that are corporeal substances, or all bodies are only true phenomena. Leibniz used the term *body* ambiguously. Sometimes he employed it to refer to any extended item whatsoever, and on other occasions he used it to refer to any extended item other than a corporeal substance. Recognition of this ambiguity is crucial in order to disarm the following argument. Throughout our texts and time period, Leibniz held the following theses: first, no substance is divisible, hence, no corporeal substance is divisible; second, every body is divisible, in fact, infinitely divided. Therefore, Leibniz was committed to the thesis that no body is a substance, hence, no body is a corporeal substance. The first thesis is correctly attributed to Leibniz; the second is only if *body* refers to extended items other than corporeal substances, in which case the conclusion, similarly construed, follows, but is devoid of interest.[20]

Surely, part of Leibniz's purpose in sending the quoted passage was to pique Arnauld's interest in the possibility that there are no corporeal substances, so that he and Arnauld might engage in a serious discussion of alternative theories, including, one would conjecture, the spiritual theory. Arnauld responded in a letter of 28 September 1686; purporting to quote the passage displayed above, he began: "In order that the body or matter not be a simple phenomenon like the rainbow. . . ."[21] In truth, in the correspondence Arnauld never gave serious consideration to the hypothesis that there are no extended items that are substances, and so never gave serious thought to the spiritual theory. Nevertheless, in order to judge Leibniz's attitude toward the various theories concerning substance in concreto, it is important to bear in mind that, at least in the early stages of the correspondence, he wished to have Arnauld consider the hypothesis that there are no corporeal substances.

In the remainder of this section I will concentrate on Leibniz's letters of 8 December 1686, 30 April 1687, and 9 October 1687. Each is in response to a letter from Arnauld; each has an associated draft, although only the draft for the 8 December letter has been published. Our investigation centers around Leibniz's responses to the following questions:

1. Are there corporeal substances? That is, are there extended entities meeting the most stringent and exacting standards of substantial unity? For example, are there extended entities that are incorruptible, ingenerable, and, most significantly, indivisible?
2. Assuming a positive answer to (1), what items in our experience qualify as corporeal substances?
3. Are bodies that lack an informing soul (or substantial form) ever substances?
4. Are souls (or substantial forms) ever substances in concreto, or are they always substances in abstracto, or do they occupy the dual position exemplified in St. Thomas's theory of the human soul?

Consider, first, the draft for the letter of 8 December and the letter itself. In his letter of 28 September 1686, Arnauld raised questions concerning Leibniz's remarks about the need for substantial forms, if there are to be corporeal substances.[22] In the draft, after responding to Arnauld's queries about the hypothesis of concomitance, Leibniz wrote: "The other difficulty is incomparably greater, concerning substantial forms and the souls of bodies; and I confess that I am not satisfied about it. In the first place, one would have to be sure that bodies are substances and not merely true phenomena like the rainbow" (LA 71). This passage is one of the last in which Leibniz thought to turn Arnauld's attention to the spiritual theory, and, since it is in a mere draft, it was never sent to Arnauld. Leibniz followed this passage with an argument intended to show that if there are corporeal substances, then those substances must have substantial forms. The argument is noted in chapter 6; relevant to our present concerns is Leibniz's manner of stating one consequence derived from its premises: "The substance of a body, if bodies have one, must be indivisible; whether it is called soul or form does not concern me" (LA 72).

Note that it is the soul or substantial form that is said to be indivisible. The soul is here referred to by the expression "the substance of——," an expression Leibniz typically used when he wished to talk about a substance in abstracto. As noted previously, this draft contains the only passage in the correspondence where Leibniz said flat out that a soul is an individual substance, although it is a consequence of many of his assertions. These passages, then, suggest that in the draft of 8 December, Leibniz favored viewing forms as occupying the dual role exemplified in St. Thomas's account of the human soul. Hence, it is relevant to our fourth question above.

The draft also includes passages relevant to some of our other questions. Consider the following passages, all from a paragraph at LA 73:

a. I do not know if the body, when the soul or substantial form is put aside, can be called a substance . . . .
b. Apart from man, there is no body about which I can declare that it is a substance rather than an aggregate of many or perhaps a phenomenon.
c. Nevertheless, it seems certain to me that if there are corporeal substances, man is not alone in that . . . .

Passage (a) suggests agnosticism with respect to our third question, whether bodies without forms are ever substances. It is an aberration; it is inconsistent with Leibniz's central negative thesis, announced in the long letter of 14 July (LA 58), that if a body lacks a form, then it is no substance. In the letter of 8 December, Leibniz set the matter straight: "Our body in itself, leaving the soul aside (i.e., the corpse), can be called a substance only by an abuse, like a machine or a heap of stones, which are only entities through aggregation" (LA 75). We may put question (3) to rest; but for (a) above, Leibniz consistently answered it in the negative in the correspondence.

Passages (b) and (c) may appear incoherent. The former seems to imply that each human being is a corporeal substance. Using this information in conjunction with (c) seems to yield that there are corporeal substances other than human beings. But (b) also seems to say that Leibniz could not then declare that there are corporeal substances other than human beings. The situation is not as chaotic as my remarks about the relation of (b) and (c) suggest. A close reading of (b), paying attention to context, suggests to me that Leibniz was expressing agnosticism there, not so much with respect to the claim that there are corporeal substances other than human beings, but rather with respect to our ability to know of any given nonhuman body that it is the body of some corporeal substance. My suggestion, then, is that (b) relates to our second question. In the letter of 8 December, Leibniz adopted a position with respect to our second question to which he remained committed throughout the remainder of the correspondence. The position is that the task of the philosopher is to provide a clear formulation of the conditions that must be satisfied for an entity to be a corporeal substance; and that what entities satisfy those conditions is a complex factual question best left to scientists, including microscopists, such as Malpighi, Swammerdam, and Leeuwenhoek—with the initial understanding that human beings are paradigms of corporeal substances.[23]

There are illuminating passages on these points in the unpublished drafts for the letter of 30 April. Consider: "It is true that I do not dare to say in a particular case whether such and such a body is a substance, or if it is only a machine. Nevertheless, it seems reasonable to me to believe that there are substances other than man in nature that surrounds us" (LBr 78v). And this passage: "I admit that I cannot demonstrate absolutely that there are substances with a true unity other than spirits. It is possible that bodies are only regulated phenomena. But that seems to me neither scarcely reasonable nor sufficiently in conformity with the perfection of God's operations" (LBr 79).[24]

We may, therefore, concentrate all our attention, in the remainder of this section, on Leibniz's remarks relevant to our first and fourth questions. Consider the following passage from the letter of 8 December: "Substantial unity requires a being that is complete, indivisible, and naturally indestructible, . . . which cannot be found in shape, nor in motion . . . but rather in a soul or substantial form. These are the only true complete beings" (LA 76). This passage clearly articulates some of the requirements Leibniz imposed on entities, in order for them to be individual substances. The condition that summarizes other required conditions is having substantial unity, which, in turn, requires being indivisible, indestructible, and a complete being.[25] Considered in isolation, one might be tempted to suppose that this passage indicates that only souls or substantial forms are individual substances, since it says that only they are complete beings. But this would be hasty. For on the very next page Leibniz drew our attention to "animate machines whose soul or substantial form brings about substantial unity" (LA 77). The next sentence makes clear that by an "animate machine" Leibniz meant a corporeal substance. And at LA 75 Leibniz asserted: "Every substantial form [or indeed every substance] cannot be destroyed or even engendered."[26]

This is the first passage in the correspondence where Leibniz explicitly asserted indestructibility of corporeal substances as well as of the substantial forms that inform them. It is worth noting that the first passage in which Leibniz explicitly asserted that corporeal substances have true unity has a similar marginated character. In the letter of 30 April 1687 (LA 97), Leibniz made note of "those substantial forms [or rather those corporeal substances] endowed with a true unity."[27] It is not until the letter of 9 October that Leibniz finally asserted outright that corporeal substances are indivisible, as all substances must be on his theory.[28] There is a clearly discernible pattern. Leibniz first asserted the relevant properties—indestructibility, true (substantial) unity, indivisibility—of substantial forms, and then claimed that substantial forms bring it about that the corporeal substances informed thereby come to have these qualities.

The letter of 30 April 1687 (and its unpublished drafts) contains Leibniz's most probing investigation in the correspondence of the notion of true unity, and the fullest statement of his reasons for requiring an entity to have true unity in order to be a substance. These are the topics of chapter 6. For our present purposes the relevant letter is that of 9 October 1687 (and its unpublished draft). As we have already noted, that letter contains Leibniz's first explicit assertion in the correspondence of the thesis that corporeal substances, since they have true, substantial unity, must be indivisible. Both the draft and the letter contain clear accounts of the idea of infinite descent that we have associated with the corporeal substance theory, modified and unmodified.[29] From our present perspective, the most important items in the 9 October letter (and its draft) bear on Leibniz's efforts to answer an objection Arnauld formulated in his letter of 28 August. By this stage of the proceedings Arnauld understood Leibniz's picture of a corporeal substance as a composite entity, consisting of a substantial form and an aggregate of extended items, although Arnauld still had not grasped Leibniz's view that the entire extended universe decomposes to such corporeal substances.[30]

Arnauld made the obvious criticism: "If a particle of matter is not one entity, but rather many entities, I do not conceive how a substantial form (which, since it is really distinct from it, can only confer on it an extrinsic denomination) is capable of causing it to cease to be many entities and to become one entity" (LA 107). Leibniz's initial response in his letter of 9 October is nitpicking: "As for this other problem that you raise, namely, that the soul joined to matter does not make an entity that is truly one, since matter is not truly one in itself, and that the soul, in your view, gives it only an extrinsic denomination, I answer that it is the animate substance to which this matter belongs that is truly a being" (LA 118).

I assume that Leibniz used the expression "animate substance" to refer to a corporeal substance, not the substantial form of a corporeal substance. So construed, the quoted passage answers the question Arnauld asked, but not the one he must have wanted to ask: given that a hunk of matter is many entities and not truly one entity, how can the composite of that hunk and a substantial form yield an entity that is truly one—that has true, substantial unity? Fortunately, in the paragraph following that quoted above, Leibniz responded to the more fundamental question: "Supposing that there is a soul or *substantial form* in beasts or other corporeal substances, one must reason with respect to them on this point as we all reason with respect to man, who is an entity endowed with a true unity that his soul gives to him, not withstanding the fact that the mass of his body is divided into organs, vessels, humors, spirits, and that the parts are undoubtedly full of an infinite number of other corporeal substances endowed with their own *forms*" (LA 120; emphasis mine).[31] This response is illuminating as much for what it does not say as for what it does. Arnauld's objection provided Leibniz with an opportunity to explain how it is that a soul or substantial form (or entelechy) produces a true unity from ingredients, some of which are divisible entities. In so doing, Leibniz would have had the opportunity to explain what relation must obtain between a form and some matter, in order for the resulting composite entity to be a corporeal substance. He did not take the opportunity. On these crucial matters he simply noted that there must be an acceptable account, because, as we all know, that is how it is with the one corporeal substance we know from the inside out, so to speak—ourselves.

It is instructive to compare the answers provided in the letter sent to Arnauld with similar efforts contained in the unpublished drafts. Leibniz wrote the following in the margin of the draft, then subsequently struck it: "I agree that a particle of matter will never become a single being, speaking in metaphysical rigor, whatever soul is given to it, but it is the soul that is truly a being." Notice that it is the soul that is here said to be "truly a being," not the animate substance, as in the passage quoted from LA 118. In the draft, Leibniz continued as follows: "Matter, in the manner in which it is commonly conceived, as a divisible mass taken without the soul, is only a phenomenon. . . . But taking matter not as the mass or extension but as the primitive passive power of a substance, it is not divisible, no more than the substance itself" (LBr 107v). It is natural to interpret this passage in the light of Leibniz's monadological theory, according to which, as we noted in section 1, even a created monad may be construed as a composite in virtue of being composed of an entelechy and matter, where the entelechy and the matter are construed as abstractions and not concrete individuals. Note that such a composite could be described as a corporeal substance in a somewhat attenuated sense; it has matter as well as form, although its matter is not divisible mass, but rather primitive passive power. The resulting composite is simple in the sense of lacking spatial parts, since not even its material component—primitive passive power—has spatial parts.

What would we then make of those passages in which Leibniz appears to treat corporeal substances in an entirely different way—as composite entities, composed of form and matter with form construed as a substantial quasi-individual entity and with matter construed as a nonsubstantial individual containing spatial parts? Surely the most plausible hypothesis would be that Leibniz introduced corporeal substances, so construed, as something akin to logical constructions, based on the ultimate metaphysical subjects —the monads. And for what purpose? In order to display to Arnauld the flexibility of Leibniz's basic metaphysical scheme in relation to the church reunion project. In the letter of 8 December, Leibniz reminded Arnauld that it was Catholic teaching, settled at the Fifth Lateran Council, that the human soul was the form of a human body. Leibniz's point was that his account provided an acceptable interpretation of this teaching and that Descartes's dualism did not.

But we are talking about a passage that was struck in its entirety. It was replaced by a passage that begins: "I agree that a particle of matter in itself will never become a true being, speaking in metaphysical rigor, whatever soul is given to it, but also, in the manner in which you take it—namely, as an extended mass composed of parts where there is only mass and extension—it does not enter into substance and is only a pure phenomenon more or less like space, time, and motion." Leibniz went on to make the following remarks that were subsequently struck: "But taking matter as the primitive passive power of corporeal substance, it is different from extension, and although body has divisible mass only because it has this passive power, matter itself, taken in this sense, is not it. A substance can lose its modes, but not its parts" (LBr 105).

This last passage is more difficult to interpret than the one previously quoted from LBr 107v. Still, it seems closer to the monadological theory than the corresponding material in the actual letter to Arnauld; note, especially, its last sentence. Now consider the passage that replaced the portion of LBr 105 that was subsequently struck; it is remarkably similar to the bracketed, marginated passage at LA 119–120, a passage not contained in Arnauld's copy of the 9 October letter: "If we take as the matter of body, the assemblage of substances of which the mass is composed, it is not essential to the substance, and we can successively lose all the parts of our body. Nevertheless, in the present state of the body, those present states are essential to it and make up its immediate requisites, and consequently they constitute a whole that has furthermore a true unity" (LBr 105). Compare the last clause here with the following remark at LA 120: "It is true that the whole that has a true unity can remain the same individual in rigor, even though it loses or gains parts as we experience in ourselves; thus, the parts are immediate requisites only pro tempore." And contrast it with the struck passage: "A substance can lose its modes, but not its parts."

The bottom line seems to be that where there is tension between variant versions of the 9 October letter—including the draft, the version sent to Arnauld, and the version retained by Leibniz—passages favoring ascription of the corporeal substance theory to Leibniz tended to survive. Passages favoring ascription of the monadological theory to Leibniz tended either to be struck or not to make the transition from draft to actual letter.

And which version of the corporeal substance theory—modified or unmodified—is favored by the texts? Without doubt, the modified theory. Aside from the passage previously cited, where Leibniz explicitly stated that the soul is an individual substance (code for a substance in concreto), there is considerable indirect evidence. Perhaps the most impressive is the fit between what Leibniz took to be fundamental truths about individual substances and what he took to be truths about souls. Consider the following necessary conditions for being a substance, according to Leibniz. In each case the citations following the condition refer to passages in which Leibniz claimed that souls or substantial forms satisfied the condition.

If x is a finite, created substance then:

1. x has a complete concept (LA 68, 76).
2. x is a complete being (LA 76).
3. x remains numerically the same over time (DM §34).
4. The doctrine of marks and traces holds of x (DM §§8, 29; LA 42).
5. The identity of indiscernibles holds of x (DM §9; LA 42).
6. x is incorruptible and ingenerable (DM §32; LA 57, 72, 76, 116).
7. x is indivisible (DM §32; LA 72, 76, 112, 116, 117).
8. x expresses its entire universe (LA 74, 76, 111, 113–114).

9. *x* is a world apart (DM §32; LA 46–47, 58, 69, 91).
10. *x* has true (substantial) unity (no citations).

All fit, with the exception of (10). What about (10)? In numerous passages Leibniz claimed that souls (and, more generally, substantial forms) convey just such unity to those corporeal substances they inform. In this context, it is unlikely that he would maintain that forms convey what they lack. I believe that Leibniz thought that the claim that souls and substantial forms satisfy (10) goes without saying. So he did not say it.

3. THE STATUS OF THE MODES OF EXTENSION

We have found that the account of substance brought to fruition in the letters of 30 April and 9 October 1687 has many of the significant features of what I called the modified corporeal substance theory. One crucial question remains. Did Leibniz then regard corporeal substances, as understood in these two letters, as the metaphysically ultimate subjects that, together with their properties, constitute the base on which all other facts of the universe supervene? It is important to recognize that the answer to this question is not settled by what we have already said of the theory of substance in these letters. Consider, again, the analysis of the components of a substance that Leibniz presented in a letter to De Volder of 20 June 1703.[32] The analysis ends with "the animal, i.e., corporeal substance, which a dominating monad makes into one machine." Yet three letters later, with no doctrinal change intervening, Leibniz wrote to De Volder (30 June 1704): "Accurately speaking, however, matter is not composed of constitutive unities, but results from them, since matter, i.e., extended mass, is nothing but a phenomenon grounded in things, like the rainbow or mock sun, and all reality belongs to unities alone" (G/2/268 [L 536]). It is clear that the unities mentioned in this passage are monads, not corporeal substances.[33] In the same vein, consider the famous "ontological chart" that supplements Leibniz's letter to Des Bosses of 19 August 1715.[34] There, under the rubric "Unum per se, complete being," we find two types of substance mentioned—simple substances (that is, monads) and composite substances (such as animals)—much as we do in the *Monadology* itself. Yet writing to Des Bosses three years earlier, Leibniz had put his metaphysical cards on the table: "I consider the explication of all phenomena solely through the perceptions of monads agreeing with each other, with corporeal substances set aside, as useful for a fundamental investigation of things" (G/2/450 [L 604]).

So we must consider whether the view Leibniz held in our time period envisaged corporeal substances as basic individuals at the deepest level of analysis, or whether he had in mind a yet more profound analysis. We pursue this question by examining what Leibniz had to say in our time period about the ontological status of extension and its modes. The issue before us is whether Leibniz then held a realistic conception of extension and its modes, or whether he looked to an idealistic, monadological analysis of extension and its modes. An argument to which Leibniz frequently appealed may be summarized as follows: whatever properties constitute a substance are objective, nonimaginary properties of it. Anything whose essence is extension is constituted by size, shape, and motion. But size, shape, and motion are not objective, nonimaginary properties of anything they constitute. Therefore, nothing whose essence is extension is a substance.[35] The conclusion of this argument is Leibniz's central negative thesis in our time period concerning the nature of substance. It is aimed at Descartes, and is intended to prepare the way for arguments supporting a positive thesis that the essence of substance is substantial form. These arguments are the subject of chapter 6. Our current concern is directed to one premiss in the argument cited: size, shape, and motion are not objective, nonimaginary properties of anything they constitute.

Note that Leibniz did not say that size, shape, and motion are not objective, nonimaginary properties of anything that has them. Had he done so, that would settle matters. If Leibniz took size, shape, and motion to be subjective, imaginary properties of whatever has them, then he envisaged an idealistic, monadological analysis of them. Those who ascribe to Leibniz a realistic interpretation of the relevant modes in our time period construe matters as follows: Leibniz was engaged in arguing that extension is not the essence of corporeal substance, that substantial form is, that the substantial form of a corporeal substance is its primitive active force, and that reference to force, active and passive, primitive and derivative, permits a realistic interpretation of size, shape, and motion.

There is much to be said for this interpretation. In numerous passages Leibniz identified the substantial form of a corporeal substance with its primitive active force. Thus, in *Specimen* (G/7/317 [MP 84–85]), he wrote: "This principle of actions, or primitive active force, from which a series of various states follows, is the form of the substance."[36] But, of course, we need to know whether a realistic, nonmonadological interpretation of primitive active force is Leibniz's last word on that subject in our time period. The following passage from the *New Essays* puts us on our guard: "I still agree with you [Locke], though, that the clearest idea of active power comes to us from the mind. So active power is only in things that are analogous to minds, that is, entelechies" (*New Essays* 172).[37] Closer to our period is the following quotation to the same effect from the *New System*. Speaking explicitly of substantial forms, Leibniz wrote: "I found that their nature consists of force and that from this there follows something analogous to feeling and to appetite; and that therefore it was necessary to form a conception of them resembling our ordinary conception of souls" (G/4/479 ([MP 116–117]). This passage strongly suggests a monadological analysis of force and, hence, tends to undercut the realistic interpretation under consideration.

The second half of the realistic strategy is the claim that reference to force, active and passive, primitive and derivative, permits a realistic interpretation of size, shape, and motion, according to Leibniz.[38] Again, there is much to be said in favor of the realistic claim. For in the very passages in which Leibniz argued for the phenomenal, imaginary status of motion in substances whose essence (*per impossibile*) is extension, he appears to argue by contrast that reference to active force permits a realistic interpretation of motion.[39]

The following passage from the unpublished draft for the letter of 30 April 1687 has the virtue of placing most of the cards on the table.

> Perhaps one will have cause to be surprised that I place shape and motion in the same rank with phenomena . . . ; as to motion, it is manifest that since it is a successive being and since it does not have its parts together, it can never exist, no more than time, which it requires. I acknowledge that force exists in bodies, namely, a state from which change will follow, but motion does not exist. And since formally and in precision motion consists in a change of location continued through some time, the subject in which the change occurs can never be determined, for an infinity of suppositions can be made, all equally satisfactory, attributing rest or motion and such a degree of speed and direction, sometimes to one object, sometimes to another. Therefore, it is necessary that there be some other real thing that is the cause of change in the subject, namely, force or action that is in the corporeal substance itself, and it is that which provides the foundation for all the reality that is recognized in motion. Otherwise, there being no reason that can be cited for one system rather than another, they will all be false, that is, the entire thing will only be apparent.
>
> And with respect to shape, I uphold another paradox, namely, that there is no shape exact and real, and that neither sphere, nor parabola, nor other perfect shape will ever be found in body. . . . One will always find there inequalities to infinity. That comes about because matter is actually subdivided to infinity. (LBr 81v)

This passage presents those advocating a realistic interpretation with two separate challenges, one with respect to motion, another with respect to shape. The realist would meet the first challenge by noting Leibniz's claim that physical force (that is, form, for the realist) is "something real and absolute" (LA 133), thereby permitting identification of those objects at rest and those in motion in a system of objects that are changing spatial relations and, thereby, saving motion from being altogether imaginary and phenomenal.[40] No such strategy will do with respect to the problem posed by Leibniz's remarks concerning shape. No one is likely to suppose that with the injection of force or form into shapeless mass, it literally "shapes up." In the remainder of this section I will concentrate on this problem.

Note that we are not dealing with a stray point in a stray text. Essentially the same remarks about shape may be found in the correspondence at LA 77, 97–98, and 119.[41] It seems to me that the realistic interpretation must be largely deflationary. There is considerable plausibility to a deflationary reading of the relevant texts. Consider the following passage from *Primary Truths*: "There is no actual determinate shape given in things, for there is none that can satisfy infinite impressions. Therefore, neither a circle, nor an ellipse, nor any other line *definable by us* is given except in the intellect" (C 522 [MP 92]; emphasis mine). According to the deflationary reading, when Leibniz asserted, somewhat mysteriously, that material objects lack determinate shape, all he had in mind was this innocuous doctrine: take your stock high-school geometrical figures, or any others "definable by us" or that "possess in full force the properties that we learn in geometry" (G/4/568 [L 583]); none of them is exemplified by real objects in nature. Of course, for any given material object, including any given corporeal substance, there exists some shape such that the object has that shape. But given the intricacies of nature, that shape will be very complex, so complex that it is not "definable by us."

This deflationary reading is plausible; all things considered, I think it deserves to be deflated and rejected, at least as a claim about what Leibniz actually believed about shape at the time of the correspondence. If we concentrate on the relevant passages from the correspondence (LA 77, 97–98, and 118–119, and the unpublished drafts LBr 81v and 105), as well as those from *Primary Truths* and *Specimen*, we find these assertions:

a. There is no fixed and precise shape in bodies (whether corporeal substances or aggregates thereof).
b. Assertion (a) is true because of the actual infinite subdivision of bodies and the fact that each body contributes to the motion and shape of every other.
c. Assertion (a) has the consequence that bodies would be "*merely* imaginary and apparent, if there existed nothing but matter and its modifications" (LA 77; emphasis mine)

I recommend the following interpretation of Leibniz's argument from (b) to (a): let x be any material object (corporeal substance or aggregate thereof). Let S be any shape of any degree of complexity. S cannot be the shape of x because, however complex it is, it represents the influence on x (via impressed motion) of only finitely many other bodies. Given the actual infinite division of matter, whatever shape we assign to x, it is not complex enough, because it fails to take into account the influence (via impressed motion) of infinitely many other bodies.[43]

Thus baldly put, Leibniz's reasoning may appear to need further buttressing. That project I leave to others. My point is that whatever the merits of Leibniz's argument, his conclusion was that finite material objects strictly speaking lack shape, not that they have (per impossibile) shape of infinite complexity. In drawing his conclusion in the draft for the letter of 30 April 1687 (LBr 81v), Leibniz contrasted extended entities with "complete being or substances." I take the locution "complete being" to be of considerable significance. My suggestion is that he then took extended entities to be incomplete entities, in the manner of phenomenal, that is intensional, objects. Robert Adams has recommended a similar interpretation: "What I assume he would say, instead of postulating infinitely complex shapes, is that for every finitely complex shape that might be ascribed to a body there is another still more complex that more adequately expresses reality. Every shape in the series of more and more adequate expressions, however, will still be only finitely complex and for that reason among others will still be an appearance, qualitatively different from the reality expressed, which is infinitely complex and does not literally have a shape at all." [44] This seems to me not only a fair representation of what Leibniz would say, but of what he did say, for example, in *Specimen*: "From the fact that no body is so small that it is not actually divided into parts that are excited by various motions, it follows that no determinate shape can be assigned to any body, . . . *although in the derivation of an infinite series certain rules are observed by nature*" (G/7/314 [MP 81]; emphasis mine). [45]

But if we adopt my interpretation, what are we to make of (c), Leibniz's claim that given that there is no precise shape in bodies, they would be "merely imaginary and apparent, if there existed nothing but matter and its modification"? I think he had the following in mind: in our texts and elsewhere, Leibniz supposed that the assignment of shape to an individual finite material object in a plenum is dependent on a proper assignment of motion and rest to the objects in the system in question. [46] But, as we have seen, according to Leibniz, a proper assignment of motion and rest among objects in a system presupposes assignments of physical forces among those same objects. According to Leibniz, force is not a mode of matter. [47] So, if there existed nothing but matter and its modifications, shape would be *purely* imaginary, not even a well-founded phenomenon. Form, according to Leibniz, permits a notion of physical force, which in turn permits a notion of shape as a well-founded phenomenon. But well-founded or not, shape and motion (and hence extension) are phenomenal in the ontologically weighty sense; as Leibniz put it in the letter of 9 October 1687, "They cannot stand up to the finest analysis" (LA 119). A full treatment of these matters would require a book on Leibniz's views about the labyrinth of the continuum. It needs to be written, but not by me. A full treatment would also include an explication of the tripartite distinction of kinds of entities, basic to Leibniz's mature metaphysics, among the real, the phenomenal, and the ideal. [48] It is important to realize that the full tripartite distinction was not consistently applied by Leibniz in our time period. [49]

I am aware that what I have said here does not settle the matter concerning the correct interpretation of the theory of substance to which Leibniz committed himself in the correspondence. One problem concerns the meaning of the phrase "extension, realistically construed." We must bear in mind that Leibniz did not regard extension as a primitive concept, that he offered an analysis of extension in terms of the primitive passive force of a substance. Such a treatment of extension should be viewed as realistic, unless it is attached to a yet deeper analysis in terms of soul-like entities.

Consider the following passage from the important paper *Specimen of Catholic Demonstrations* (dated 1683–1686 in the *Vorausedition*): "I will show that matter no more consists in extension than force in action; therefore, just as force is that from which action follows unless something impedes, so matter is the passive force or force of resistance in any body whatever, from which a certain extension of body follows, unless the Author of things wills otherwise" (Grua 29). Here we find Leibniz outlining his view that extension arises from the passive force of resistance and is to be analyzed in terms of that force. Those who ascribe the corporeal substance theory, realistically construed, to Leibniz in our period will be inclined to interpret the passages concerning shape, noted above, in a different manner from the one I recommend. They will be inclined to see these passages as calling for an analysis of shape—as a mode of extension—in terms of passive forces, unaccompanied by a supplementary analysis in terms of soul-like entities.

I do not have a refutation of this suggestion. Still, I do not accept it. It seems to me an account that would fit better with an analysis of determinate shape as applied to specific bodies, rather than what we find in the texts (or so I say): an argument to the conclusion that there is no determinate shape in specific bodies. It might be taken as a condition of adequacy for an analysis of shape in terms of some variety of physical force that it make sense to ascribe determinate shapes to specific bodies. If, on the other hand, the ultimate metaphysical base is entirely nonphysical—of a different ontological type—then we might expect a replacement analysis, where no such condition of adequacy need hold.[50] And, of course, my claim is that a replacement analysis is what is lurking in the background. Perhaps the idea that there must be some such replacement analysis is what lurks in the background. The details of the *Monadology* are not to be found here. It is not part of my claim that Leibniz really had the view of the *Monadology* in mind at this time.

In chapter 6 we will consider two theses about substances that occupy a central place in the correspondence: a negative thesis that there is no individual substance whose essence is extension, and a positive thesis that every individual substance includes a substantial form. Obviously, these theses are more easily established if individual substances are construed monadologically. In the correspondence Leibniz set out to establish the truth of these theses even in the case where corporeal substances, realistically construed, are taken to exist and to be basic individual substances. I have suggested that his motivation here was related to his church reunion project. Whatever his motivation, Leibniz's effort in this regard produced numerous difficulties with which he struggled during the time of the correspondence. That effort, as much as anything else, has caused commentators (incorrectly, I believe) to attribute the corporeal substance theory, realistically construed, to him.

Chapter 6

❖❖❖❖❖❖❖❖❖

SUBSTANTIAL FORMS

There are two central theses concerning the composition of corporeal substances—one negative, the other positive—to which Leibniz held fast in the *Discourse* and the correspondence. The negative thesis is that nothing whose essence is extension is an individual substance. The positive thesis is that each created individual substance, hence each corporeal substance, includes a substantial form. Leibniz saw these theses as connected. He often wrote as if establishing the negative thesis were tantamount to establishing the positive thesis.

In section 3 of chapter 5 we considered one of Leibniz's major arguments for the negative thesis: that whatever properties constitute an individual substance are objective, nonimaginary properties of it. But size, shape, and motion—the chief modes of extension—are not objective, nonimaginary properties of anything they constitute. So extension cannot constitute the essence of any individual substance, including corporeal substances. In section 1 of this chapter we will concentrate on the following argument for the negative thesis: anything whose essence is extension is such that all its contingent properties are modes of extension, that is, identifiable with some mode characterizable in terms of size, shape, and motion. Every individual substance has force. But force is not identifiable with a mode characterizable in terms of size, shape, and motion. So nothing whose essence is extension is an individual substance.[1] In section 2 we will consider a number of Leibniz's arguments for the negative thesis that bear on the notion of substantial (true) unity. Section 3 contains speculation concerning the positive thesis.

1. FORCE AND EXTENSION

In *DM* §18 Leibniz said: "Force is something different from size, shape and motion and it can be judged from that that all that is conceived in body does not consist uniquely in extension and its modifications, as our moderns are persuaded." The opening remarks of *DM* §18 make clear that Leibniz took the results of *DM* §17 as either establishing or at least going a long way toward establishing that force is not identifiable with any mode characterizable in terms of size, shape, and motion. In *DM* §17 Leibniz presented the argument of the *Brevis demonstratio* to the effect that Descartes erred in measuring force in terms of the product of mass and velocity, rather than in terms of the product of mass and the square of the velocity.[2] On the whole, commentators on Leibniz have not been sufficiently puzzled by what bearing this result could possibly have on the thesis that force is not identifiable with any mode characterizable in terms of size, shape, and motion. A plausible initial reaction would be that if Leibniz were right—if force were measurable in terms of the product of mass and the square of the velocity—then force would be characterizable in terms of size (mass) and motion. But this seems to be just the opposite of what Leibniz did conclude. After stating in outline the argument of *DM* §17, I will speculate on the inference from its conclusion to the thesis that force is not identifiable with any mode characterizable in terms of size, shape, or motion.

Consider the following propositions:

1. God always conserves the same quantity of motive force in the world.
2. The quantity of motion of a body B at time t is the product of its size at t—perhaps its weight, measured in suitable units—and its speed at t, measured in suitable units.
3. Quantity of motion is a suitable measure of motive force.
4. God always conserves the same quantity of motion in the world.

Leibniz attributed all of these propositions to Descartes. Since (2) is a definition of "quantity of motion," Leibniz had no quarrel with it. Like Descartes, he accepted (1). But he rejected (3) and, hence, (4). Leibniz's argument against (3) goes as follows. Consider these propositions:

5. The motive force acquired by a body free-falling n feet is the same as the motive force required to lift that body n feet.
6. The motive force required to lift a body weighing m pounds n feet is the same as the motive force required to lift a body weighing n pounds m feet.

Leibniz accepted (5) and (6) and assumed that Cartesians would as well. His argument, based on (5) and (6), may be put as follows: consider body A, weighing one pound, free-falling four feet, and body B, weighing four pounds, free-falling one foot. In virtue of (5) and (6), A and B have the same motive force just prior to impact. But do they have the same quantity of motion? They would, were the speed of A just prior to impact four times that of B, since the size of B is four times that of A. But as Galileo taught us, the speed of A just prior to impact is only twice that of B. Therefore, (3) is false—quantity of motion is not a suitable measure of motive force. Leibniz added that whereas (1) is correct, (4) is mistaken.

Our problem is to determine what bearing Leibniz took this to have on the thesis that motive force cannot be identified with any mode characterizable in terms of size and motion. I have found a passage from a letter written to Bayle in 1687 helpful in understanding Leibniz's thinking on this topic in our time period. After stating the argument formulated above concerning a suitable measure of motive force, Leibniz waxed metaphysical. "I will add a remark of consequence for metaphysics. I have shown that force must not be estimated by the composition of speed and size, but rather by the future effect. Nevertheless, it seems that force or power is something already real and the future effect is not. From which it follows that it will be necessary to admit something in body different from size and speed, unless you wish to refuse all power to act to bodies" (G/3/48).

I construe the argument of this passage in the following manner: the proper way to determine a suitable measure of the motive force of a body B at a time t is by determining what work B would do under suitable conditions at some subsequent time t'. Corresponding to this measure there will be a dispositional property that body B has at t—a property in virtue of which B will have a certain effect at t', if placed in appropriate conditions. But there must be some intrinsic occurrent property that B has at t that is the basis for this dispositional property. Otherwise, we refuse force to everything corporeal, which is just to deny the existence of corporeal substances.[3] Of properties identifiable with some mode characterizable in terms of size, shape, and motion, the only plausible candidate is what Leibniz called impetus in the *Specimen dynamicum*, that is, the composition of mass (size) and velocity (speed) at a given instant.[4] But the point of the argument at *DM* §17 is just that this identification yields incorrect results. So there is no property identifiable with a mode characterizable in terms of size, shape, and motion that yields the right results, which is the conclusion Leibniz set out to establish here. So motive force is not a physical mode of corporeal substance, if by physical mode we mean a mode of extension. The product of a body's mass at t and the square of its velocity at t serves to measure its motive force at t. But no one who utilized the machinery of a substance-mode ontology in our time period would have viewed the abstract composite entity consisting of a body's mass at t and the *square* of its velocity at t as a mode of anything.[5]

At the close of the long letter to Arnauld of 14 July 1686, Leibniz wrote: "I am as corpuscular as one can be in the explanation of particular phenomena. . . . One must always explain nature along mathematical and mechanical lines, provided one knows that the very principles or laws of mechanics or of force do not depend upon mathematical extension alone but upon certain metaphysical reasons" (LA 58). In light of the interpretation of Leibniz's remarks to Bayle sketched above, we would construe these comments written to Arnauld in this manner. Given a closed system of bodies, a knowledge of position, mass, and velocity at a given time t yields knowledge of the same features at any subsequent time t', in virtue of knowledge of relevant laws. The relevant laws are propositions whose nonlogical concepts are either mathematical or concepts of modes of extension, or composed thereof. The point of Leibniz's comment to Bayle is to argue that the composite concepts employed in correct formulations of the relevant laws—especially the composite concept measuring motive force—presuppose something in corporeal substances that is not physical, in the sense characterized above. It is beyond physics, hence, metaphysical.

2. UNITY

The arguments for the negative thesis limned in section 3 of chapter 5 and in section 1 of this chapter failed to pique Arnauld's critical instincts. In this section we focus on those arguments for the negative thesis to which Arnauld did respond, that is, those employing the notions of substantial (true) unity, divisibility, and beings by aggregation. It is important for the reader to bear in mind the conclusions reached in section 3 of chapter 5. I concluded there that in the correspondence Leibniz did not intend to commit himself to the corporeal substance theory, realistically construed. I also concluded that, nonetheless, Leibniz intended to demonstrate in the correspondence that the corporeal substance theory, realistically construed, could be so understood that corporeal substances met the relevant requirements having to do with substantial (true) unity and divisibility. These are contentious conclusions. If they are mistaken, then the interpretation of Leibniz's arguments offered in this section is systematically askew. Nevertheless, I believe that the following treatment of Leibniz's arguments may hold some interest even for those who reject my contentions.

Consider the following argument, which I will call the "true unity argument":

i. Every substance has true (substantial) unity.
ii. Anything whose essence is extension is divisible.
iii. Anything that is divisible is a being by aggregation.
iv. Nothing that is a being by aggregation has true (substantial) unity.

v. Hence, anything whose essence is extension lacks true unity.
vi. Therefore, nothing whose essence is extension is a substance.

Versions of this argument, variously compressed, may be found in the draft for the letter of 8 December 1686 (LA 72), the letter itself (LA 76), the draft for the letter of 30 April 1687 (LBr 81), the letter itself (LA 96ff.), and the letter of 9 October (LA 119).[6]

Following our usual practice, we commence with Arnauld's critical reaction. It is formulated in his letter of 4 March 1687. Arnauld conceded (ii). He saw no need to reach (v) via a connection between divisibility and being an entity through aggregation. Thus, he was prepared to admit this premiss: whatever is divisible lacks true unity. So he accepted (v), but denied (i) in the sense Leibniz attributed to it, and rejected the conclusion (vi).[7]

His claim was that Leibniz was relying on a purely stipulative definition of substance, in effect securing his conclusion by arbitrarily defining substance in terms of a trumped up standard of unity, which items whose essence is extension have no chance of satisfying. Arnauld supplemented these critical remarks by two further points. First, he offered what he took to be a proper, nonstipulative account of an individual substance. It amounts to this: an individual is a substance just in case it is neither a mode nor a state of something else. Second, since many items whose essence is extension— or, at any rate, many items that lack organizing substantial forms, such as a block of marble—are, nonetheless, not modes or states of other things, they are substances. Unfortunately, Arnauld put this second point in a manner equivalent in boxing to thrusting one's jaw forward, while ostentatiously dropping one's hands to one's side. He said: "this block of marble is not the state of being of another substance; . . . One might say . . . that it is not a single substance but many substances mechanically joined together" (LA 86).

Arnauld made it unmistakably clear that he was, indeed, guilty of the error that seems to lurk here. He added: "In the whole of corporeal nature there are only machines and aggregates of substances, because of none of these parts can one say, accurately speaking, that it is a single substance" (LA 87). Leibniz appended the following remark to his copy of Arnauld's letter: "If there are aggregates of substances, there must also exist true substances from which all the aggregates are made." Surely Leibniz was right.

A close analysis of Arnauld's comments in subsequent letters suggests to me that what he wanted to affirm was something like this: any item that is not a mode or state of something else is a substantial item. It is arbitrary, a matter of convention, how we decompose those substantial items that are extended into individual substances. But (Arnauld might have concluded) we do it, since we (Leibniz included) talk about *one* sun, *one* earth, without supposing that there is a substantial form of the sun or earth.[8] In suggesting that "in the whole of corporeal nature there are only . . . aggregates of substances," Arnauld perhaps only wanted to remind us that whatever scheme we adopt for decomposing the substantial into substances is conventional and has alternatives.[9]

Leibniz disagreed with everything of substance that Arnauld offered on these matters, including the words I have put in Arnauld's mouth. In his letter of 30 April 1687, Leibniz admitted that there are "degrees of accidental unity," as he called it, where "our mind notices or conceives of certain genuine substances which have various modes; these modes embrace relationships with other substances, from which the mind takes the opportunity to link them together in thought and to enter into the account one name for all these things together, which makes for convenience of reasoning" (LA 101). He recognized that, as Arnauld insisted, we do talk about *one* sun, *one* earth, *one* army, although none of these entities is a substance. They have what Leibniz called accidental unity, phenomenal unity.[10] And he agreed that phenomenal unity involved human convention. After admitting that various composite bodies have phenomenal unity, he added, "it can therefore be said of these composite bodies and similar things what Democritus said very well about them, 'they exist by opinion, by convention' " (LA 101).

Think of the unity conditions for a type of entity as those conditions that permit enumeration of entities of that type; think of the identity conditions for a type of entity as those conditions in virtue of which an entity of that type at one time is identified with an entity of that type at another time. Leibniz insisted that at the level of substance, unity conditions and identity conditions must not be matters of convention or matters of degree. In the letter of 8 December (LA 76) and, again, in the letter of 30 April (LA 101–102), he formulated an important argument for his negative thesis that we may state as follows: any entity whose essence is extension is such that its unity and identity conditions are a matter of degree, a matter of convention. No substance is such that its unity and identity conditions are a matter of degree, a matter of convention. So, no entity whose essence is extension is a substance. The second premiss of this argument may well be a basic presupposition for Leibniz. It expresses an attitude that has had a remarkable hold on Western thought. The idea is that the fundamental individuals of an acceptable metaphysical system must have their unity and identity conditions independent of human convention; otherwise, our metaphysical analysis has not reached bedrock. Leibniz was its advocate. When he waxed most eloquent about substance, in contrast to various pretenders, it is this fundamental intuition that is generating the steam: "I maintain that one cannot find a better way of restoring the prestige of philosophy and transforming it into something precise than by distinguishing the only substances or complete entities, endowed with true unity . . . ; all the rest is mere phenomena, abstractions or relationships" (LA 101).

What about Arnauld's claim that Leibniz's account of substance involved pure stipulation, and that a correct account of substance is consistent with the claim that some substances are entities whose essence is extension? Leibniz offered two important responses.

First, in the crucial letter of 30 April, Leibniz reacted by defending the true unity argument for the negative thesis, and supplementing it with a line of reasoning in support of the positive thesis—that every created substance must include a substantial form. He insisted on premisses (ii) and (iii) of the true unity argument; that is, that anything whose essence is extension is divisible, and that whatever is divisible is a being through aggregation. He then set out to show that, therefore, any entity that is divisible must have a decomposition containing entities that are not divisible. His main argument for the latter thesis employs the following principle:

> THE GROUNDING PRINCIPLE. For any x, if x is a being through aggregation, then there exists a decomposition D of x such that, for any y, if y is an element of D, then y is not a being through aggregation.[11]

Leibniz applied the grounding principle to extended entities that he regarded as aggregates. It is a consequence of premisses (ii) and (iii) of the true unity argument that any entity whose essence is extension is an aggregate. Consider the components of an extended aggregate. In the draft for the letter of 30 April, Leibniz said:

> It is at this point where the process to infinity cannot hold, just as it cannot hold in logic concerning reasonings. Consequently, if there is nothing in bodies except extension, in continuing the resolution one necessarily arrives at atoms, like those of Epicurus or Cordemoy, or it is necessary that bodies are composed of mathematical points, i.e., those that lack parts, or, finally, it will be necessary to hold that bodies are only phenomena, where there is nothing real. I do not believe that these atoms exist in nature and even less that bodies can be composed of points; and, if you agree, then there remains therefore that there are substantial forms if bodies are something more than phenomena. (LBr 81)

Obviously, Leibniz favored the last alternative. Assuming that bodies are not pure phenomena, he saw just two alternatives to introducing substantial forms: that bodies are composed of mathematical points or that bodies are composed of atoms. He rejected the first alternative—decomposition to mathematical points—on the ground that mathematical points are not parts, but rather limits, of whatever they compose. He rejected the other alternative—decomposition to atoms—on the ground that physical theory requires that every item whose essence is extension, hence every atom, is not only infinitely divisible but, in fact, infinitely divided.[12]

The passage quoted above from the draft for the letter of 30 April is useful because in it, unlike the corresponding passage in the letter itself, Leibniz displayed awareness that ruling out "a process to infinity" needed some support. Unfortunately, the only support offered in the quoted passage consists in noting a supposed analogy in the present case with some version of foundationalism in the case of reasoning; but for the details of the alleged analogy, we are on our own. Arnauld's response in his letter of 28 August 1687 is useful on some topics, but on the grounding principle and related matters his comments are desultory. After a few sallies wide of the mark, he changed the subject.[13]

In part, Leibniz came to the grounding principle from a consideration of our intuitions with respect to clear-cut cases of aggregates. His favorite examples in texts from our time period were a pile of stones (LA 58, 76; *Specimen* G/7/314 [MP 81]), an army (LA 97; *General Notation* [Grua 322]); a pile of sticks (*LH* IV 7C Bl. 70, 109–110); a herd of sheep (LA 76). Consider a herd of sheep—the Spey herd. There may be a decomposition of the Spey herd into the Knockdhu, Macduff, and Macallan herds; and perhaps the Macallan herd may be decomposed into the Glenlivet, Cardhu, and Tamdhu herds, but ultimately you must reach some sheep.

We can obtain a deeper understanding of Leibniz's commitment to the grounding principle for aggregates by exploring his second major response to Arnauld's allegation that his account of substance involves pure stipulation. In the letter of 30 April, Leibniz set out to show that no aggregate is an individual substance, without making use of the notion of true unity in his argument. It is seldom noted, but nonetheless true, that Leibniz was prepared to accept Arnauld's account of a substance as an individual entity *x* such that there is no individual entity *y* such that *x* is a mode or state of *y*. Presupposing this characterization of an individual substance, Leibniz then asserted the premiss he needed to reach the relevant conclusion: "What constitutes the essence of an entity through aggregation is only a state of being of those entities from which it is composed; for example, what constitutes the essence of an army is only a state of being of the men who compose it" (LA 96–97).

A question that deserves our attention is this: what did Leibniz take to be the relation between an entity through aggregation and the entities that compose it, in virtue of which the entity through aggregation can be said to be "a state of being of those entities from which it is composed"? Little in either the *Discourse* or the correspondence is helpful on this point. Fortunately, *General Notation* is extremely helpful. After a number of paragraphs in much the same spirit as the *Discourse* and correspondence, Leibniz wrote:

> It is worth investigating in what way an entity through aggregation, such as an army or even a disorganized multitude of men, is one; and in what way its unity and reality differ from the unity and reality of a man. It seems that the chief difference is to be observed in their attributes and operations. Some attributes are said equally of the whole as of its parts, as, for example, that the army is located in the fields of Marathon, which is true of each individual soldier. Other attributes can be said only of the whole, as, for example, that the army is 30,000 strong, and that it is disposed in a lunar-shaped battle line. Nevertheless, all these things can be stated and expressed even if the multitude is not viewed as a single entity. Thus, I can say that 30,000 soldiers are present and that one soldier is situated with respect to another just as the battle line mentioned requires, so that certain ones are distanced from a fixed point by so much, others by so much. . . . The chief point is this: an army accurately considered is not the same thing even for a moment, for it has nothing real in itself that does not result from the reality of the parts from which it is aggregated; and since its entire nature consists in number, figure, appearance and similar things, when these change it is not the same thing." (Grua 323)

I take the view being expressed in this remarkable passage to be the following: an aggregate is a state of being of those entities that compose it, in the sense that any truths about the aggregate can be expressed in propositions that ascribe modes and states to the composing entities without any need to refer to the aggregate itself. In other words, I take Leibniz to be claiming that aggregates are logical constructions from the modes and states of the entities aggregated. Given this view of aggregates, it is easy enough to see why Leibniz would accept the grounding principle.

Once we see Leibniz's rationale for the grounding principle, it is clear that considerable weight must be borne by premiss (iii) of the true unity argument, the thesis that whatever is divisible is a being through aggregation. On this point, the quoted passage from *General Notation* is also helpful. The last sentence indicates that a characteristic feature of a being by aggregation for Leibniz is this: a being by aggregation does not remain numerically the same, given any alteration in any member of its grounded decomposition set.[14] Leibniz made similar remarks about items whose essence is extension, that is, items that are divisible. In *DM* §12, considering the hypothesis that extension and its modes constitute body, Leibniz wrote: "If there were no other principle of identity in bodies than what we have just said, a body would never subsist more than a moment." Similar remarks occur in the long letter of 14 July (LA 53–54) and in *Mira de natura substantiae corporeae* (*Wonders Concerning the Nature of Corporeal Substance*), where Leibniz wrote: "If mass is of the essence of a human substance it can not be explained in what way a man remains the same" (*LH* IV 1, 14c Bl.11).

A straightforward presentation of his ideas on this topic is given in a paper entitled *Definitiones notionum metaphysicarum atque logicarum* (Definitions of metaphysical and logical concepts).[15]

> If many things are posited, then by that very fact it is understood that some single thing is immediately assumed. The former are said to be the parts; the latter, the whole. It is not necessary that they exist at the same time or in the same place; it is sufficient that they be considered at the same time. Thus, from all the Roman emperors together we construct a single aggregate. Actually, however, no entity that is truly one [*Ens vere unum*] is composed of parts. Every substance is indivisible and whatever has parts is not an entity, but only a phenomenon. From these considerations the ancient philosophers correctly attributed substantial forms, such as minds, souls, or primary entelechies, to those things that they said made up an Unum per se. And they denied that matter by itself is a single entity [*Unum Ens*]. Certainly those things that lack these [substantial forms] are no more a single entity [*Unum Ens*] than a pile of sticks; indeed, they are no more real entities than rainbows or mock suns. Certainly, these things do not remain the same more than a moment, whereas, by contrast, true substances remain through changes.[16]

Thus, Leibniz saw an intimate connection between entities that are divisible and entities through aggregation. An entity through aggregation is an entity whose existence depends upon those entities from which it is aggregated, in such fasion that a change in entities aggregated means a different entity through aggregation. But any entity whose essence is extension depends for its existence on a collection of parts that compose it; different parts composed mean a different extended entity. The feature common to divisible entities and entities through aggregation, to which Leibniz wished to draw our attention, is this: such entities are wholes composed in such fashion that their identity conditions require a different whole for every change in composition.

As we noted in section 2 of chapter 5, Arnauld was particularly concerned with the question of how, on Leibniz's theory, a substantial form could produce an entity—a corporeal substance—that is not divisible from ingredients that are divisible. Surely the point of Arnauld's query is the suspicion that the corporeal substance theory, realistically construed, is vulnerable to the very objections Leibniz had been pressing against the view that there are substances whose essence is extension. Let us pursue the point on Arnauld's behalf.

I use the term *composite entity* to refer to any individual, one proper component of which is another individual. In that sense corporeal substances, realistically construed, are composite entities, whereas monads, for example, are not. On the corporeal substance theory I am a corporeal substance, composed of a soul that informs a certain organic body, which, in turn, is an aggregate of corporeal substances. I intend to use *component* so broadly that not only are the corporeal substances that are aggregated to form my body components of me, but so is my left index finger, although it is no corporeal substance, but only an aggregate of such. Now, my index finger is separable from my body, so my body is divisible. I grant the obvious point: from the fact that my body is divisible and is a component of the corporeal substance that is identical with me, it does not follow that that corporeal substance is divisible. So there is room for the claim that a divisible entity is ipso facto no substance, whereas an entity with many components, some of which are divisible, may yet be a substance.

By itself, surely this is a slim point. It is hard to believe that so much metaphysics could hang on it. After all, even if I am not divisible, I am still deconstructible component-wise, so to speak. If being divisible is not compatible with being a substance, why isn't being deconstructible component-wise? That, I take it, is the point of Arnauld's query about the worm cut in half.[17] Say, if you want, that the worm is not divisible; still, it is plain as day that the worm is deconstructible component-wise. We can think of Arnauld as claiming that the following line of reasoning is as plausible as Leibniz's true unity argument: If there are corporeal substances, then there are substances that are extended. Whatever is extended is deconstructible component-wise. Whatever is deconstructible component-wise lacks true unity. But whatever lacks true unity is no substance. Therefore, there are no corporeal substances. Of course, Arnauld rejected the conclusion of this argument. His point was that the premiss to reject is the thesis that whatever lacks true unity is no substance. But if that premiss is rejected, Leibniz's true unity argument collapses. Leibniz would claim that whereas the thesis that whatever is divisible lacks true unity is true, the thesis that whatever is deconstructible component-wise lacks true unity is not. Our problem is to grasp the rationale for his acceptance of the one and rejection of the other. What is the operative difference between being divisible and being deconstructible component-wise on which Leibniz wished to build so much metaphysics?

The real test is this: does the composite entity in question depend on each and every one of its components for its existence? If the answer is yes, then we have no substance; if the answer is no, we may have a substance. So divisibility is not really the vital matter here; the vital matter is whether the particular entity in question can remain the same entity over time while undergoing change of components. Leibniz's claim amounts to this: given a substantial form suitably related to various components, we have a composite entity that can pass the test of remaining the same through change of components; absent the form, we do not.

Our task, then, is to explain Leibniz's reasons for supposing that a composite entity whose essence is extension cannot persist through changes of components, whereas a composite entity, one component of which is a substantial form, can. I believe that unearthing that explanation will show a link between the negative thesis and the positive thesis with which we began this chapter. The key, I think, is coming to grips with the following enigmatic passage from Leibniz's draft for the letter of 8 December: "But also the general concept of individual substance, which you seem inclined to accept, Sir, proves the same thing [that is, the negative thesis]. Extension is an attribute that cannot make up a complete entity; no action or change can be deduced from it—it expresses only a present state, not at all the future and past as the concept of a substance must do." (LA 72).[18]

3. IDENTITY

A version of the argument contained in the enigmatic passage above constitutes Leibniz's first round on substance in the correspondence. Consider the following from the long letter of 14 July:

> Moreover, if with respect to some person and even with respect to this universe something were to proceed differently from the way it went, nothing would prevent saying that it would be another person or another possible universe that God would have chosen. It would thus truly be another. There must also be an a priori reason (independent of my experience) that makes one say truly that it is I who was in Paris and that it is still I, and not another, who am now in Germany, and consequently the concept of myself must connect or include these different states. Otherwise, one could say that it is not the same individual, although it appears to be. And, in fact, certain philosophers who were not sufficiently acquainted with the nature of indivisible entities or entities per se have thought that nothing remained truly the same.

And it is because of that, among other things, that I judge that bodies would not be substances if there were nothing in them except extension. (LA 53–54)

It is instructive to compare this passage from Leibniz's letter of 14 July 1686 with its analogue in the draft for the letter. The analogous passage in the draft commences with an exposition of the same problem—a question about our right to claim that we remain the same entity over time. It looks for a solution in the same place—the nature of the concept of an individual substance—but it elaborates on the positive solution, and does not draw the negative conclusion about extension.

Let there be a straight line ABC representing a certain time. And let there be a certain individual substance, for instance myself, who remains or subsists throughout this time. Let us first take the I that subsists during the time AB, and then the I that subsists during the time BC. Since, then, the assumption is that it is the same individual substance that endures, or that it is I who subsist in the time AB, who am then at Paris, and that it is still I who subsist in the time BC, and who am then in Germany, there must necessarily be a reason that makes it true to say that we endure, i.e., that I who was in Paris, am now in Germany. For if there were none, we would have as much right to say that it is another person. It is true that my internal experience convinces me a posteriori of this case of identity, but there must also be an a priori reason for it. Now, it is not possible to find another, except that my attributes and state in the preceding time as well as my state and attributes in the later time are predicates of one and the same subject: *insunt eidem subjecto* [they are in the same subject]. Now, what is meant by saying that a predicate is in a subject, except that the concept of the predicate is included in some fashion in the concept of the subject? And since from the time when I began to be it was possible to say of me truly that this or that would happen to me, it must be acknowledged that these predicates were laws included in the subject or in my complete concept, which makes that which is called I, which is the foundation of the interconnection of all my different states, and which God knew perfectly from all eternity. (LA 42–43)

Surely these passages sound like a runaround. I claimed that one virtue of approaching Leibniz through Arnauld's criticisms is that those criticisms sometimes caused Leibniz to dismount from his metaphysical high horse and explain himself. This passage sounds like someone on a metaphysical high horse. Still, there can be no doubt that Leibniz regarded it as extremely important; in the draft he preceded the quoted passage with the plea "I hope that what I am going to say will be able to convince even Arnauld" (LA 42). What I have to say is speculative in the extreme; if ever there were important passages in Leibniz that are difficult to interpret, they are these. Much is at stake here. If our analysis of Leibniz's arguments for the negative thesis is correct, then the conclusions established in this passage must bear considerable weight. It is here, if anywhere, that we will find an explanation for the fact that some composite entities persist through change of components, while others—the beings through aggregation—do not. Furthermore, the quoted passages—both in the draft and the letter of 14 July—are intended to convince Arnauld that any alteration in the properties of Adam (draft)— or, indeed, any person (letter of 14 July)—would yield a different person. So, the quoted passages are intended to provide a convincing basis for super-intrinsicalness; the stakes are high. It is important to note one thing that Leibniz was not trying to establish in those passages. He was not trying to establish that there are created entities that persist over time as numerically the same and that are the fundamental individuals of the universe. That is, he is not trying to prove that there are created substances. His aim here was to analyze the notion of an individual substance.

Taking the two passages together, two extraordinary items cannot fail to capture attention. First, the remark, boldly stated in the letter of 14 July, that if things were to proceed differently with respect to some individual, then nothing would *prevent* our saying that it would be another person, in which case, Leibniz concluded, "it would thus truly be another." This sounds like the principle of sufficient reason run amok. Generalizing the reasoning apparently involved, one dreads the case where nothing prevents saying p and nothing prevents saying not p. But the culprit—the principle "For all p, if nothing prevents saying p, then p"—is not involved here. I think the point Leibniz had in mind is that remaining numerically identical over time is a basic condition that the metaphysically ultimate individuals of an acceptable substance ontology must satisfy. The requirements that must be satisfied for that condition to be met must be rigorous, objective, and independent of convention, thus yielding genuine units. The burden of proof is on someone who claims to have formulated suitably rigorous criteria for persistence of numerically the same individual. The point is not epistemological; it has nothing to do with problems that may arise in attempting to decide whether x at t and y at t' satisfy the stated criteria and, hence, are one and the same individual.[19]

The second striking item is contained in the draft: "And since from the time when I began to be it was possible to say of me truly that this or that would happen to me, it must be acknowledged that *these predicates were laws* included in the subject" (emphasis mine). "These predicates were laws"— a strange locution that immediately brings two things to mind. First, we are reminded of Leibniz's doctrine of marks and traces, which comes to this: if some substance x has property f at some time t, then at every moment of its history, there is some set of intrinsic denominations of x, in virtue of which x has f at t.[20] Second, we are reminded of numerous passages, especially from the later writings, in which Leibniz asserted an intimate connection between an individual substance and its developmental law, that is, a law yielding its states throughout its history.[21]

Consider the following samples (in each case the emphasis is mine):

> This law of order . . . *constitutes* the individuality of each particular substance.[22] For me nothing is permanent in things except the law itself, which involves a continuous succession and which corresponds, in individual things, to that [law] which is of the whole universe. . . . The fact that a certain law persists, which involves the future states of what we conceive to be the same—this is the very fact, I say, that *constitutes* the same substance.[23]

Similar passages occur in our time period. In the letter of 1690 to Arnauld, summarizing his position, Leibniz wrote, "Each substance contains in its nature the law by which the series of its operations continues and all that has happened or will happen to it" (LA 136). And in *General Notation* he wrote: "A thing can remain the same, even if it changes, if it follows from its own nature that numerically the same thing must have successive diverse states. Certainly, I am said to be the same who existed before, because my substance involves all my states, past, present, and future" (Grua 323). But the passages from our time period do not assert that the law governing the successive states of a substance *constitutes* a substance, as do those quoted from later periods. Is this a significant difference? I don't think so. The fact is that Leibniz was willing to assert that a developmental law governing the successive states of a substance constitutes a substance only if the law itself meets certain quite rigid requirements. In the passages quoted from later periods, Leibniz took it for granted that the requisite rigid requirements were built into the relevant developmental law. But the account of substance involved was fresh in our period; hence, Leibniz tended to emphasize the requirements themselves, rather than the law.

Among the presupposed constraints on developmental laws are those that preclude unacceptable juxtapositions, for example, the states constituting Leibniz's history up to high noon of 1 January 1700, followed by the sequence of states constituting Malebranche's life thereafter. The doctrine of spontaneity yields the desired results. Throughout the texts from our period it is clear that the series of states, constituting the history of an individual substance, must be generated by a relation of causality, applied to its initial state.[24] In the draft for the long letter of 14 July, Leibniz put it this way: "Every present state of a substance occurs to it spontaneously and is only a consequence of its preceding state" (LA 47). It is crucial to the interpretation I am recommending that "is a consequence of" be read as "has as a real cause." There are no passages in our texts where Leibniz denied this; the letter of 9 October contains a clear affirmation that the relation in question between relevant states of an individual substance is real causation.[25]

Some commentators have suggested that, according to Leibniz, the states of a substance are caused by (or, at least, consequences of) its complete concept. As support for that interpretation, consider *DM* §33: "Everything that happens to . . . each individual substance is a consequence of its concept." Similar passages occur at *DM* §§14 and 32; LA 75; and *Specimen* (G/7/312 [MP 79]). Perhaps LA 74 might be put forward as a compromise; it says of a particular state of a particular substance that it "is a natural consequence of its state *or* concept." But we should not compromise. That every property included in the concept of individual substance is intrinsic to that substance is a consequence of the concept of an individual substance, shared by Leibniz and Arnauld (among others). That an entity is an individual substance only if its series of states may be generated by a relation of real causality applied to its first state is a consequence of Leibniz's extraordinarily rigorous conception of what is involved in being an individual substance.

With those ideas in mind, we may avoid compromise as follows: although the topic of real causality, as employed, for example, by Descartes, Arnauld, Malebranche, and Leibniz, deserves a book unto itself, we may be sure that the notion involved is strong, involving a correlative concept of nonlogical necessity with real teeth in it. For our speculative purposes here we need to suppose that Leibniz regarded it as preserving intrinsicalness, so that whenever some state f of x is a real cause of state g of x, then if x has f intrinsically, x has g intrinsically. Some textual evidence supports this speculation. In the draft for the long letter of 14 July, Leibniz argued that the properties of a substance are intrinsic to it. He termed Arnauld's denial of this thesis a "prejudice." He then offered a diagnosis of the source of this alleged prejudice: "These things seem undetermined to us only because the advance indications or marks of them that occur in our substance are not recognizable to us" (LA 45). The diagnosis clearly presupposes a strong link between a property's being intrinsic to a substance and its being causally determined in a certain way.

We need one more assumption—a plausible one: that Leibniz supposed that the initial state of any substance is intrinsic to it. Putting together these assumptions with those previously noted, we may attribute the following view to Leibniz: every noninitial state of a substance has as its real cause some preceding state of that substance; and, since every state of an individual substance thereby turns out to be intrinsic to that substance, every state of that substance (including its initial state) is included in, and in that sense a consequence of, its concept.

Let us take stock of what ground has been covered and remains to be covered. Our first concern was how Leibniz differentiated between composites that are divisible and those that are not. Careful scrutiny of Leibniz's arguments in the correspondence suggested that that distinction turned on another—the one between composite individuals that remain numerically the same through changes over time and those that do not. So our question became: What conditions must an entity satisfy according to Leibniz in order to remain numerically the same over time? Our answer is that this condition obtains, according to Leibniz, if each noninitial state of an individual has as its real cause some predecessor state of that individual. On this interpretation, the doctrine of spontaneity is built into the notion of an individual substance, according to Leibniz. Given the thesis that the relation of real causality preserves intrinsicalness and the thesis that the initial state of a substance is intrinsic to it, we reach the doctrine of superintrinsicalness. Attempting to derive so much of Leibniz's doctrine concerning individual substances from his conception of what is required for real unity—unity consistent with remaining numerically identical through change—may seem excessive. But I take heart from a letter from Leibniz to l'Hospital, dated July 1695. After rehearsing the doctrines of spontaneity, world-apart, and marks and traces, Leibniz concluded, "The key to my doctrine on this subject consists in this consideration of what is properly a real unity, Monas" (GM/2/294–295).

Recollect that we reached these conclusions in the context of trying to grasp Leibniz's reasons for his negative thesis—that there is no individual substance whose essence is extension. It is clear that Leibniz thought that no entity whose essence is extension could satisfy the rigid requirements for remaining the same through changes in composition. But why? The answer seems to be that on Leibniz's principles there must be some aspect or component of an individual substance that persists through time, in virtue of which its developmental law holds of it—that is, in virtue of which its states are so related as to satisfy the principle of spontaneity. And, of course the internal generator, in virtue of which a substance produces its states in accord with its developmental law, is its primitive active force. In *Specimen*, after noting that an individual substance must have a complete concept and a power of acting, Leibniz identified its power of acting with its primitive active force. In section 1 of this chapter we studied Leibniz's reasons for supposing that force is distinct from extension and its modifications. Clearly, he held that whatever has force essentially is not such that its essence is extension. And the doctrine from *Specimen* seems to yield an account of Leibniz's reasoning in support of the positive thesis, that each corporeal substance includes a substantial form. The argument is that in order to be a corporeal substance, an entity must have primitive active force. Its primitive active force is its substantial form. Therefore, each corporeal substance includes a substantial form.

If the corporeal substance theory, realistically construed, were Leibniz's basic theory regarding created substances at the time of the correspondence, our investigation of his primary views concerning substantial forms might have reached closure. But in section 3 of chapter 5, I argued that, all things considered, the evidence indicates otherwise; that in our period Leibniz's deepest view was that primitive active force, physically interpreted, is a phenomenal representation of something yet more basic—a substantial form construed as a soul-like entity.[26] Similarly, I would argue that Leibniz regarded the developmental law of an individual substance as dependent on something yet more basic.

The deep thesis involved is the doctrine of marks and traces; as Leibniz put it in the draft for the long letter of 14 July: "Every individual substance always contains traces of everything that has ever happened to it and indications of what will ever happen to it" (LA 39). In *General Notation*, when explaining how a composite can have true unity, Leibniz wrote: "What makes these parts a unity in the case of man has attributes that cannot be made known without something that binds them together, namely, the faculty of perceiving and desiring" (Grua 323). I think that these passages fit together in a significant way. Since past and future states of a substance (or anything else) do not literally exist in the present, they can be contained in the present state of a substance only intensionally, past states as the objects of memory, future states, as the objects of desire, or at least expectation. But, of course, only a soul, or soul-like entity, is capable of having such states. Hence, only an entity that is a soul, or at least contains a soul, can satisfy the condition imposed by the doctrine of marks and traces and, hence, reach the level of an individual substance.

In this section I have attempted to extract considerable mileage from the attribution of an analysis of substantial persistence to Leibniz. Baldly put, the analysis amounts to this: substance x at t is identical with substance y at t' (with t′ later than t) just in case some state of x at t is a causal ancestor of some state of y at t'. The mileage extracted is my doing, but I owe the idea of the analysis to Louis Loeb.[27] Behind the analysis is the idea that the order of derivation is from spontaneity to superintrinsicalness to the concept-containment account of truth.

4. PROBLEMS OF INTERPRETATION

The preceding section is rampant with speculation. In this section I will note three problems related to this speculation, leaving their detailed resolution to others.

In the preceding section I quoted from Leibniz's letter to De Volder of January 1704, in which he claimed that a substance is constituted by its developmental law. The passage quoted is preceded by the following: "If it is claimed that substances do not remain the same, but that different substances which follow upon prior ones are always produced by God, this would be to quarrel about a word, for there is no further principle in things by which such a controversy can be decided" (G/2/264 [L 535]). Here Leibniz appears to suggest that whether we adopt an ontology of transitory individuals or an ontology of persisting substances is a matter of convention—a decision not grounded in the nature of things. Compare the passage from the

De Volder letter quoted above with the following, somewhat heated passage from *Theodicy* §393:

> It is good to take care, moreover, that by confounding substances with accidents, by taking away action from created substances, one does not fall into Spinozism, which is exaggerated Cartesianism. What does not act, does not merit the name of substance: if accidents are not distinguished from substances; if created substance is a successive being, like motion; if it does not endure beyond a moment, and is not the same (during some assignable part of time) no more than its accidents; if it does not operate any more than its accidents; if it does not operate any more than a mathematical figure or number: why shall we not say, like Spinoza, that God is the only substance, and that creatures are only accidents, or modifications?[28]

Did Leibniz take the scheme of transitory individuals to be metaphysically impossible, or did he have other grounds for favoring the scheme of created substances persisting through changes? I lean toward the latter. I believe that Leibniz's primary intellectual motivation here was theological, since he took various theological doctrines concerning the relation of God to creatures, especially creatures who are moral agents, to require persisting individuals.

In summing up the main points contained in his letter of 9 October, Leibniz began: "Every substance contains in its present state all its states, past and future" (LA 126). My recommendation, stated at the close of the preceding section, is that we should take this remark literally, provided that the containment mentioned is construed intensionally, that is, that containment of the past occurs through memory; of the future, through desire and expectation. But a problem arises here. At *DM* §34 Leibniz seems to hold that having memory is one feature that distinguishes spirits from nonspiritual substantial forms. But the doctrine of marks and traces applies to all substances, hence to all substantial forms. So the suggested gloss on the doctrine of marks and traces appears in jeopardy.[29] Moreover, in *New Essays* 114, after asserting the doctrine of marks and traces, Leibniz added, "Memory is not necessary for this." Nonetheless, I stand by the proposed gloss. What is needed is a distinction formulated, for example, in *New Essays* 161, where Leibniz wrote: "I shall say then that it is sensation when one is aware of an external object, and that *remembrance* [*reminiscence* in the French] is the recurrence of it without the return of the object; but when one knows that one has had it, this is *memory* [*souvenir*]" (emphasis mine).[30]

What we need is a distinction between remembrance—the sheer reoccurrence of a previous perception, unaccompanied by consciousness of past perception—and memory, which is remembrance accompanied by consciousness of past perception. My suggestion is that remembrance is all that my gloss on the doctrine of marks and traces requires with respect to containment of the past in a present state of a substantial form, and that Leibniz held that every form has remembrance. (For a source of this distinction in our time period, see *LH* IV 1, 14c Bl.9). The distinction is important for Leibniz; it occurs in texts from diverse periods. But, as is so common in Leibniz, the distinction is expressed in various terms. In his response to Bayle in 1702, Leibniz noted that spontaneity must be located in an entelechy because it, unlike matter, has memory ("souvenir, pour ainsi dire") and premonition.[30] In his notes preparatory to his published response to Bayle, Leibniz claimed that this "memory, so to speak" extends to all the preceding states of the entelechy, just as the doctrine of marks and traces requires (G/4/543). "Souvenir, pour ainsi dire" is remembrance, as explained in the *New Essays*.

In section 3 we considered Leibniz's problem about the content of the claim that substance x at time t is identical to substance y at time t' (with t' later than t). I suggested that Leibniz's analysis comes to this: substance x at t = substance y at t' if and only if, for some states S and S', x is in state S at t and y is in state S' at t' and S is a causal ancestor of S'. Removed from the context of Leibniz's metaphysics of causation, this analysis does not look promising. Were there intersubstantial causal relations, it would be disastrous. But our context includes Leibniz's metaphysics of causation, in particular the doctrine of spontaneity; its initial formulation in the correspondence is this: "Every present state of a substance occurs to it spontaneously and is only a consequence of its preceding state" (LA 47).[31] This formulation of the doctrine of spontaneity fits the analysis of substantial identity that I have ascribed to Leibniz.

Unfortunately, this formulation of the doctrine of spontaneity appears incomplete in relevant respects when compared with more elaborate versions. Consider the following carefully crafted version from the letter of 30 April: "Everything happens in each substance in consequence of the first state that God gave it in creating it, and, extraordinary concourse aside, his ordinary concourse consists simply in the conservation of the substance itself, in conformity with its preceding state and with the changes that it carries with it" (LA 91–92). The doctrine formulated in this passage is exemplified in another, written in Latin and struck from Leibniz's copy of the letter of 30 April. In the struck passage (LBr 90), Leibniz employed the scholastic distinction between immanent causation (intrasubstantial causation) and transeunt causation (intersubstantial causation). He claimed that, in metaphysical rigor, transeunt causation is restricted to God's operations and comes in three forms: creation, conservative causation, and the production of miracles. The same scholastic terminology occurs in the unpublished draft for the letter of 30 April, in which Leibniz wrote: "I accord only immanent actions and passions (speaking in metaphysical rigor) to created substances, always putting aside the universal cause" (LBr 78).

Consider Leibniz's threefold classification of God's transeunt operations.

God's conservative causation (that is, his "ordinary concourse," as understood by Leibniz) may create problems for the doctrine of spontaneity, but it seems to pose no special problems for the proposed analysis of substantial identity over time, so we put it aside for now.[32] By contrast, God's creative causation does pose a problem. Unless we restrict the proposed analysis to created substances, all states exemplified in the world will turn out to be states of God, according to Leibniz. Yet, again, we face the bleak possibility of lapsing into Spinozism. Let us then take the proposed analysis to be restricted to created substances.

The third mode of God's intersubstantial activity—the production of miracles, his "extraordinary concourse"—is where some have claimed that a difficulty for the proposed interpretation arises. In section 6 of chapter 4, we noted that Leibniz distinguished between the nature of a substance—what it brings about through its own active force—and the concept of a substance, which includes those states brought about by its own active force, plus any that it possesses that exceed that force. According to Leibniz, states in the latter category are miraculous, hence presumably due to God's transeunt operation in the miraculous mode.[33] Now we have the alleged problem. Take some (noninitial) state S' of some created substance x at time t', where x's being in state S' at t' is miraculous. The natural interpretation of Leibniz's remarks in our period has this consequence: x's being in state S' at t' is not a causal consequence of some prior state S of substance x; rather, it is a causal consequence of God's transeunt operation in the miraculous mode. Does this have the unfortunate consequence that miraculous intervention would "disrupt" a substance's identity over time? No, since our recommended analysis of the identity of a created substance over time only requires that *some* state of x at t' have as causal ancestor some state of x at t. Still, my effort to explain Leibniz's thesis that a substance has all its properties intrinsically requires that every noninitial state of a substance have some preceding state of that substance as a causal ancestor.

So a problem remains; it is clearly formulated and discussed by Robert Adams in "Predication, Truth, and Transworld Identity in Leibniz."[34]

He suggests that we stick to the idea that, according to Leibniz, each noninitial state of a substance is a consequence of the primitive active force of that substance. We must then distinguish between natural outcomes of that active force and miraculous outcomes of that force, utilizing Leibniz's epistemological characterization of a miraculous state as one that "cannot be foreseen by the reasoning of any created mind, however enlightened it might be" (*DM* §16). The textual support is thin, but the idea is worth pursuing. I have a contribution to make to it. Take a humdrum, nonmiraculous, noninitial state S' of some substance x at t', which, Leibniz would claim, is a consequence of (that is, is caused by) some state S of x at t. According to Leibniz's doctrine of conservative causation, even in such a case God makes a crucial contribution, for God produces whatever there is of perfection in x's being in S' at t', whereas x's own contribution consists in whatever there is of limitation in x's being in S′ at t′.[35] Hence, even in humdrum, nonmiraculous immanent causation, God makes a causal contribution. So it is not a matter of contrasting a nonmiraculous case, where God makes no causal contribution, with a miraculous case, where God makes the sole causal contribution. With this in mind we may amplify Adams's suggestion and assume that there is a natural connection between what the created substance contributes on the limitation side and what God contributes on the perfection side. In the case of a miracle, the created substance still makes its causal contribution on the limitation side. But in the case of a miracle, God's contribution on the perfection side exceeds what is natural, given the created substance's contribution.

Chapter 7

❖❖❖❖❖❖❖❖❖

ACTION

The *Discourse on Metaphysics* begins and ends with God; in between comes the metaphysics—the metaphysics of created substances. It commences in article 8, whose heading reads: "In order to distinguish the actions of God and of creatures, we explain in what the concept of an individual substance consists." Leibniz began the text of article 8 thus: "It is difficult enough to distinguish the actions of God from those of creatures [and also the actions and passions of those same creatures]; for there are some who believe that God does everything, and others imagine that all he does is to conserve the force that he has given to creatures. The sequel will show how far the one or the other can be said. Now, since actions and passions properly belong to individual substances [*actiones sunt suppositorum*], it will be necessary to explain what such a substance is."

In an important sense, then, the main problem motivating the metaphysics of the *Discourse* is quasitheological, an effort to provide an adequate account of the provenance of the actions performed by creatures in this world. Clearly, this problem of provenance of actions bears on the general problem of evil and the special problem of the distribution of grace. Leibniz harvested some of the consequences of his theory for these crucial theological problems in articles 30 through 33 of the *Discourse*. Some of that harvest has been discussed in previous chapters. Now our task is to come to grips with the theory itself.

Article 8 of the *Discourse* contains both the concept-containment account of truth and the complete-concept theory of individual substance. Article 9 draws consequences from these two theses, the "notable paradoxes." The paradoxes come in two groups, the second containing doctrines that Leibniz took to be relevant to formulating a proper answer to the problem of the provenance of actions. The relevant "paradoxes" are here identified using language close to Leibniz's own, in virtue of which they take on the aura of advertising slogans.

1. Each created substance is like an entire world, a world apart, independent of every other substance, except God.
2. The phenomena of each created substance are only a consequence of its being.
3. Each created substance expresses the whole world and/or God, and the past and future, as well as the present.
4. Each created substance accommodates itself to every other substance, thereby generating a concomitance or harmony among substances.

Some of what is involved in (1) and (2)—the doctrine that each created substance is a world apart, and the doctrine of spontaneity—has been discussed in the previous chapter. What remains to be said about (1) and (2) concerns aspects of Leibniz's doctrine of causality. Paradoxes (1), (2), and (4), taken together, yield the doctrine Leibniz usually referred to in our texts as the theory of concomitance or harmony, and in subsequent works as the theory of the pre-established harmony. How (3), the doctrine of universal expression, is supposed to be related to (4) is a puzzle which, on the whole, has failed to puzzle Leibniz scholars.

Paradoxes (1), (2), and (4) conjoined—the theory of concomitance or harmony—are intended by Leibniz as a general account of causality, the foundations of the orderliness in the universe, and the relation of mind to body. As such, he envisaged the theory as in competition with, and a distinct improvement on, all its rivals, which Leibniz took to be the scholastic theory of influx, Malebranche's occasionalism, and, in the special case of mind-body interaction, Descartes's alleged "change the direction, but keep the same quantity of motion" view. Each of these theories constitutes a purported solution to a metaphysical problem. Consider two humdrum situations. In the first, one billiard ball A strikes another billiard ball B, which was stationary and now is in motion, in circumstances where we would say that at that time, B would not have moved had it not been struck by A. In the second, a philosophy professor wishes to illustrate his free will to skeptical students, so he raises his arm voluntarily, in circumstances in which we would all say that had he not decided to raise his arm, his arm would not then have been elevated. The metaphysical problem—as it was understood in our time period—was to provide an adequate account of the ontological structure of these humdrum situations. It is true that the accounts offered by Malebranche and Leibniz both make essential reference to the activity of God. Still, the problem is essentially metaphysical; one can imagine theories that attempt to solve it without reference to God.

However, in the late seventeenth-century context, a complete theory of causation was expected to shed light on a theological problem as well. As is to be expected, the alleged data requiring explanation in the case of the theological problem are not so humdrum. There was a consensus at the time that God not only creates the world but conserves it, and, furthermore, that God's conservation of the created world amounts to something like his continual re-creation of it. There was, then, a near-universal consensus that created entities depend on God for their properties as well as for their existence. But the actions of creatures are properties of them. Yet some creatures are responsible for some of their actions. The theological problem was to provide an account of divine and creaturely causality adequate to account for the total dependence of creatures on God, yet consistent with attributing responsibility for actions to creatures. Both Malebranche and Leibniz struggled with this problem. The results of those struggles—their respective solutions to the theological problem—are not strictly components of, respectively, occasionalism and the theory of concomitance, not as I understand these doctrines. Bits and pieces of Leibniz's solution to the theological problem are to be found in the *Discourse* and in the correspondence, but no coherent statement of it is contained therein. This is mildly surprising, since the heading for section 8 of the *Discourse* and the first paragraph of that section raise the theological problem as much as the metaphysical. Unfortunately, Arnauld let the theological problem go. We will include a brief account of Leibniz's favorite solution.

Not surprisingly, Leibniz thought that his own solution to the metaphysical problem of causality was the solution of choice. He thought the scholastic theory of influx and the Cartesian account of mind-body interaction ultimately unintelligible and, hence, unacceptable. So he viewed occasionalism, primarily in Malebranche's version, as the chief competitor. In section 1, we will focus on Leibniz's criticism of the influx theory and the Cartesian theory, as allegedly applied to the mind-body problem. We will also consider Leibniz's application of his own theory of concomitance to his favorite illustrative example, the mind-body problem. In section 2, attention is directed to Arnauld's objections to Leibniz's theory of concomitance. Arnauld's major claim is that concomitance amounts to occasionalism, when expunged of certain metaphysical excesses. Hence, in section 3 salient aspects of Malebranche's version of occasionalism will be discussed, followed, in section 4, by exposition of Leibniz's principal objections to Malebranche's occasionalism. Section 5 concerns the structure of Leibniz's reasoning, whereby he inferred the theory of concomitance from its foundations, with particular attention to the relation between the doctrine of universal expression and the theory of concomitance. In section 6 we will consider a radical version of world-apart. Section 7 concerns Leibniz's favorite solution to the theological problem.

1. INTERSUBSTANTIAL CAUSATION

When a substance acts, it causes changes to occur, either in itself, in which case Leibniz would say we have an instance of immanent causation, or in another, in which case Leibniz would say we have an instance of transeunt causation.[1] In the second half of the seventeenth century it would have required a conscious act of disengagement to discuss the topic of action and causation without at least an obiter dictum on the problem of mind-body interaction. Leibniz was not thus disengaged. Since the problem in its then current form was largely a reaction to aspects of Descartes's philosophy, it is natural for us to start with Leibniz's comments on Descartes on mind-body interaction in our time period. In a letter to Malebranche, dated 23 January 1679, Leibniz wrote: "I am entirely of your opinion concerning the impossibility of conceiving that a substance that has nothing but extension without thought, could act on a substance that has nothing but thought without extension." (A/2/1/455 [L 209]). But Leibniz held that Descartes was committed to the relevant theses—that body was extension without thought, whereas mind was thought without extension; and, further, that mind and body appeared to interact, particularly in perception (where the body seems to act on the mind) and some cases of voluntary action, where the mind seems to act on the body. So Leibniz held that Descartes had a problem.

Curiously, in our texts Leibniz appears to have held two seemingly incompatible attitudes towards what measures, if any, Descartes took to resolve the problem. At LA 94 (letter of 30 April 1687) Leibniz set out a criticism of an explanation of how the mind acted on the body, which explanation Leibniz attributed to Descartes. The explanation in question is the "change the direction, but not the quantity of motion" account, previously mentioned. By contrast, in the draft for the letter of 8 December 1686, after noting the facts to be explained, and after outlining the two serious candidates for consideration, Leibniz wrote: "Perhaps Descartes favored concomitance rather than the hypothesis of occasional causes, for he did not express his opinion upon this matter, as far as I know" (LA 70). The same agnosticism about Descartes's treatment of the difficulty is expressed more explicitly in the unpublished draft for the short letter of 14 July 1686. Leibniz noted one of the most important consequences of his account of truth and the nature of individual substances: "It is the explication of the manner according to which substances have commerce among themselves, and particularly how the soul perceives what takes place in the body and, in return, how the body follows the wishes of the soul. Descartes was content to say that God willed that the soul receive some sensations following certain movements of the body, but he has not wished to undertake to explain it; his disciples have had recourse to the universal cause, and have claimed that God produces in the soul sensations appropriate to the movements of the body, but that is to have recourse to a miracle" (LBr 69, 69v). This passage is particularly interesting for our present purposes. Notice that mention of the phenomena purportedly explained by the "change the direction, not the quantity of motion" view— that is, the body following the wishes of the will—is followed immediately by a declaration that Descartes simply noted the facts and, piously affirming their concordance with God's will, offered no explanation.

This same odd pairing occurs elsewhere in Leibniz's work. For example, in the *New System*, published in 1695, after outlining his basic principles, Leibniz wrote: "After having established these things, I thought I had reached port; but when I set myself to meditating on the union of the soul with the body, I seemed to be cast back into the open sea. For I could find no way of explaining how the body causes something to happen in the soul, or vice versa, nor how one created substance can communicate with another. Descartes threw in the sponge, as far as can be judged from his writings" (G/4/483 [MP 121]). Compare this with the following from a reply to Foucher's objections to the *New System*:

> You know that Descartes believed that the same quantity of motion is conserved in bodies. It has been demonstrated that he was mistaken in this. I have shown that it is always true that the same motive force is conserved, rather than the same quantity of motion, as he thought. Even so, the changes that take place in the body as a consequence of the modifications of the soul caused him embarrassment, because they seemed to violate this law. Hence, he thought that he had found a way out, which is surely ingenious, by saying that it is necessary to distinguish between motion and direction of motion; and that the soul can neither augment nor diminish the motive force, but that it changes the direction of the course of the animal spirits, and it is in this way that voluntary motion takes place. (G/4/497 [MP 129–130])[2]

Leibniz's claim that "Descartes threw in the sponge, as far as can be judged from his writings" suggests that Descartes recognized a problem needing solution and yet did not provide a solution that can be located in his writings. Leave aside the first part of this claim. The second part seems right, at least to this extent: nothing comparable to the "change the direction, not the quantity of motion" view can be found in Descartes's extant writings. In fact, they indicate a rather blasé attitude toward the problem of interaction, though not the union, of mind and body. The following remark, contained in Descartes's last letter to Arnauld (29 July 1648), is typical: "Moreover, that the mind, which is incorporeal, can impel the body, requires no reasoning or comparison with other things, but, in fact, is shown to us daily by the most certain and most evident experience; indeed, this is one of those things known per se, which, when we propose to explain it by other things, we obscure" (AT/5/222). This leaves us in a mild quandary about what led Leibniz to attribute the "change the direction, not the quantity of motion" view to Descartes. Maybe Leibniz knew something we don't about what was contained in Descartes's writings; after all, the only source for some of Descartes's extant writings is copies made by Leibniz. At least as likely, Leibniz was attributing to Descartes a view held by followers of Descartes, but not by Descartes himself.[3]

Let us consider the "change the direction, but not the quantity of motion" view, and Leibniz's objections thereto, even though the view may not be Descartes's.[4] The basic ideas are these. As noted in section 1 of chapter 6, Leibniz assumed that Descartes assumed the following:

1. The quantity of motion of a body B at time *t* is the product of its size, perhaps its weight, measured in suitable units, and its speed, again measured in suitable units.
2. God always conserves the same quantity of motion in the world.

Now consider a case in which alterations in the pineal gland bring about alterations in the animal spirits, thereby initiating a physical causal chain leading to a case of arm elevation. How can the mind bring about alterations in the pineal gland, having such striking consequences, without thereby falsifying (2)? By altering the *direction* in which the pineal gland is moving without altering either its size or speed, where its speed, of course, is not a function of its direction. The whole thing depends on the distinction between speed and velocity, where the latter is a vector quantity, determined both by speed *and* direction. Leibniz thought this scheme ingenious, but, like so many ingenious schemes in philosophy, ultimately unacceptable.

In the first place, as noted in chapter 6, Leibniz rejected (2). In the second place, Leibniz thought that even if (2) were acceptable, another conservation principle of which Descartes was not aware ruled out the "change the direction, not the quantity of motion" gambit, with its clever use of a multidirectional pineal gland. In a letter to Bayle Leibniz pointed out that the basic insight required is that motive force is to be measured by the amount of work that its possession permits its possessor to do. Hence, he wrote, properly formulated conservation principles are consequences of a general metaphysical principle—the entire effect is exactly equivalent, in relevant respects, to its full cause.[5] Leibniz thought that, whatever measure of motive force turned out to fit the facts, the general principle had as a consequence that in an aggregate of bodies, closed to outside forces, not only is motive force conserved, but so is direction of motion of elements in the aggregate relative to some fixed point in the aggregate.[6]

Understandably, expounding this criticism of Descartes gave Leibniz considerable pleasure. But the fact is that it is not crucial to his rejection of Descartes's alleged account of mind-body interaction. Suppose further investigation convinced Leibniz that while he was right about the measure of motive force, the principle of conservation of direction of motion was mistaken. Leibniz would then have brought out his major objection; namely, that no account is given, and no account can be given, of how the mind manipulates the pineal gland, even if its manipulations are confined to changing the gland's direction of movement. Perhaps, then, this is what Leibniz meant when he claimed that Descartes threw in the sponge: the "change the direction, not the quantity of motion" view tells an interesting (if, in the end, physically impossible) tale, but it does no more than delay the time at which the sponge is tossed. Thus, in the letter of 30 April 1686, after outlining the "change the direction, not the quantity of motion" view, but before arguing that it involves the physically impossible, Leibniz wrote: "It will still be quite difficult to explain what connection there can be between the soul's thoughts and the paths or angles of the body's direction" (LA 94). Similar remarks are to be found in Leibniz's response to Foucher's objections to the *New System* (G/4/497 [MP 130]). In later writings on this topic, Leibniz's language became even more forceful. Commenting on Locke's suggestion that the idea of the mind moving the body can be as clearly and distinctly conceived as the idea of extension, Leibniz said: "This hypothesis is not intelligible" (*New Essays* 220). In the *Theodicy*, Leibniz wrote: "That the soul changes the quantity of force and that it changes the line of direction, those are two things equally inexplicable" (*Theodicy* §60).

As we have seen, Leibniz sometimes attributed the "change the direction, but not the quantity of motion" view to Descartes. Throughout his philosophical career he attributed the influx theory to "the schoolmen" and frequently referred to it as "the common philosophy," rarely deigning to specify a particular schoolman as advocate of the theory. When he did, the usual culprit was Francisco Suarez. In his introduction to an edition of Nizolius's work, commenting on various figures of speech employed by Scholastics, Leibniz mentioned the verb "to flow in" (*influere*), and said: "On the invention of this last word Suarez prides himself not a little. . . . Introducing the phrase 'flow in' ('influx'), he defined cause as what flows being into something else—a quite barbarous and obscure expression" (A/6/2/418 [L 126], 1670).[7] There are numerous references to the influx theory (or, alternately, the way of influence) in our texts, all disparaging. Here are some examples, beginning with one that says what the theory is:

> Some have believed that something or other passes from the soul to the body, and conversely—this is the hypothesis of real influx. From the concept of an individual substance it follows in metaphysical rigor that all the operations of substances, both actions and passions, are spontaneous, and that with the exception of the dependence of creatures on God, no real influx from one to the other is intelligible.

> Nothing enters into our spirit naturally from outside; our soul does not receive "messenger species," as if it had doors and windows. (*DM* §26)

> It is useless to require the influence of another . . . substance, not to mention that this influence is absolutely inexplicable.

The exact nature of the influx theory, as Leibniz understood it, may be unclear, but the basic structure of his critical reaction to it is straightforward. First, he argued that it is "inexplicable," "impossible . . . except by Divine omnipotence" (G/4/484 [MP 122]). Second, he argued that the nonmiraculous actions of a created substance are all consequences of its nature or concept, and hence that in these cases there is no need for a cause external to the substance itself. Leibniz's argument seems to presuppose that the states of a substance are not overdetermined. We have construed the doctrine of spontaneity as requiring that each noninitial (nonmiraculous) state of a created substance have a predecessor state of that substance as a real cause. To reach the desired conclusion—the doctrine that we have called world-apart, that is, that finite substances do not causally interact—a premiss ruling out overdetermination is required.

Consider the following: "Anything capable of having many causes is never a complete entity" (LA 72).

At present, I want to focus attention on Leibniz's manner of closing out the argument in hand. A sample case of that closure occurs in *DM* §33. Having argued for the relevant thesis of intrasubstantial causal determination, and having assumed that causal overdetermination does not apply in the case of substances, Leibniz concluded that, therefore, mind and body do not interact causally. The same argument occurs in *Specimen* (G/7/313–314 [MP 80–81]) and in the correspondence (see LA 47 and 69). Stated fully, the argument appears to require these premisses: minds are substances, some bodies are substances, and no mind is identical with a body. Moreover, "some bodies are substances" would have to be read as "some extended items lacking soul-like components are substances." We *know* that the conjunction of what is required yields a proposition Leibniz did not accept. In his letter of 28 September 1686, Arnauld said: "Our body and soul are two substances that are really distinct. Now, by putting a substantial form into body in addition to extension, one cannot imagine that they are two distinct substances" (LA 66). Leibniz replied: "In my opinion our body itself, leaving the soul aside . . . can be called a substance only by an abuse" (LA 75). In his copy of Arnauld's letter, above the phrase "by putting a substantial form into body" Leibniz wrote: "the soul itself is this substantial form."[8] Of course, this is old-hat by now. And it is not only this one argument that appears at risk. If we go back to the beginning of our discussion, to the letter to Malebranche, in which Leibniz parsed the problem of commerce between the mind and the body in terms of two totally different kinds of substance, every argument considered appears to share the same presuppositions, presuppositions that we know Leibniz rejected.

In *From Descartes to Hume*, Loeb notes that Leibniz's solution to the mind-body problem—the pre-established harmony—presupposes a dualist framework, which is lacking in Leibniz's "mature metaphysics, within which there are no extended or material substances."[9] We have left open the possibility that in our time period Leibniz had not reached the position of his mature metaphysics—that he was then committed to some version of the corporeal substance theory. The theory of corporeal substance obviously involves the existence of "extended or material substances," but, for all that, it is not a dualistic theory, not in its unmodified form.

We need to engage in some damage assessment. We will concentrate on the unmodified form of the corporeal substance theory—a "worst case" scenario. Two points seem noteworthy. First, even if, in the end, we have to accept the conclusion that there really is no mind-body interaction problem for Leibniz, there remains a problem about the proper explanation of the regularities—apparent causal interactions—holding among corporeal substances. With respect to that problem, at least, Leibniz's overdetermination argument will be applicable. Moreover, his theory of concomitance constitutes a viable competitor to Malebranche's occasionalism.

Second, we should remind ourselves that Spinoza took the problem of the relation of the mind to the body seriously and proposed a solution that has important similarities to that of Leibniz—minus God's purposeful behavior —even though he admitted only one substance. The problem to which Spinoza offered parallelism as a solution was generated for him by a guiding intuition concerning a deep conceptual division between accidents falling under the attribute "thought" and those falling under the attribute "extension."[10] Surely, it is a variant of that intuition that moved Descartes to postulate two ultimate kinds of finite substances. As Bennett says: "He [Spinoza] never questioned the truth of a doctrine that I shall call property dualism, which says that the properties of things can be cleanly split into two groups, mental and physical, with no property belonging at once to both groups; this being so understood as to rule out any defining of mental terms through physical ones. When I speak of Spinoza's dualism, I allude to that doctrine which he shares with Descartes. He rejects Descartes's stronger substance dualism, which adds to property dualism the thesis that no one thing can have properties of both kinds."[11]

Bennett notes that Spinoza coupled this intuition with a thesis about the nature of causality, and thereby derived the result that there could be no causal interaction between the mental and the physical.[12] Leibniz shared the intuition concerning a division into two groups of properties, mental and physical, so construed as to denigrate the possibility of causal interaction between mental and physical states of affairs. It can be doubted that he understood the division so as to preclude defining physical terms through mental terms; resolution of that doubt turns, in part, on how broadly we are prepared to stretch the notion of a definition. In his mature metaphysics, Leibniz might view the idea that there are genuine causal relations holding between states of affairs wholly characterized by mental properties, and states of affairs wholly characterized by physical properties, as involving a kind of category mistake.

To this point, our damage assessment has been limited to the suggestion that a problem with respect to apparent causal interaction between the mental and the physical may persist for Leibniz, even if he remained committed to the notion of corporeal substance as the basic individual unit in the created world. Furthermore, we could resuscitate his reasoning as contained in the overdetermination argument, for example, were we to find that he applied the world-apart doctrine and the thesis of spontaneity to souls and to (some) bodies. We have already noticed that Leibniz did assert the relevant doctrines of souls.[13] And he asserted the relevant doctrine of bodies in a passage contained in the letter of 9 October 1687 to Arnauld, which was bracketed by Leibniz with a notation in German for the copyist that it not be sent. Here is the passage: "Bodies, speaking rigorously, are not pushed by others when impact occurs, but by their own movement, that is, by their own elasticity, which is still a movement of their parts. Every bodily mass, large or small, has already in it all the force that it will ever acquire, but the collision with other bodies only gives it its determination, or rather, this determination occurs only at the time of the collision" (LA 116). Exactly the same doctrine is stated in the unpublished draft for the letter of 9 October (see LBr 107v). And it is to be found in *Specimen* (G/7/313 [MP 79–80]) and *Primary Truths* (521 [MP 90]). It is elegantly formulated in part 2 of *Specimen dynamicum* (1696):

> From what has been said it also follows, wonderfully, that every passion of body is spontaneous, that is, it originates in an internal force, although on occasion of the occurrence of something external. However, here I understand its own individual passion, which arises from percussion, that is, that which remains the same, whatever hypothesis is finally assigned or to whatever we finally ascribe absolute rest or motion. For, since the percussion is the same, whatever the real motion belongs to, it follows that the effect of percussion is distributed equally between both, and thus in the collision both suffer equally, and both act equally; and thus half the effect comes from the action of one, the other half from the action of the other. And since half the effect or passion is also in one and half in the other, it suffices to derive the passion that is in one from the action in it; we require no influence of one upon the other. (GM/6/251)

It seems likely that Leibniz would say that the bottom line of our damage assessment report ought to read: "Contrary to initial appearances, no damage." For me to issue such a report, I would have to know much more than I now know about the fit of Leibniz's physics with his metaphysics in our time period. In the next section we will compare occasionalism with concomitance, as accounts of apparent causal interaction among substances. Much of the discussion concerns apparent mind-body interaction. We will treat this as an illustrative example, which, in Leibniz's case, may be off the mark.

2. ARNAULD'S OBJECTIONS

The long letter of 14 July 1686 served as Leibniz's transition letter, bringing to Arnauld's attention features of the *Discourse* other than those directly bearing on freedom and necessity. What concerns action is stated at the close of that letter. Having reviewed his theory of individual substance and having concluded that real physical influence between substances is impossible, Leibniz wrote:

> The hypothesis of occasional causes does not satisfy a philosopher, it seems to me. For it introduces a kind of continual miracle, as if God

were constantly changing the laws of bodies, on the occasion of thoughts of minds, or changing the regular course of thoughts of the soul by exciting in it other thoughts, on the occasion of movements of the body; and generally as if God ordinarily intervened other than by conserving each substance in its course and according to the laws established for it. There is then only *the hypothesis of the concomitance or harmony between substances* that explains everything in a conceivable manner and worthy of God, and that is even demonstrative and inevitable, in my opinion, according to the proposition that we have just established. It seems to me also that it agrees much more with the freedom of rational creatures than *the hypothesis of impressions or that of occasional causes*. God first created the soul in such a way that, in its ordinary course, he has no need of these changes; and what happens to the soul is born to it from its own depths, without its having to accommodate itself subsequently to the body, any more than the body to the soul. Each one following its laws, the one acting freely, the other without choice, agrees, one with another, in the same phenomena. (LA 57–58)

Let us begin by extracting what we can from Arnauld's questions and criticisms, and Leibniz's responses. We have three letters from Arnauld to consider: those of 28 September 1686, 4 March 1687, and 28 August 1687. Fortunately for us, Arnauld made his points with respect to two examples throughout the correspondence:

Example 1. Arnauld is wounded in the arm, that is, certain alterations occur in his arm which are conjoined with his soul's immediately feeling pain. Arnauld added the following data with respect to this example: first, he (his soul) did not know of the physical wound prior to feeling the pain, that is, he came to learn of the wound via the pain; second, he would not have felt the pain had his arm not been wounded (LA 64–65).

Example 2. Arnauld wanted to take off his hat, so he raised his arm as a beginning. That is, his soul had a certain wish, which was accompanied by certain movements in his body. Arnauld added the following data with respect to this example: first, the arm has no cognitive mechanism adequate to inform it of the soul's wishes, in order to respond appropriately thereto (LA 106); second, his arm would not have elevated, had he not wanted it to do so (LA 65).

In the letter of 28 September, Arnauld argued as follows with respect to the first example. For every event, there is some real cause of that event. The pain that accompanied his wound is an event, so it has a real cause. On Leibniz's view, unlike that of an occasionalist like Malebranche, God is not the real cause of an ordinary event in the course of nature, of which Arnauld's pain is an example. On Leibniz's view, like that of Malebranche, an event in one created substance (Arnauld's body, in this case) cannot be the real cause of an event in another created substance (Arnauld's soul). But on Leibniz's view, Arnauld's body and Arnauld's soul are distinct substances.[14] So, no event in Arnauld's body (or any other body, for that matter) is the real cause of Arnauld's pain. So according to Arnauld, no plausible candidate remains except some event in Arnauld's soul. Arnauld asked, rhetorically: "But what reply can you make to those who object that it would then be necessary for the soul to know that its body is indisposed before being sad about it: whereas it appears that it is the pain that warns it that its body is indisposed?" (LA 65). This last argument comes in the context of consideration of St. Augustine's theory that bodily pain is simply the soul's sadness in virtue of distress to its body. St. Augustine's theory was a familiar stalking-horse in the seventeenth century. Assertions of it in our time period are hard to come by; for a limited defense by Leibniz, see LA 70–71.

It is unfortunate from our point of view that Arnauld's argument peters out in this fashion. For, clearly, the last alternative considered—that Arnauld's pain was caused by some preceding event in Arnauld's soul—is exactly what Leibniz held. Notice that Arnauld's objection in this case is based on the first item of the alleged data of the case; no appeal is made to the second item of the data. But it is clear to me that Arnauld took the second item —that the pain would not have occurred had the wound not occurred—as inconsistent with the claim that a causal history of the occurrence of the pain could include only states of Arnauld's soul. At any rate, Arnauld made an analogous point with respect to the second example.

As in the case of the first example, Arnauld set out to show that Leibniz's views had the consequence that a certain event lacked a cause; in this case, the event is Arnauld's arm elevation or some physical event occurring in a causal history of that event. Again, on Leibniz's view, unlike that of an occasionalist like Malebranche, God is not the real cause of an ordinary event in the course of nature, of which Arnauld's arm elevation is an example. Like Malebranche, Leibniz would deny that a physical event like an arm elevation could have as its real cause a mental event like a human volition. Hence, Arnauld argued, there is nothing left but some physical event preceding the arm elevation. He said: "If I wish to take off my hat, I raise my arm. This upward movement of my arm is not in accordance with the ordinary rules of movements. What, then, is the cause?" (LA 65).

Consider the second item of the data in this case—that Arnauld's arm would not have elevated had he not wanted it to do so. Arnauld took this alleged datum to be inconsistent with the claim that an extended causal history of the arm elevation in question need mention only physical events. That, I take it, is what led him to conclude that the event in question was not "in accordance with the ordinary rules of movements." Leibniz, of course, denied that. Indeed, on his copy of Arnauld's letter, above "is not in accordance with the ordinary rules of movements," Leibniz wrote, "I believe that it is." [15]

Arnauld based one criticism on the first datum under the second example (LA 106). He asked rhetorically: "Since [my arm] is without consciousness, how could it know when I wanted it to move?" This is an argument we may safely ignore.

Arnauld raised one last objection that deserves attention. In the letter of 8 December 1686, Leibniz responded to Arnauld's criticisms, insisting that in the first example the pain was, in fact, caused by a preceding state of Arnauld's soul; and in the second example that the arm elevation was, in fact, caused by a preceding state of Arnauld's body. Expanding on his response to Arnauld's reasonings in connection with the second example, Leibniz claimed that precisely when Arnauld willed that his arm elevate, just then the laws of motion, applied to a preceding state of Arnauld's body, had as a consequence the occurrence of the wanted elevation, "since God took it [the willing] into consideration in advance, when he made his decision about this succession of all things in the universe" (LA 74).

Consider an extended causal history of Arnauld's pain and an extended causal history of Arnauld's arm elevation (in the cases noted in our examples). As far as Leibniz is concerned, the histories may extend as far back in time as you like, provided you do not reach creation. In general, when we talk about an extended causal history of some mentioned event, let us stipulate that the history in question starts (so to speak) with some post-creation event. In the cases in question, let us think of the first extended history as going back at least as far as some event preceding the wounding of Arnauld's arm; and let us think of the second extended history as going back at least as far as some event preceding Arnauld's decision to raise his arm. Leibniz claimed that no physical event belonged to the first history and that no mental event belonged to the second history. Arnauld simply could not bring himself to believe that Leibniz meant what he said in this context. In particular, he could not bring himself to believe that Leibniz believed that in every single case in which some created being successfully wills that a bodily event occur, there is an extended causal history of that bodily event of which no mental event is a member. After all, Arnauld reasoned, sometimes a creature successfully wills a body to move, where (a) no other body then strikes the creature's body, and (b) the creature's body, just subsequent to the willing, was not in motion. But no body not in motion can cause itself to move. Surely, Arnauld argued, what holds in this case must hold generally; so he concluded: "It remains, therefore, that it is this 'consideration by God' that is the real and efficient cause of the movement of my arm. Now, you yourself call this consideration by God 'his decision,' and decision and will are the same thing: therefore, according to you, every time I wish to raise my arm, it is God's will that is the real and efficient cause of this movement" (LA 85). This argument is a crucial link in Arnauld's effort to show that, insofar as Leibniz's theory of concomitance is coherent, it reduces to occasionalism. This became one of the major themes in subsequent criticism of Leibniz's theory of concomitance during his lifetime—that when some of Leibniz's metaphysical excesses are deleted, concomitance reduces to occasionalism.

While Arnauld's major effort was to argue that Leibniz's theory reduces to occasionalism, Bayle employed some of the same observations as Arnauld with the intent of reducing the theory of concomitance to absurdity.[16] Bayle's objection is based on his understanding of Leibniz's explanation of the causal structure of cases like Arnauld's first example. The letter of 9 October 1687 contains an account of that structure.[17]

Applied to the case in hand, here are the details: Arnauld's body is punctured at t; some perception of the puncture exists at t in Arnauld's soul (whether he is aware of it or not). The puncture causes the wound (that is, the separating of flesh with attendant physical changes) to occur at t'; the perception of the puncture at t causes the pain to occur at t'.

The point of Bayle's objection is this: according to Leibniz, the perception of the puncture is the real cause of the pain; by contrast, the puncture itself is not a real cause of the pain; indeed, it is not even a real cause of the perception of the puncture. It is neither causally necessary nor causally sufficient for either the perception of the puncture or the pain. Therefore, Bayle reasoned, in making the counterfactual assumption that Arnauld's arm was not punctured at t, we remove no condition that is causally relevant to Arnauld's pain; so the envisaged state of affairs, which still includes the real cause of Arnauld's pain (according to Leibniz), is causally possible. Bayle inferred that would warrant the following assertion:

1. Even if Arnauld's arm had not been punctured at t, Arnauld would have been in pain at t'.[18]

But Bayle, like Arnauld, took it to be a datum of the case described that the following conditional holds:

2. If Arnauld's arm had not been punctured at t, Arnauld would not have been in pain at t'.

But (1) and (2) are inconsistent. Since the theory of concomitance implies (1), it must be false. That, I take it, is Bayle's argument.

The doctrine of superintrinsicalness generates special problems for Leibniz in ascribing sense to counterfactual conditionals.[19] Nonetheless, Leibniz formulated a reply to this argument (see G/4/519 (493) for his response in 1698, and G/4/530–532 for his response in 1702). The reply consists in arguing that concomitance, plus the envisaged facts, do not imply (1). Leibniz asks us to consider this state of affairs: Arnauld's arm is not punctured at t, yet his soul contains a perception of the puncture and subsequent pain. It is crucial to Bayle's argument that this state of affairs be both metaphysically and causally possible, on Leibniz's view. In his initial comments Leibniz claimed that the state of affairs in question is "a metaphysical fiction . . . contrary to the order of things . . . that cannot occur naturally" (G/4/518–519 [L 493]). We may then suppose that Leibniz rejected (1) because the relevant state of affairs is contrary to the nature of things. What did Leibniz intend by calling the imagined state of affairs "a metaphysical fiction"?

A metaphysical impossibility? I do not think so. In notes preparatory to his reply to Bayle in 1702, Leibniz said of the state of affairs in question (or, rather, one relevantly similar) that it is "a metaphysical possibility . . . that does not agree with the facts and their reasons" (G/4/530). This is a standard way in which Leibniz characterized a state of affairs that he regarded as metaphysically possible but contrary to the nature of things. Part of the force of Bayle's criticism derives from the fact that, on Leibniz's view, the state of affairs in question is causally as well as metaphysically possible. A concept of causal possibility, fashioned in terms of a notion of real causality, which is limited (among creatures) to *intra*substantial causality, will yield the result that all sorts of disorderly *inter*substantial states of affairs are causally possible. Leibniz aimed to recoup his losses by introducing the concept of what is natural, which includes a certain level of intersubstantial orderliness. Hence, Leibniz must argue that (1) is inconsistent with the nature of things, even though the corresponding state of affairs is both metaphysically and causally possible. An investigation of the basis of Leibniz's position here would take us far afield. In sections 3 and 4 we will return to Arnauld's major objection to concomitance. In section 6 we will consider a radical version of the doctrine of world apart, suggested by Leibniz's response to Bayle.

3. MALEBRANCHE'S OCCASIONALISM

When Leibniz spoke about occasionalism, he almost always had Malebranche's version in mind. When not harassed by critics claiming that concomitance really reduced to occasionalism, Leibniz was generous in praising what he took to be Malebranche's insights. Thus, writing to l'Hospital on 30 September 1695, Leibniz, having noted some respects in which Malebranche's occasionalism differed from his theory of concomitance, said of the latter: "It can be said that it is not so much an overthrow of his doctrine, as an advancement, and that it is to him [Malebranche] that I am indebted for my foundations on this subject" (GM/2/299).

Indeed, Leibniz at first was prepared to use the language of occasional causes. Early versions of *DM* §32 read as follows: "In the language of metaphysics, God alone operates on me and alone can do good or evil to me, other substances being only occasional causes, because God, having regard for all, shares his blessings and obliges them to accommodate themselves to one another." (The underlined words were subsequently replaced by "contributing only by reason of these determinations.") And: "But in practice one attributes actions to occasional causes." (The underlined words were subsequently replaced by "particular reasons.") [20]

The letter to l'Hospital, quoted above, continues in the following interesting way: "We agree that the mind and the body have no influence on one another, and that all the perfections of things are always produced by the operation of God. I only add that what he produces in A, conforming to what he produces in B, conforms also with its own laws that he has established for A, which has not been considered sufficiently" (GM/2/299). The important point to extract from this passage is that Leibniz took it that he and Malebranche agreed on a distinction between primary and secondary causes, where God is taken to be the primary cause, the creator and conserver of the universe and everything in it, whose operations are responsible for whatever perfections are exemplified by creatures. What is involved in the distinction between primary and secondary causes, and attendant theses, is discussed briefly in section 7 of this chapter. The remainder of this section concerns differences between Malebranche and Leibniz with respect to secondary causes, that is, the causal activity of creatures.

Consider, to begin with:

i. For any alteration e, there is some real cause of e.
ii. For any created substances x and y, if $x \neq y$, then there are no states S and S' such that S is a state of x and S' is a state of y and the occurrence of S is a real cause of the occurrence of S'.

Proposition (i) is a straightforward application of the principle of sufficient reason, construed causally, and (ii) represents Leibniz's claim that each substance is a world apart. Leibniz and Malebranche accepted both (i) and (ii).[21] But when we reach Leibniz's thesis of the spontaneity of substance—that is, that each nonmiraculous state of a created substance (with the exception of its original state) has as its real cause, some predecessor state of that very substance—we reach the parting of the ways. And the parting is dramatic, for Malebranche held the following:

iii. No created entity is ever the real cause of any alteration.

Malebranche's commitment to (iii) may seem to undercut my remarks above about the extent of his agreement with Leibniz. I said that Malebranche and Leibniz agreed on a distinction between primary and secondary causes. But how much real agreement is there, given that, according to Malebranche, the primary cause—that is, God—is the only real cause? Moreover, is it true, after all, that there is some proposition p such that Malebranche and Leibniz would agree that (i) expresses p and that p is true? The distinction between a concept and some particular analysis thereof, to which a particular philosopher may subscribe, is relevant here. For Malebranche, as for Leibniz, the idea of a real cause is the idea of something that brings about change.[22] This is easily obscured by the fact that Malebranche usually rushed past his intuitive idea of a real cause in order to state and defend his major thesis with respect to the idea; namely, (iii).

Malebranche offered a number of arguments for (iii). We should note two of them. First, Malebranche held that in order for x to be a real cause of y, there must be a necessary connection between x and y. But among the cases of alleged causation, the only cases where we see the requisite necessary connection are those where the connection is between God's willing that an event occur (or object exist) and that event's occurring (or object's coming into existence).[23] Therefore, only God's will is a real cause. Second, Malebranche argued that a proper understanding of the doctrine that God's conservative causation amounts to continual creation implies that God is the sole real cause. The argument may be summarized as follows: the doctrine of conservative causation implies that at each instant at which some substance x exists, God wills that x then exist. But God's will is always determinate; that is, God does not simply will that x exist at time t. Rather, with respect to each property f that x has at t that requires a cause, God wills that x have f at t. But God's will is always effective. So, for every feature of every created substance that requires a cause, God's will serves as its real cause. Assume a principle excluding causal overdetermination in the case of real causes, and there is simply nothing left over for anything else to cause.[24]

I believe that there is room for genuine debate here between Leibniz and Malebranche, because the underlying intuitive idea of a real cause is one they shared. Unfortunately, that debate did not take place. I have found only one passage where Leibniz took on the first argument noted above—a private reading note, not intended for publication or correspondence.[25] Leibniz took his theory of concourse between God and created substances to constitute a reply to Malebranche's second argument.[26] The relevant ideas are outlined in section 7 of this chapter.

In the remainder of this section I will concentrate on some details of Malebranche's version of occasionalism that are germane to understanding Leibniz's criticism of that system. We will consider two topics in turn: the distinction between God's acting by particular volitions and God's acting by general volitions, and the nature of occasional causation.

General versus particular volitions. For Malebranche, an investigation of real causality is an investigation of the ways of God with respect to his willing. An investigation of secondary causation, according to Malebranche, is an investigation of the role of occasional causes in relation to one of the ways of God's willing. Malebranche formulated a basic distinction with respect to the ways of God's willing in the first elucidation to the *Traité*.

a. I say that *God acts by general volitions*, when he acts in consequence of general laws that he has established. For example, I say that God acts in me by general volitions when he makes me feel pain when I am pricked [by a pin], because in consequence of the general and efficacious laws of the union of the soul and the body that he has established, he makes me suffer pain when my body is ill-disposed (*OM*/5/147; emphasis is mine).

b. I say, on the contrary, that *God acts by particular volitions* when the efficacy of his will is not determined by some general law to produce some effect. . . . Thus, supposing that a body begins to move without being pushed by another, or without changes in the will of some mind, or without some other creature who determines the efficacy of some general law, I say that God would move this body by a particular volition (*OM*/5/147–148; emphasis is mine).

On the basis of this distinction between God's acting by general volitions and God's acting by particular volitions, Malebranche characterized the notions of occasional cause and miracle.

c. In order that the general cause [God] may act by laws or by general volitions and that his action may be regular, constant and uniform, it is absolutely necessary that there be some *occasional cause* that determines the efficacy of these laws (*OM*/5/67; emphasis is mine).

d. Whether an effect is common or rare, if God does not produce it in consequence of his general laws, which are natural laws, it is a *true miracle*. . . . Thus I say that God acts by particular volitions only when he brings about a miracle (*OM*/8/696).

Comprehending this scheme presents various problems, some serious, some not so serious. We begin with one that has received considerable attention, but that is not so serious. Malebranche's frequent remark that an occasional cause "determines the efficacy" of a law, or of God's will, caused needless controversy. Arnauld asked how something utterly lacking in real causal power can determine the efficacy of anything.[27] What Malebranche had in mind may be explained as follows: a general law is the propositional content of one of God's general volitions. An examination of the various items that Malebranche took to be laws suggests that they all may be construed as having the following form: for any x and y, if x is f and x bears R to y, then y is g. To say that a's being f and bearing R to b is the occasional cause of b's being g is just to say that a is f and bears R to b, and there is a law G of the relevant form. It is as simple and harmless as that.[28]

Now let us consider a serious problem that has received less attention. Note the importance to Malebranche's scheme of his claims that God does not always act by particular volitions and that God's acting by general volitions "spares him, so to speak, a great number of particular volitions" (*OM*/5/202). These claims ground his distinction between miraculous events and natural occurrences, and are at the heart of his theodicy. Malebranche's idea is that God's acting by general volitions is simpler than the alternative, hence, other things being equal, preferable, even though acting by general volitions sometimes yields outcomes that are inferior to what might have been achieved through a particular volition.[29] Arnauld raised the following objection: "It cannot be said, unless one strangely abuses . . . the meaning of terms, . . . that God brings about something by general volitions. For everything that happens, happens in particular, and not in general. . . . And thus, all that can be said, speaking exactly, is that God acts by particular volitions in consequence of general laws" (*OA*/39/175).

In responding to Arnauld's objection, Malebranche drew a distinction between two types of volitions: practical volitions and what we might call simple volitions.[30] A simple volition may be expressed by preceding its propositional content by something like "Would that it were the case that. . . ." A practical volition may be expressed by preceding its propositional content by something like "Let it be the case that. . . ." When God wills that p with a practical will, then p obtains. God has a simple will that p whenever he would prefer that p be the case, were other things equal—which they often are not. If the volition—simple or practical—is general, then its propositional content is as previously specified, that is, for any x and y, if x is f and x bears R to y, then y is g. If the volition—simple or practical—is particular, then its propositional content is expressed by something of the form "the x such that x is f is also g." Consider, for example, Malebranche's claim that God wills that all humans are saved. Since not all humans are saved, the volition in question must be simple. We can express the relevant general volition by reading "x is f" as "x is human"; "y is g" as "y is saved"; "x bears R to y" as "x is identical with y"; and preceding the result by "Would that it were the case that . . . ."

The distinction between simple and practical volitions in God is useful for a number of purposes germane to Malebranche's scheme. But the distinction is of no use in meeting Arnauld's objection noted above, because that objection has to do only with God's practical will, particular or general. We may develop Arnauld's objection in the following manner.

Consider a general law G of the form "For all x and y, if x is f and x bears R to y, then y is g." Let G be the propositional content of some practical general volition VG of God. Consider two individuals, a and b, where b is g in virtue of a's being f and bearing R to b. Arnauld asked: what, according to Malebranche, is the real cause of b's being g? Malebranche's main thesis about real causality implies that the real cause of b's being g is some practical volition of God. VG? Apparently not. Malebranche's main argument for his main thesis about real causality employs the principle that there must be a necessary connection between a real cause and any effect thereof. But there is no necessary connection between God's willing G,—that is, having VG—and b's being g. Some have suggested in discussion that perhaps Malebranche thought that, given that a is f and bears R to b, there is a necessary connection between God's having VG and b's being g. But this is too egregious an error to attribute to Malebranche without compelling textual support, which seems lacking.

Others have suggested in discussion that Malebranche took the real cause of b's being g to be the complex state of affairs consisting in God's having VG and a's being f and bearing R to b. A defect of this suggestion is that on this account God's will is no longer the only real cause, although God's will would be at least a real partial cause of every alteration. Moreover, God's will would be the total real cause of some alterations—those where God acts by a particular volition. But, on this account, occasional causes, like God's will in the case of general volitions, would be real partial causes. And that consequence seems to me something Malebranche rejected. It is true that he often made note that in explaining particular phenomena we must make reference to the relevant natural agents, that is, occasional causes. Typically, he went on to add that reference to God's will is relevant to explain the operation of occasional causes.[31] Hence, a complete explanation of a particular event, according to Malebranche, will often involve reference to occasional causes, as well as to the will of God. But it would be a blunder to infer that Malebranche held that occasional causes are ever real causes, even real partial causes.[32] It is just that full explanations of natural phenomena typically involve reference to occasional causes, as well as real causes.

Leibniz, like Arnauld, assumed that if some volition of God is the real cause of a particular event, then the volition must be particular.[33] But unlike Arnauld, Leibniz did not draw the inference that, therefore, on Malebranche's scheme, God must act by particular volitions whenever he brings about a particular event. This reading of Malebranche appears to depend on drawing a distinction between God's *acting* by a particular volition and a particular volition of God's being the real cause of the occurrence of some particular event. This distinction is plausible if we attribute the following analysis of acting by a particular volition to Malebranche.

e. God acts by a particular volition in bringing it about that y is g just in case:
(i) God has the practical volition that y be g, and
(ii) there is no general law G of the form "For all x and y, if x is f and x bears R to y, then y is g", such that God has the practical volition that G, and y's being g instantiates the consequent of G at a time when there is some x that is f and bears R to y.

This analysis permits us to distinguish between God's acting by a particular volition and God's acting by a general volition, even though every alteration has as its real cause some particular practical volition of God.

Construed as an analysis of Malebranche's intentions, there are some things to be said for (e) and, unfortunately, some things to be said against it. One thing to be said for it—something that is of importance to our inquiry —is that it seems in accord with Leibniz's understanding of Malebranche on this matter. Consider this passage from a reading note concerning Bayle's *Réponse aux questions d'un provincial*, written at a time when Leibniz was preparing the *Theodicy*: "I do not believe that miracles and particular volitions are the same thing. In my opinion all the volitions of God with respect to a particular thing are particular. But they are the consequences of the application of universals, i.e., they are reasonable."[34] I take it that in this passage Leibniz was agreeing with Arnauld that God can bring about a particular event only by means of a particular volition. Furthermore, he understood Malebranche's distinction between God's acting by a particular volition and God's acting by a general volition in a manner consistent with the analysis proposed above.

Leibniz then went on to criticize Malebranche's thesis that God sometimes acts by particular volitions—whenever he performs a miracle. The criticism is developed in paragraph 206 of the *Theodicy*: "I agree with Malebranche that God brings things about in the manner most worthy of him.

But I go a little further than he with respect to general and particular volitions. Since God cannot bring anything about without reasons—even when he acts miraculously—it follows that God has no volition about individual events that is not a consequence of a truth or general volition. Thus I would say that God never has a particular volition such as Malebranche understands it, i.e., a primitive particular volition." Given Leibniz's commitment to the principle of sufficient reason, this objection was to be expected. For Leibniz, acting reasonably is acting in accordance with some general principle. Hence, acting by a particular volition—as that notion is analyzed in (e)—is acting without a reason, that is, unreasonably.

As a by-product of understanding Malebranche, we have located one of Leibniz's central objections to Malebranche's scheme, namely, that on it all miraculous behavior on God's part would be irrational. My current interest is in emphasizing the point that Leibniz seems to have understood Malebranche in the manner proposed above. However, it should be noted that some textual evidence goes against the analysis proposed in (e), understood as an analysis of Malebranche's considered view. In various passages Malebranche explicitly stated that God does not *have* a practical particular volition with respect to those events that are brought about by a general volition, that is, those that have occasional causes. Here is an example: "I claim that God does not will with a practical particular volition those effects that are produced by occasional causes" (*OM/*7/577).[35]

There is an alternative interpretation of Malebranche according to which, when God acts by a general volition, not only does he not act by a particular volition, but he does not even have a practical particular volition with respect to the relevant events. In various texts Malebranche proposed an interpretation of the biblical account of God's six-day labor at creation followed by rest, which we might characterize as follows:[36] God brought about the initial state of the universe by various particular volitions, which we may combine into one—the initial-state volition. God also willed that certain laws obtain, which we may combine into one general volition—the law volition. Thereafter (so to speak), but for an occasional particular volition for the sake of a miracle, no more divine volitions are required. We may combine all the particular volitions associated with miracles (subsequent to the initial state of the universe) into one—the miracle volition. Except for our efforts to economize by combining like volitions into one, our characterization has a textual basis.

We might be tempted to try to solve our problem by saying that the real cause of *b*'s being *g* according to Malebranche is the complex state of affairs consisting in the initial-state volition, the law volition, and the miracle volition, or, at any rate, some components of that complex state of affairs. The merits of this interpretation are considerable. Real causes, even partial real causes, are all volitions of God. Moreover, there is a necessary connection between the alleged cause and its effect. Furthermore, God is thereby "spared" having the practical particular volition expressed by "Let it be that

the *x* such that *x* = *b* is *g′*. It may be that something like this is what Malebranche had in mind, but if so, he was adept at concealing it. Note that on
this interpretation, as well as on its predecessor, Malebranche would appear to remain vulnerable to Leibniz's criticism that when God performs a
miracle, he acts by primitive practical particular volitions—a violation of the
principle of sufficient reason, by Leibniz's lights.

In fairness, we should note that on occasion Malebranche offered a more
detailed account of a miracle, one that may not be vulnerable to Leibniz's
criticism. Consider the following passage from the *Dialogues on Metaphysics*:

> When God performs a miracle and does not act in accordance with the
> general laws that are known to us, I claim that either he acts in accor-
> dance with other general laws that are unknown to us, or what he does
> then is determined at that time by certain circumstances that he had
> in view from all eternity in forming that simple eternal, invariable act
> that contains both the general laws of his ordinary providence and also
> exceptions to these very laws. But these circumstances should not be
> called occasional causes in the same sense that, for example, impact of
> bodies is the occasional cause of motion, because God did not make
> general laws to regulate the efficacy of his volitions uniformly on the
> occurrence of these circumstances. For in the exceptions to the general
> laws, God acts sometimes one way and sometimes another, although
> invariably in accordance with what is required of him by that one of
> his attributes that is, so to speak, most valuable to him at the time
> (*OM*/12/177 [Doney 175]).

I think that a plausible way to understand Malebranche here is to suppose
that he was drawing a distinction between reasons and causes. He applied
the term *general law* (in this context, at any rate) to universal generalizations that are causal in character. Given this reading, when God acts by a
particular volition, he may have reasons for his action—reasons that could
be formulated by universal generalizations that are not causal in character.[37]
Such volitions would not be primitive particular volitions, in Leibniz's sense.
My own sense is that a full and fair exposition of Malebranche's theory
would show that he is not vulnerable to Leibniz's criticism noted above.[38]

Occasional causation. Malebranche saw the system of occasional causes as
the key to understanding causality in its theological setting, as well as in the
realm of nature. The full system is described in dialogue 13 of the *Dialogues
on Metaphysics*. There we are told that occasional causes may be organized
into five categories, or sets of laws.[39] The fivefold scheme comprises the
following:

1. The laws of the communication of motion, where the occasional causes
   are impacts of bodies and the effects are changes in the velocity of bodies
   impacted.[40]
2. Laws of the union of mind and body, where the occasional causes are

brain traces and the effects are thoughts in the soul, or vice versa; or the occasional causes are emotions or volitions of the soul and the effects are movements of animal spirits in the body, or vice versa.[41]

3. Laws of the union of finite minds with Universal Reason (that is, ideas in God's mind), where the occasional causes are our desires for illumination and the effects are perceptions of ideas in God's mind.[42]
4. Laws in virtue of which angels act on bodies (including human bodies), where the occasional causes are angelic desires and the effects are movements of bodies angelically desired.[43]
5. Laws of the distribution of internal grace, where the occasional causes are the desires of the human nature of Jesus Christ, and the effects are those states of pleasure or revulsion that constitute internal grace.[44]

According to Malebranche, laws of the first three types govern the realm of nature; they may be known through reason and experience.[45] Laws of the last two types govern the realm of grace, according to Malebranche; to the extent to which they are known at all, it is through revelation. Malebranche's seventeenth-century colleagues tended to put considerable emphasis on the laws purporting to govern the realm of grace. Malebranche employed the fourth set in order to account for various historical phenomena usually attributed to the miraculous intervention of God. More significantly, he employed the fifth set in order to solve a special version of the problem of evil: the inequitable and uneconomical distribution of that internal grace presumed necessary for salvation. Essentially, he argued that God wisely selected a simple means for distributing the relevant grace, namely, the desires for such distribution that are attributable to the human nature of Christ. But the human nature of Christ does not have infinite actual knowledge of the relevant situations at any one time. This is the source of the inequitable and uneconomical distribution of internal grace.[46] It was Malebranche's contribution with respect to the distribution of grace that first roused Arnauld's opposition.

We need not engage in a full analysis of Malebranche's account of an occasional cause. But we do need to settle one issue of special relevance to a comparison of Malebranche with Leibniz. The issue is whether Malebranche required an occasional cause to be a necessary, as well as sufficient, condition of its effect.[47] Numerous passages suggest that he did. Thus, in the *Traité*, speaking of occasional causes, Malebranche wrote: "These causes have their effect always and very promptly, and without them the effect is never produced. For example, since the impact of bodies is the occasional cause of the change that occurs in their motion, if the two bodies do not collide, their motions do not change, and if they change, one can be sure that they collided" (*OM*/5/69). Arnauld based his account of Malebranche's analysis of occasional causation on this passage.[48] He took it to imply something like the following: Event e is the occasional cause of event e' only if (1) events of the same type as e are always followed by events of the same type as e'; (2) e is causally sufficient for e', (3) e is causally necessary for e'; and (4) some component of e temporally precedes every component of e', and some component of e is simultaneous with some component of e'.

Clearly, Arnauld took it that Malebranche supposed that in order for one event e to be an occasional cause of another event e', e must be causally necessary for e'. But in responding to Arnauld, Malebranche indicated that he did not accept this condition, and, indeed, careful consideration of his system makes it clear that he could not.[49] Consider, again, the case of Arnauld's raising his arm voluntarily in order to remove his hat. Focus attention on the first motion of animal spirits, which, according to Malebranche, initiated the physiological side of this action. On Malebranche's scheme, there are at least four distinct ways in which motion of the type involved might have come about. First, it might be a case of God's acting by a particular volition, that is, it might be a miracle. We may leave that case aside; we are concerned here only with events that have occasional causes. Second, it might have as its occasional cause the desire of some angel. We may leave that case aside as well. We want to concentrate on the operation of occasional causes in the realm of nature. Third, it might have as its occasional cause impact with some body that is in motion. And fourth, it might have as its occasional cause Arnauld's volition concerning his arm.

By Malebranche's lights, in the case in hand, the last possibility is the actual occasional cause. But the point is, even if we restrict ourselves to non-miraculous events in the realm of nature, we cannot consistently attribute to Malebranche the claim that each occasional cause is a necessary condition of its effect. And Malebranche was well aware that the laws of the union of mind and body allow a means of generating motion that is totally foreign to the laws of the communication of motion. Consider this passage from the first elucidation to the *Traité*: "According to the general laws of the communication of motion, heavy bodies fall toward the earth. My arm is heavy and nevertheless I raise it toward the sky, because I will it. Certainly God, who determines the motion of the animal spirits in order to raise my arm according to my desires, acts then only in consequence of the general law of the union of the soul and the body, by which law I have the power to move my arm. Nevertheless, this movement would pass for miraculous, if we did not recognize other natural laws than those of the communication of motion" (*OM*/5/198–199).[50]

There are numerous passages where Malebranche seems to say that impact is a necessary condition of nonmiraculous change of velocity. I believe that close attention to context will show that Malebranche generally had in mind a proviso that the change of velocity in question does not have as its occasional cause some volition of a created mind.[51] Similar considerations apply, I believe, to a proper understanding of the content of Malebranche's conservation principles. In the tenth of the *Dialogues on Metaphysics*, Malebranche summarized his thoughts on the laws of the communication of motion thus: "In a word, God chose the simplest laws derivative from that single principle that the stronger must overcome the weaker, with the condition that there always be in the world the same quantity of motion in a given direction" (*OM*/12/243 [Doney 243]). Prudence suggests that we should take it that Malebranche intended the conservation principle to apply to "the purely material world," thus leaving aside those motions whose occasional causes are volitions.

4. AGAINST OCCASIONALISM

We want to focus on the debate between Malebranche and Leibniz on causality in "the realm of nature." We need to concentrate on what each would regard as nonmiraculous events in the realm of nature. Once again, contrary to initial appearances, there is adequate agreement for meaningful debate. Although Leibniz and Malebranche had different conceptions of the miraculous, they were in remarkable agreement on the classification of individual cases. This is not a trivial matter. The ordinary seventeenth-century Christian intellectual would have regarded many more events as miraculous than Malebranche or Leibniz did. Both were men of science who had faith in the idea that, on the whole, God works his wonders through natural occurrences, with only rare recourse to the miraculous.

What follows is not intended as an impartial, balanced assessment of the relative merits of Leibniz's theory of concomitance and Malebranche's theory of occasionalism. The context of our discussion is more circumscribed. In the *New System*, having outlined the theory of concomitance and compared its virtues with those of its chief competitors, Leibniz wrote, rather weakly: "This hypothesis is very possible." A page later, he was more bold: "Besides the fact that this hypothesis is recommended by all these advantages, it may be added that it is something more than a hypothesis, since it seems hardly possible to explain things in any other intelligible way" (G/4/486 [MP 123–24]). The claim involved in this passage is what Leibniz sometimes meant when he said that the theory of concomitance could be demonstrated. Thus, in a letter to Lady Masham, he formulated an argument that he later called a *demonstration* of the theory of concomitance, but which then (1704) went under the name "the hypothesis of pre-established harmony."[52] The outline of the argument is this: either influx theory or occasionalism or concomitance is true; but neither influx theory nor occasionalism is acceptable. Therefore, concomitance is the correct theory.[53] On other occasions, Leibniz contrasted this argument via the elimination of competing theories with an alleged a priori proof of concomitance based on his account of substance.[54] The a priori proof from the account of substance is the subject of section 5 of this chapter. In this section we will focus on the argument from elimination.

Usually, Leibniz made no effort to prove that the three theories exhaust the viable alternatives.[55] Still, in what follows I assume that something near to that was his goal. We will consider his effort to establish that occasionalism is unacceptable, construing occasionalism quite broadly but keeping Malebranche's version in mind. Obviously, the less specific content we ascribe to occasionalism, the more difficult it is to prove it false and, yet, the closer Leibniz comes to establishing the disjunctive premiss. I believe that Leibniz had essentially three distinct arguments against occasionalism in our time period: an argument against the occasionalist's conception of individual *natures;* a general argument, based on the occasionalist's alleged positing of continual *miracles;* and a specific argument, based on an alleged need for God to disturb (*troubler* in French) certain laws in the case of mind-body interaction—the "*troubler* argument," as I call it.

Natures and miracles. As noted in section 6 of chapter 4, Leibniz carefully distinguished the nature of a thing—its primitive force—from its concept. He regarded what depends on the nature of a created substance as nonmiraculous. A miracle, then, was defined by Leibniz as an event occurring to some created substance that exceeded its nature, that is, its own causal powers. Laws of nature are then characterized as generalizations that are true of created substances in virtue of their natures. Malebranche, of course, denied that created substances have natures in Leibniz's sense. Malebranche's first sustained discussion of the restriction of real causality to God occurs in book 6, part 2, chapter 3 of the *Search after Truth.* Before presenting his own theory, Malebranche began:

> If we assume . . . that there are in bodies certain entities distinguished from matter, having no distinct idea of these entities, we can easily imagine that they are the true or principal causes of the effects that we see occur. That is even the general opinion of ordinary philosophers, for it is primarily in order to explain these effects that they think that there are substantial forms, real qualities, and other similar entities. If next we consider attentively the idea we have of a cause or of a power to act, we cannot doubt that this idea represents something divine. . . . Therefore, we admit something divine in bodies around us, when we admit forms, faculties, qualities, virtues, or real beings capable of producing certain effects by the force of their nature. (*OM/2/309* [LO 447]).

Given Leibniz's definition of a miracle and Malebranche's denial of natures (in Leibniz's sense) in created substances, criticisms of Malebranche's occasionalism from Leibniz's point of view were ready to hand. Any event that occurs to any created substance exceeds the force of the nature of that substance, since, according to occasionalism, it has none. So every event in the created world is miraculous by definition. Clearly, Malebranche rejected Leibniz's definition of a miracle; the real issue here is the alleged existence of natures—real causal powers—in created substances. We have already reviewed Leibniz's major argument for his view in chapter 6: no natures, no finite substances, a line of reasoning that leads to Spinoza. Similar treatment should be accorded to Leibniz's claim that occasionalism is inconsistent with ascribing freedom to created substances.[56] He argued that an action is free only if it is spontaneous. An action is spontaneous only if some state of the agent is a real cause of the action. But, according to occasionalism, no state of a created substance is a real cause of anything. And so on. Obviously, Malebranche would reject the condition imposed on spontaneity. In section 3 of chapter 3, we noted some features of his alternative—the theory of consent.[57]

Leibniz was aware that Malebranche and other occasionalists would reject his definition of a miracle. He knew that Malebranche defined a miraculous event as one with respect to which God acts by a particular volition. As noted in section 3 of this chapter, Leibniz took this to imply that Malebranche held that whenever God acts in accordance with a general rule, whatever results is natural and, hence, nonmiraculous.[58] Leibniz formulated three responses to Malebranche's retort. First, he argued that it had the unacceptable consequence that when God acts miraculously, he acts irrationally. In section 3, I concluded that in its most subtle form, Malebranche's theory is probably immune to this criticism. Second, he claimed that since God acts in accord with general principles whenever he acts, Malebranche's definition (as understood by Leibniz) would preclude miraculous events. Our discussion in the previous chapter suggests that the most subtle version of Malebranche's theory may escape this criticism, too. Third, he held that Malebranche's theory has the unacceptable consequence that any true universal generalization, meeting certain minimal conditions, must be a law of nature, true of nonmiraculous (hence, natural) occurrences.

Leibniz's most penetrating discussion of this aspect of occasionalism occurs in notes for a response to criticisms of his own view in Lamy's *De la connaissance de soi-même*:

> In reasoning in this way, one lacks a proper sense of what a miracle is. For following this idea, the laws of nature would be arbitrary, and those that God would have willed to establish would be the nature of things, just as exceptions to them would be miracles. Consequently, the natural and the miraculous would not differ in themselves, but only by an extrinsic denomination. . . . But it must be known that not every sort of rule or law is appropriate to constitute a law of nature, and that there is an essential difference between the natural and miraculous, so that if God acted continually in a certain manner, he would bring about perpetual miracles. For example, if God had established that a planet must always go on its own in a line curved like an ellipse, without adding anything explicable that caused or maintained this elliptical movement, I say that God would have established a perpetual miracle and that it could not be said that the planet proceeded thus in virtue of its nature or following natural laws, since it is not possible to explain this, nor to provide a reason for such a phenomenon. (G/4/587–588)

The same example occurs in support of the same point in our texts at LA 93. Here we have Leibniz's rationalism in as naked a form as we ever find it,

Leibniz insisted that only certain modes of activity are suited to constitute the natural. He also insisted that there must be a perfect fit between those mechanisms that are natural and the epistemic capacities of the human intellect. Thus, in *DM* §16 Leibniz stated: "Miracles and the extraordinary concourses of God have this peculiarity: that they cannot be foreseen by the reasoning of any created mind, however enlightened it might be, . . . whereas everything that is called natural depends on less general maxims that creatures can understand." This involves another doctrine to which Leibniz steadfastly adhered from our time period on. The doctrine involved is to be found in *New Essays* §65 and *Theodicy*, Prel. Dis. 23, among others. Indeed, sometimes it sounds as if Leibniz intended the doctrine to be a definition of the miraculous. All things considered, I think it best to view Leibniz as defining a miracle as something that occurs to a created substance, but that cannot be brought about by the powers available to created substances, supplementing that definition with a postulate: Since created intellects are exactly suited to understanding natural phenomena, miracles are those phenomena whose comprehension exceeds their grasp.

Leibniz's definition of a miracle may appear to give him an advantage over Malebranche in formulating criteria for deciding whether some recalcitrant event is a genuine miracle, or simply a nonmiraculous counterexample to what we previously took to be a law of nature. Leibniz had an answer ready to hand: the event in question is a genuine miracle just in case its occurrence exceeds the powers of the relevant substance (or substances). But, of course, we learn about what powers things have by determining what laws of nature hold of them. Here is where the postulate may prove useful. It may now be called in to decide whether the event in question exceeds natural powers and, hence, is a miracle. According to the postulate, the event in question does exceed natural powers (and hence is miraculous) just in case it was not predictable nor explicable by any created mind, however enlightened. But Leibniz's conception has no clear-cut advantage over that of Malebranche. Malebranche could simply accept the postulate, without the intervening theory about natures and powers. And, indeed, our discussion in the preceding section suggests that something along these lines was the course Malebranche actually followed.

The troubler *argument.* Speaking of the commerce between substances, especially the mind and the body, at the close of his draft for the long letter of 14 July, Leibniz wrote: "It does not conform . . . to the hypothesis of occasional causes, as if God were to intervene ordinarily in any other way than by conserving each substance in its course, and as if God on the occasion of occurrences in the body aroused thoughts in the soul that would change the course that the soul would have taken without that" (LA 47). The argument that occasionalism, especially in what it affirms concerning intersubstantial occasional causation, implies that God alters the laws of nature, was a favorite of Leibniz. In addition to the passage from the draft for the long letter of

14 July, it may be found in the letter itself (see the quotation at the beginning of section 2 of this chapter) and in the letter of 30 April (LA 93–94).[59]

It will prove useful to concentrate on a specific instance of purported intersubstantial occasional causation to which Malebranche would have subscribed. If asked to give a causal history of Arnauld's voluntary arm raising, Malebranche would have talked about muscle contractions induced by the flow of various animal spirits, which were, in turn, induced by a nonphysical event—Arnauld's desire to take his hat off. In this case, then, Malebranche believed that there was a causal history, terminating in the arm elevation, which included a mental event—Arnauld's desire to remove his hat manually. Clearly, Leibniz thought that something Malebranche believed in this case was inconsistent with some important truths about the physical world. A number of the passages previously cited indicate that the physical truth allegedly disturbed is the principle of the conservation of motive force (see the letters to l'Hospital and Basnage, and the passages from *Considerations on Vital Principles* and the *Theodicy*, mentioned in note 59). Since Malebranche and Leibniz remained at odds for some time over the correct measure of force, and hence over an exact statement of the principle of the conservation of motive force, it would be helpful to have some more basic truth about the physical world with respect to which Malebranche's views were alleged by Leibniz to be inconsistent. Fortunately, one such is noted in *Considerations on Vital Principles*. Once again touting the virtues of the theory of concomitance, Leibniz wrote: "This system also has the advantage of preserving in all its rigor and generality the great principle of physics that a body never receives a change in motion except by another body in motion that pushes it" (G/6/541 [L 587]).

From this passage we may extract the basic truth about the physical world that Leibniz thought occasionalism put at risk. Furthermore, we may safely assume that the very general idea involved is one Leibniz accepted in our time period. Before we attempt to formulate the principle, we need to introduce some quasitechnical terminology, with the aim of preserving neutrality between Leibniz and Malebranche, so far as possible. Consider a case where a cue ball, having been put in motion by impact with a pool stick, subsequently strikes the eight ball, which then moves toward the near corner pocket. Neither Leibniz nor Malebranche would view the impact of the cue ball with the eight ball as the real cause of the subsequent motion of the eight ball.[60] Both Leibniz and Malebranche would have agreed that there is something counter-intuitive about denying a causal relation in this case; both sought to explain a notion of quasi-causality that did hold in this case and others, where real causality does not. For Malebranche, the relevant notion of quasi-causality is just occasional causality. Leibniz, too, explained a notion of quasi-causality—in our texts, for example at *DM* §§14 and 15; LA 47, 69, 71, 91–92, 95, and 133; *Specimen* (G/7/312 [MP 79]); and *Primary Truths* 521 (MP 90). Consider two passages:

In order to speak like other men, who are right when they say that one substance acts upon another, we must give another concept to what is called action. (LA 133)

The action of one finite substance on another consists only in the increase in the degree of its expression conjoined with the diminution of that of the other. (*DM* §15)[61]

Leibniz's theory, like Malebranche's theory of occasional causation, is meant to apply to those phenomena that seventeenth-century scientists would regard as causal in character in the order of nature. We said something about Malebranche's understanding of quasi-causality in section 3 of this chapter. Leibniz's standard way of characterizing the relevant pre-analytic idea is this: "What we call causes are, in metaphysical rigor, merely concomitant requisites" (C 521 [MP90]). That surely sounds like necessary and sufficient conditions. We have already seen that Malebranche's theory is best understood as not requiring that quasi-causes be necessary conditions. The difference between Leibniz and Malebranche on this point turns out to be significant. But it does not preclude meaningful debate, because the underlying difference turns out to be factual, not conceptual.

Malebranche held that no quasi-cause is a real cause. I believe Leibniz did not, but in Leibniz's case matters are a bit complex. Consider, once again, a case of the impact of two substances—say, two hedgehogs, where the motion of hedgehog A at impact is a quasi-cause of the resulting motion in hedgehog B. By Leibniz's lights, the real cause of the resulting motion in B is some prior state S of hedgehog B. So, if we ascribe to Leibniz the view that real causes are also quasi-causes, then we must be prepared to ascribe to him a principle permitting overdetermination with respect to quasi-causes. In the case in hand, both S—the real cause of the motion of B—and impact with A would be regarded by Leibniz as quasi-causes of the motion of B. If we ascribe the possibility of overdetermination of quasi-causation to Leibniz, as I think we must, then we allow for the possibility of diverse extended quasi-causal histories terminating in the same event. Notice that in that case Leibniz's "great principle of physics," as formulated in *Considerations on Vital Principles*, has two distinct formulations in terms of quasi-causality:

P_1. For any motion M, there exists an extended quasi-causal history H, such that:
(a) H terminates at M, and
(b) for any x, if x is a member of H, then x is a motion of a body.
P_2. For any motion M and any extended quasi-causal history H, if H terminates at M, then, for any x, if x is a member of H, then x is a motion of some body.[62]

Consider again the case of Arnauld voluntarily raising his arm. Clearly, Malebranche believed that there is some extended quasi-causal history H terminating in the motion of Arnauld's arm, such that some mental event

(Arnauld's desire to take off his hat manually) is a member of H. No doubt Malebranche and Leibniz believed that Arnauld's desire is not a motion of some body.[63] So, if (P$_2$) is the correct formulation of Leibniz's physical principle, then Malebranche believed something inconsistent with it, as Leibniz claimed. But, then, so did Leibniz. In the draft for the letter of 8 December 1686, Leibniz wrote: "Nevertheless, one is quite right to say that my will is the cause of this movement of my arm . . . for the one expresses distinctly what the other expresses in a more confused way, and one must attribute the action to the substance whose expression is more distinct" (LA 71; see also LA 95–96).

Suppose, then, that the correct formulation of Leibniz's physical principle in terms of quasi-causation is (P$_1$), and that he held that every case of real causation is also a case of quasi-causation. Then Leibniz would have held that there is an extended quasi-causal history of Arnauld's arm raising that satisfies (P$_1$). Our investigation in section 3 indicates that Malebranche believed that every extended quasi-causal history of Arnauld's arm raising has Arnauld's desire as a member. Apparently, then, Malebranche held beliefs inconsistent with (P$_1$); if (P$_1$) is true, then he had beliefs about intersubstantial quasi-causality that are false. But the problem would not be his occasionalism, but rather his ignorance of physiology. Further research might have convinced Malebranche that there are diverse extended quasi-causal histories terminating in Arnauld's arm elevation, one of which contains Arnauld's desire, another of which contains no such mental event. The point is this: the facts are either consistent with (P$_1$) or they are not; if not, the *troubler* argument cannot get started. If they are, occasionalism can accommodate those facts so as to remain consistent with (P$_1$). It may be that Malebranche held empirical beliefs about mind-body interaction that are inconsistent with (P$_1$). But that has nothing to do with his occasionalism.[64]

Perhaps I have been led astray by Leibniz's examples. We know that in a strict formulation of his physics Leibniz would trade in (P$_1$) for something like the following:

P$_3$. For any motion M of body B at time t, there exists a motion M' of body B' at time t' such that:
(a) B' and B are components of the same substance, and
(b) t' precedes t, and
(c) M' is a quasi-cause of M.

Would (P$_3$) have caused Malebranche troubles? It need not. Either (P$_3$) is true or it is not. If not, it causes Malebranche no problems. If it is true and Malebranche did not know it, then he may have had some false beliefs about causal relations, not only about the physiology of voluntary actions, but about physics as well. But that is irrelevant to occasionalism. Occasionalism, as formulated by Malebranche, is a potent metaphysical theory in what it claims about real causation. But it is no more than a descriptive theory in what it claims about the distribution of occasional causes. Various advocates of occasionalism may have made factual mistakes about the distribution of occasional causes; but no particular distribution is built into the theory.

Leibniz would find one aspect of the response outlined on Malebranche's behalf unacceptable. Suppose we settle for two distinct quasi-causal histories, each terminating in Arnauld's arm elevation, one composed solely of motions of matter, the other including at least one mental event, namely, Arnauld's desire that his arm elevate. Suppose that we set up a correspondence between these two histories, pairing items occurring at the same time. Then there will be some motion of matter paired with Arnauld's desire that his arm elevate. Both the motion of matter so paired and the desire are occasional causes of the elevation. We have assumed that Malebranche's notion of an occasional cause included the idea of temporal priority of cause relative to its effect. Therefore, the relevant motion of matter is not an occasional cause of the desire, nor the desire an occasional cause of the motion. Yet their correspondence would be vital to the theory herein attributed to Malebranche. But it is exactly this sort of unexplained correspondence to which Leibniz objected. In notes for a reply to Bayle in 1698, Leibniz wrote: "Thus it is not enough that God order the body to obey the soul, and the soul to perceive what happens in the body, it is necessary that he give them a means to bring it about, and I have explained this means" (G/4/533).

The important point here is that this is not a new criticism of occasionalism. The *troubler* argument may draw our attention to some empirical failings of Malebranche's occasionalism, but Leibniz's real message comes after the response that occasionalism, being no more than a descriptive theory about the distribution of occasional causes, can adjust to avoid the *troubler* argument. One of Leibniz's deep points connected with the *troubler* argument is that occasionalism deprives laws of nature of a rational foundation, thus violating the principle of sufficient reason.

Thus, Leibniz saw occasionalism as at odds with a basic metaphysical truth—the principle of sufficient reason. He also saw occasionalism as inconsistent with a proper account of finite substances, in virtue of its denial of the thesis of spontaneity. And he saw a crucial connection between occasionalism's denial of spontaneity and what he took to be its theological inadequacies. In *De la connaissance de soi-même*, Lamy argued that the pre-established harmony, unlike occasionalism, is inconsistent with the essential dependence of creatures on the Creator and with the supreme power of the Creator. Leibniz replied:

> But you do not indicate why and in what respect my supposition is contrary to these doctrines. In order for a creature to be weak and dependent, must it be without any power? And in order for the Creator to be supremely powerful, must he alone be powerful and active? Because God is infinitely perfect, would he allow no perfections in creatures? You would prove in the same way that because he is the supreme Being, he is the only Being, or at least the only substance.

I agree that God acts on creatures at every moment by conserving them; but if he alone acts, what perfection has he given them? I really wish that you would specify it, because you will find none of them that does not indicate some action. And if he has given them no perfections, his work would be unworthy of him. (G/4/586–587)[65]

Leibniz made numerous efforts to engage Malebranche in meaningful debate on fundamental matters. After a series of letters to l'Hospital in 1695, Leibniz, using l'Hospital as intermediary, brought the theory of concomitance, as outlined in the *New System*, to Malebranche's attention. Leibniz awaited Malebranche's reaction. It is the subject of l'Hospital's letter to Leibniz of 3 September 1695:

Malebranche, to whom I said that you wished to have his opinion, requested that I assure you for his part that he has a very special esteem for you, that, with respect to your metaphysical meditations, they did not seem to him sufficiently explained, and that it would be quite difficult to philosophize by letter on these matters that are in themselves so abstract. It must be admitted that demonstrations of this sort do not have the same evidence as those in mathematics, for it seems to me that ordinarily one remains attached to the view that one embraced in the first place, and, between us, I do not believe that Father Malebranche intends to abandon his system of occasional causes. (GM/2/296)

After publication of the *Theodicy*, Leibniz tried again to engage Malebranche in discussion. This time the intermediary was Father Lelong, a close friend and colleague of Malebranche, through whom Leibniz forwarded a copy of the *Theodicy* to Malebranche. Malebranche responded in December 1711, pointing out some of the differences between his account of God's choice of a world to create and that of Leibniz, differences noted in chapter 3.[66] Leibniz replied at once, pressing his own account.[67] Malebranche never wrote to Leibniz again, but Lelong did. The letters between Lelong and Leibniz in February and March 1712 are deep, the beginning of what might have been a profound discussion of the issues. Lelong signaled disengagement in a letter of April 1712 with these words, which must have had a familiar ring to Leibniz: "It is difficult to reason by letter on metaphysics, especially when we do not agree on principles, for that exposes us to engaging in useless writings" (*ML* 424).

Suppose that an extended debate between Malebranche and Leibniz had taken place. What would have been the central issues? I believe that debate would have begun with some quasi-theological matters concerning the politics of omnipotence, Malebranche claiming that it denigrates God's power to suppose that he shares it with created substances in order to bring about his ends, and Leibniz claiming that it denigrates God's power to suppose that he is unwilling (or unable) to share it with created substances in order to bring about his ends. The debate would then have revolved around three metaphysical matters: (1) the exact nature of the necessary connection that both Leibniz and Malebranche believed must obtain in order for one thing to be a real cause of another; (2) the exact nature of God's conservative causation, without which, Malebranche and Leibniz agreed, the world would cease to be; and (3), last and foremost, a detailed analysis of exactly what occurs, according to a substance/mode ontology, when something brings it about that a substance comes to have a mode that it previously lacked, Malebranche arguing that what then occurs is creation pure and simple, which, both Leibniz and Malebranche agreed, is God's prerogative. What a debate it would have been.

5. EXPRESSION AND ACCOMMODATION

In section 4 we considered Leibniz's purported proof by elimination of the theory of concomitance. We noted that in some statements of the elimination argument Leibniz referred to an independent a priori proof.[68] That proof is the subject of this section. It is whatever line of reasoning Leibniz had in mind when he asserted at the beginning of the draft for the letter of 8 December: "The hypothesis of concomitance is a consequence of the concept I have of substance" (LA 68). In the same draft he wrote: "The hypothesis of concomitance or of the accord of substances among themselves follows from what I said that each individual substance envelops forever all the accidents that will occur to it, and expresses the entire universe in its own manner" (LA 70). The same thesis, accompanied by arguments, varying as to detail, may be found in our texts at *DM* §§8–9, 33; LA 47, 57–58, 74–75, 95–96, 113–114; *Specimen* (G/7/312–313 [MP 79–80]); and *Primary Truths* (520–521 [MP 90–91]). Many of these passages include the idea contained in the passage quoted above from LA 70—that the argument is intended to go from the complete-concept theory to the thesis of universal expression, and then to the hypothesis of concomitance.

A terminological matter requires attention here. Consider the following theses: (a) spontaneity; (b) world-apart; (c) universal expression, that is, the thesis that each created substance expresses every other; (d) universal accommodation, or the thesis that each created substance accommodates to, accords with, or harmonizes with every other; and (e) the thesis that God brings it about that (a) through (d) obtain. Sometimes Leibniz took the hypothesis of concomitance or harmony (that is, the theory of pre-established harmony) to consist in the conjunction of (a) through (e). So, construing the hypothesis of concomitance, we might plausibly understand Leibniz's remark at LA 68 quoted above—that concomitance is a consequence of his concept of substance—as involving a two-stage argument. The first stage would involve arguing that a proper concept of substance yields (a) and (b), spontaneity and world-apart. The second stage would involve arguing from (a) and (b) to (c), and then from (c) to (d) and (e).

In this scheme the heavyweight metaphysics occurs in the first stage. It was the subject of section 3 of chapter 6. In this scheme, only the second stage remains for our consideration. On other occasions Leibniz took the hypothesis of concomitance to consist in (d) or the conjunction of (d) and (e). So construed, Leibniz's frequent remark that the hypothesis of concomitance is a consequence of his concept of substance would plausibly be interpreted to mean that spontaneity and world-apart yield (d) and (e), with (c), expression, playing some mediating role in the argument. The result is that on either interpretation of Leibniz's claim, what remains for our consideration is the move from (a) and (b) to (d) and (e) via (c). Hence, for simplicity, I take the hypothesis of concomitance to consist in (d), or, on occasion, the conjunction of (d) and (e).[69]

I will concentrate on some elementary questions about what Leibniz took to be the logical relations among the relevant doctrines, particularly universal expression and universal accommodation. I believe that such an examination sheds some light on what Leibniz had in mind by these doctrines. Moreover, it indicates that in their general forms, texts from our period leave them in an inordinately vague state. Perhaps it would be more accurate to say that what follows indicates that my understanding of Leibniz's views on expression and accommodation remains in an inordinately vague state. I have wrestled with these matters for some time and I have lost. My hope is that what follows will motivate someone to step forward and explain these topics properly.

It is useful to focus on three relations that Leibniz took to be universal among created substances—compossibility, expression, and accommodation. Thus, Leibniz held the following to be universally true, where our variables range over actual created individual substances:

1. x is compossible with y.
2. x expresses y.
3. x accommodates to y.

An elementary question worth asking with respect to each of the above is whether Leibniz took it to be a necessary truth, bearing in mind that he took those propositions he believed to be strict metaphysical consequences of the complete-concept theory of substance to be necessary truths. In brief, I suggest that Leibniz took (1) to be a necessary truth, and it is quite clear why he did so. Leibniz's arguments for (2) treat it as a necessary truth, indeed, a triviality; it is not clear that Leibniz understood (2) as the triviality his arguments made it. It is not so clear how he took (3), since it is not clear what meaning he ascribed to it. All things considered, I lean toward the view that in our time period, at least, Leibniz did not take (3) to be a necessary truth, and hence did not take it to be a strict metaphysical consequence of the complete-concept theory of substance. Since he said, in quite plain language, that (3) is a consequence, in some sense, of his concept of substance, this leaves me with some explaining to do. Moreover, the claims noted above would be in jeopardy if there were good reason to suppose that Leibniz held either that (1) entails (3)—that is, that compossibility entails accommodation—or that (2) entails (3)—that expression entails accommodation. Yet both claims have their supporters.

Consider my thesis that Leibniz did not take compossibility to entail accommodation; the contrary view is clearly stated by Jacques Jalabert in a recent comparative study:

> Malebranche appealed to the notion of an occasional cause, in order to explain the correspondence of substances and the harmony of phenomena in nature. For Leibniz, the correspondence and harmony exist already at the level of the possibility of things, as they are conceived by the divine understanding. Each possible universe includes such a correspondence; phenomena that are not harmonious cannot constitute the same universe. So the universal harmony is not pre-established solely in the sense that it is realized once for all in the act of creation, willed for all eternity; it is also pre-established in the sense that it is already constituted, from the possibility of things, that God contemplates prior to his decision to create.[70]

But surely this cannot be right. Part of the problem of interpreting Leibniz on concomitance is the obscurity of the notion of accommodation that is central to it. We need some guidelines for our discussion. A reasonable one is that whatever accommodation amounts to, it is stronger than mere compossibility. In his letter to Arnauld of 9 October 1687, Leibniz wrote: "This mutual correspondence of different substances . . . is one of the strongest proofs of the existence of God" (LA 115; underlining Leibniz's).[71] In the *New System*, after expounding the facts of agreement and accommodation of substances, Leibniz added: "Also, here is a new proof for the existence of God, which is of surprising clarity" (G/4/486 [MP 124]).

It is clear that Leibniz did not intend the argument as yet another version of the first way, that is, as an argument based on the requirement of an uncaused cause, outside the series of finite substances constituting the world. It is based on special features of the actual world—a version of the argument from design. I am assuming that compossibility is construed by Leibniz in the manner noted in section 1 of chapter 4: a set of possible individuals is compossible just in case it is possible that all its members jointly exist. Recently, it has been suggested that the Leibnizian notion of compossibility has considerably more content, something like consistency relative to some fixed set of laws of nature.[72] Such a reading would undercut my claim that compossibility does not imply accommodation. Leibniz used the notion of compossibility frequently; there are remarkably few passages known to me where he set out to define it. It is included in a set of definitions (so called by Leibniz) tentatively dated 1679–1685 in the *Vorausedition*, which commences thus:

Being—possible term.
Possible—what does not imply a contradiction.

Existing—compossible with the most perfect.
Compossible—what, when taken with another, does not imply a contradiction. (Grua 324–325)

Leibniz may have employed more stringent notions of compossibility on occasion. But this seems to be the basic notion employed in his thinking about possible worlds.

We consider next the relation of expression to accommodation. I think there is little doubt that Leibniz regarded it as necessarily true that every individual substance expresses every other, that is, that the universal closure of (2) holds in every possible world. There is no question that Leibniz thought the doctrine of universal expression was a fundamental element of his system of thought. In a letter to Jaquelot in 1704, Leibniz claimed that all the rest of his system is only a consequence of universal expression (G/3/464–465).[73] In some texts we find associated with universal expression a doctrine that Leibniz put thus in a draft for his letter to Arnauld of 30 April 1687: "Our soul has some confused sentiment of the entire universe, and of the entire past, present, and future, and . . . *its entire individual essence consists in nothing but this expression of the universe*" (LBr 78; emphasis mine). This is a stronger doctrine than universal expression; it suggests that there is nothing to substances except representations from a certain point of view. See *DM* §14, where a point of view is, in turn, characterized in terms of quality of representings on the confused-distinct-perception scale. The thought that there is something viciously impredicative about this structure is sure to come to mind.

Mates and Rescher have made good use of the idea that, according to Leibniz, each substance expresses all *and only* those substances in its world, in order to provide ingenious constructions of possible worlds in the manner of Leibniz.[74] It is worth noting that in our time period Leibniz was not of a settled mind on this topic; in particular, in the *Discourse* (paragraphs 26 and 29), Leibniz claimed that souls express not only all the actual substances of this world, but all possible substances as well.[75]

Let us restrict our attention to universal expression, free from attendant doctrines. That is, let us concentrate on (2), leaving aside questions about what items other than actual created substances may be expressed by actual created substances, and leaving aside problems engendered by the idea that the expression of a created substance constitutes "the entire individual essence" of that substance. Questions arise about what Leibniz meant by the doctrine, as well as why he accepted it. On these matters we receive less help than before from Arnauld's probing. In his letter of 4 March 1687, Arnauld raised a question about the basis of Leibniz's claim that the soul expresses its body more distinctly than other bodies. This is an interesting topic, involving a level of detail that we will not reach in this commentary. Fortunately for us, Leibniz's response to Arnauld's question made clear to Arnauld that he did not grasp the notion of expression Leibniz employed.

And so, in his last letter to Leibniz (28 August 1687), Arnauld said what somebody needed to say: "I have no clear idea of what you mean by the word 'expression,' when you say '. . . that our soul expresses more distinctly, other things being equal, what pertains to its body, since it even expresses the entire universe in a certain sense'" (LA 105). Leibniz responded: "One thing *expresses* another (in my terminology) when there is a constant and fixed relationship between what can be said of one and of the other. This is the way that a perspectival projection expresses its ground plan. Expression is common to all forms, and it is a genus of which natural perception, animal sensation and intellectual knowledge are species. In natural perception and in sensation, it is enough for what is divisible and material and dispersed into many entities to be expressed or represented in a single indivisible entity or in substance, which is endowed with true unity" (LA 112; emphasis mine).[76]

There is an obvious problem about how to understand the phrase "constant and fixed relation" in Leibniz's characterization of expression. One might suppose that Leibniz had in mind some kind of isomorphism, or partial isomorphism, of structure whose careful delineation would yield a single relation that holds in every case of expression—*the* relation of representation. Two considerations weigh heavily against this idea. First, as Kulstad has shown, the full range of cases that Leibniz presented as cases of one thing expressing another makes it unlikely that a unique relation of representation was intended.[77] Second, as will be made clear below, Leibniz's major metaphysical argument in favor of the thesis of universal expression suggests quite the opposite—that the existence of any relation mapping truths about y onto truths about x yields that x expresses y. Leibniz's major metaphysical argument may assume that, but surely he had something more in mind, for in various texts Leibniz noted conditions, admittedly rather minimal, that relations must satisfy in order to be relations of expression. Thus, in *Theodicy* §356 Leibniz stated that representation has a natural relation to what is represented, so that the idea of a square is an unsuitable representation of a round object.[78] And the following argument, employed by Leibniz to establish that matter is full of organisms, utilizes the premiss that if x expresses y and y is organic, then there is something organic in x: "The general and exact connection of all things among themselves proves that all parts of matter are full of organisms. For, since each part of matter must express the others and since there are many that are organic among the others, it is clear that there must be something organic in that which represents the organic" (LH I 20 Bl. 206).

The unclarity concerning the nature of expression infects Leibniz's account of perception, which is based on expression. Indeed, according to the passage from LA 112 where we find Leibniz's definition of expression, perception comes to nothing more than the expression of the divisible by an indivisible substance. This is a serious matter. If we were forced to produce a single sentence from the Leibniz corpus to stand as an epitome of his final philosophy, surely it would be this from a letter to 1704 to De Volder:

"There is nothing in things except simple substances, and in them perception and appetite" (G/2/270 [L 537]). Appetites turn out to be tendencies to pass from one perception to the next. Appetites and perceptions are the only intrinsic denominations characterizing the only things there really are, according to Leibniz's final position.

Independent of its obscurity, Leibniz's conception of perception has troubled commentators from the beginning. Bayle was perplexed by how a simple substance—a soul—could produce the diversity of operations that Leibniz's theory seems to require.[79] Leibniz responded that although the soul is simple, in the sense of lacking parts, its internal state at any time contains many perceptual states, indeed, infinitely many perceptual states, of which the soul is aware of only a small selection.[80] More recently, commentators have been bothered by the relational nature of the account of perception attributed to Leibniz, given his attitude toward relations noted in section 5 of chapter 4. Here, Leibniz's response to Bayle is relevant. Corresponding to the relational account of perception noted above, there is an "inner state" form of perception. As Leibniz put it in *The Principles of Nature and of Grace*, "Perception . . . is the inner state of the monad representing external things" (G/6/600 [MP 197]). A full account of the relation between the inner-state form of the account of perception and the relational form would require a full treatment of Leibniz on relations. It will not happen here. Still, some of the relevant material emerges through a consideration of Leibniz's main metaphysical argument for universal expression in our time period, to which we now turn.

A number of texts from our time period purport to provide a proof of universal expression: *DM* §§8 and 9; Leibniz's draft for the long letter of 14 July (LA 41); the actual letter (LA 57); and *Primary Truths*, wherein the argument is presented in a particularly pellucid form. A premiss common to most versions of the argument is "the connection of things." In *Primary Truths* it is so stated as to fit perfectly with a reading of Leibniz's definition of expression, in virtue of which it turns out to be a near triviality: "There is nothing on which some true denomination cannot be imposed from another, at all events a denomination of comparison and relation" (C 521 [MP 90]). Thus, whatever is true of a given substance y at a time t forms the basis for a relation between it and any other substance x, in virtue of which there is a corresponding truth about x. Taken in its most trivial form, that gives us universal expression, but in a form that would not support the internal-state form of universal perception without a thesis concerning the reducibility of relational properties to intrinsic denominations. Now comes the wolf in sheep's clothing: Leibniz casually added, "But there are no purely extrinsic denominations" (C 521 [MP 90]). The same sequence of moves can be found in *Specimen*: "Nothing happens in one creature of which some exactly corresponding effect does not reach all others. Nor, again, are there any absolutely extrinsic denominations in things" (G/7/311 [MP 78]).

As we noted in section 5 of chapter 4, there are two candidates for Leibniz's thesis of intrinsic foundations, one stronger than the other. All things considered, it appears more plausible to attribute the weak thesis to Leibniz than the strong thesis. We also noted in section 5 of chapter 4 that the weak thesis of intrinsic foundations, combined with the trivial version of universal expression, will not yield all that Leibniz wanted. It will not suffice to meet the charge of concept packing. Independent of that charge, other considerations suggest that Leibniz intended a stronger thesis of universal expression than the trivial thesis supported by his arguments. Recall that Leibniz defined perception as the expression of what is divisible by an indivisible substance. Clearly, Leibniz intended the definition to characterize a broad range of phenomena. But with expression understood in the manner of the trivial, weak thesis of expression, the resulting notion of perception contains no cognitive component whatsoever. And we have already noted that some of Leibniz's reasoning about expression presupposes more content to the notion of expression than the weak thesis of expression attributes to it. Undoubtedly, Leibniz had in mind a stronger thesis according to which each substance in a world perceives every other in a sense of perception involving low-level cognition. Let us call the stronger version the thesis of universal perception.

Unfortunately, while the thesis of universal perception may be presupposed in texts from our period, it is neither explained nor justified there. In fact, I do not know of any Leibnizian texts that adequately motivate, explain, and justify the relevant idea. Some have suggested to me that the key is a proper understanding of Leibniz's intended use of a premiss stating "the connection of things." [81] The idea seems to be this: we know from physics (a) that "the least motion of the smallest particle in the universe affects the entire universe" (LBr 69). We know from metaphysics (b) that there is no real intersubstantial causal influence, and (c) that the proper analysis of apparent intersubstantial causal influence is in terms of correlative changes on the confused-distinct perception scale between agent and patient. Putting together what we know from physics and from metaphysics, we reach the thesis of universal perception. But something is awry here. Surely the proposed analysis of apparent intersubstantial causal influence in terms of relevant changes in the quality of perceptions is plausible only if we presuppose universal perception. It cannot be employed to argue for that thesis.

In considering the relationship between universal expression and accommodation, we have two versions of universal expression to consider, one of which—universal perception—is a will-of-the-wisp. Our primary question is whether in our time period Leibniz thought universal accommodation is a metaphysical consequence of universal expression. I think he did not, no matter which version of universal expression is considered. Throughout the discussion that follows I will use the term *universal expression* to refer to the weak version. At the close of my discussion of what accommodation is according to Leibniz, I will consider whether universal perception implies universal accommodation.

I am fully convinced that Leibniz took accommodation to presuppose expression, so that he understood universal expression to be a strict metaphysical consequence of universal accommodation.[82] But I think that he rejected the inference in the other direction. I can put my misgivings concerning the relevant inference in terms of one of Leibniz's most dramatic examples of accommodation or harmony. In his letter of 30 April 1687, the notion of harmony occurs literally: "This concomitance I uphold is like many different bands of musicians or choirs, playing their parts separately, and so placed that they cannot see or even hear each other, but can nevertheless harmonize perfectly, by each one following his own notes" (LA 95). Whether the separate bands succeeded in producing a euphony or a cacophony, there would be a "constant and fixed relation" between the two based on certain "inner states" of the two groups—the notes and silences produced at a given time. So one would express the other, whatever strange sounds were forthcoming, that is, whether they succeeded in harmonizing or not.

But these are my misgivings about the validity of the relevant inference. Is it so clear that Leibniz shared them? The passage from LA 70 quoted at the beginning of this section comes close to asserting that expression implies accommodation. I agree. But when we meticulously examine it, and others like it, we find that the text begins by favoring the thesis that Leibniz accepted the inference from expression to accommodation and then adds a comment that undercuts that suggestion. The text from LA 70 is followed by this: "And *if it happens* constantly that certain thoughts are joined to certain movements, the reason is that God first created all substances so that subsequently all their phenomena might correspond" (LA 70; emphasis mine). The correspondence envisaged here is not just any arbitrary correspondence; accommodation apparently requires something more. Thus, according to Leibniz, if my arm moves upward just when I will to raise it, that is accommodation. Other outcomes would not be, although other outcomes would be consistent with the correlative claim about expression.

Having reached the conclusion that Leibniz did not think that expression entails accommodation, I will now consider what he meant, in our time period, by accommodation. Unfortunately, on this matter, we receive no help, belated or otherwise, from Arnauld. There appear to be four prima facie, distinct accounts of accommodation in the *Discourse* and the correspondence.

1. In *DM* §32 we find the following account of the relation among substances required for accommodation: "God brings about liaison and communication of substances, and it is through him that the phenomena of one meet and agree with those of others and *consequently that there is reality in our perceptions*" (emphasis mine). A similar remark occurs at *DM* §14. Leibniz's views about what the "reality of our perceptions" requires varied from

a commitment to external objects to something like what we would count as phenomenalism. In either case, we obtain an interesting account of accommodation. Perceptions of substances are related in the relevant way in case they have sufficient constancy, coherence, and the like to render meaningful a distinction between appearance and reality, however that distinction is ultimately construed. I take it that Leibniz had this relation in mind in the letter of 9 October 1687, when he said that if the phenomena of different substances failed to harmonize, "there would be as many systems as substances. . . . The entire concept that we have of time and space is based on this harmony" (LA 115). Accommodation, on this account, is that relation which makes meaningful our distinction between appearance and reality, and which permits us to have concepts of space and time. Some will prefer to see here a thesis about accommodation, explicated in some other manner, rather than an analysis of what accommodation is. That claim is suggested by the fact that what appears to be an alternative analysis of accommodation immediately precedes the quoted passage in the letter of 9 October 1687.

2. Substances accommodate to each other just in case they are related *as if* one acted on the other. This is the account Leibniz offered in *Monadology* §81: Speaking of the pre-established harmony, he wrote: "Under this system, bodies act as though, per impossibile, there were no souls: and souls act as if there were no bodies, and both act as if each influenced the other." There is a serious problem with the idea of taking this as Leibniz's primary account of accommodation. The notion of influence involved is one that Leibniz characterized as "inexplicable" (LA 70) and "inconceivable" (LA 57), as we noted in section 1 of this chapter. It would be an unhappy state of affairs were Leibniz's chief account of a notion that was as central to him as accommodation to make use of an idea that he regarded as inconceivable, even when proceded by an "as if."

3. A third account of accommodation found in our texts is particularly suited to the monadological view: One substance y accommodates to another substance x just in case y behaves in such fashion as to satisfy some desire of x.[83] Note that when Leibniz wanted a clear example of two entities behaving as if they interacted causally, in a manner that constituted accommodation of one to the other, he utilized the idea of the body responding to the will. There is an obvious virtue to this approach. It is built into the description of an agent's desire that p obtain what state of affairs would constitute accommodation to that desire; namely, the state of affairs consisting in p's obtaining.[84]

4. We have been concentrating on an account of accommodation peculiarily suited to Leibniz's ultimate monadological view. The last account I want to mention is more general; many will suppose that it is quite plainly Leibniz's central notion of accommodation. It is most easily applied to a system of entities, whatever its size, including a possible world. The entities of a system universally accommodate just in case there are natural laws to which their behavior is subject.[85]

Using texts from our time period, can we not establish that in this sense Leibniz took universal accommodation to be a necessary truth? This is a difficult question. In many places Leibniz affirmed that nothing happens (or could happen) out of order; that there is always a general law in accordance with which phenomena occur.[86] But in all the cases cited and in others like them where Leibniz amplified these remarks, it turns out that what he was referring to are the developmental laws of the relevant substances, system, or world. But now consider the following from Leibniz's draft for the long letter of 14 July: "Since there is an infinity of possible worlds, there is also an infinity of laws, some peculiar to one world, some to another, and each possible individual of any world includes in its concept the laws of its world" (LA 40). The context makes clear that Leibniz was referring to laws of nature, not developmental laws. Some have suggested to me that in this passage Leibniz was claiming that universal accommodation holds in all possible worlds, hence is a necessary truth, and hence is implied by universal expression. The passage does not strictly imply this. It says that universal accommodation (in the relevant sense) holds in infinitely many possible worlds. Moreover, it says that in any world in which universal accommodation does hold, the laws of that world are contained in its complete individual concepts. But that is consistent with there being infinitely many possible worlds in which universal accommodation does not hold. In addition, the passage quoted is unusual; it may be an aberration. Its analogue in the letter of 14 July sent to Arnauld (LA 51) makes similar points about the inclusion of the laws of a world in the concepts of the individuals of that world. But the laws are clearly identified as primitive free decrees of God, that is, developmental laws.

Consider accommodation in the sense of number 4. Is it plausible to argue that it is implied by the thesis of universal perception? I don't think so. Laws of nature may be construed as governing apparent intersubstantial causal relations. As we have already noted, in our period Leibniz analyzed the notion of apparent intersubstantial causal relations in terms of correlative changes on the confused-distinct perception scale between the related substances. But universal perception would only guarantee that every substance perceives (and, hence, has at least low-level cognition of) every other. It would in no way guarantee that the requisite correlations on the confused-distinct perception scale held, in order to guaranntee law-like behavior.[87]

What, then, is to be said about those passages quoted at the beginning of this section in which Leibniz said, in so many words, that concomitance is a consequence of his notion of substance? I take his claim to be that if his conception of substance is true—that is, if spontaneity and world-apart hold—then for any possible world composed of created substances, where there is accommodation among substances, the theory of a pre-established harmony produced by God provides the proper account of the occurrence of accommodation in that world. And of course, given the theses of spontaneity and world-apart, any accommodation produced by God must be produced in a particular way—not by God's acting as chief puppeteer, but by God's producing automata, individual substances acting out their own programs in virtue of their own primitive active force. Part of what is involved here is a special version of the argument from design. Curiously, in the letter to Arnauld of 9 October 1687, Leibniz seemed to recognize that for the argument to reach its conclusion, "pure chance" needs to be ruled out.[88] Leibniz said no more about "pure chance." Perhaps its inconsistency with the principle of sufficient reason was so obvious that he saw no need for further discussion.

6. *RADICAL WORLD-APART*

We have construed world-apart as asserting the causal independence of created substances with respect to everything other than God. Our discussion of Leibniz's response to an objection formulated by Bayle (see section 2 of this chapter) suggests that Leibniz considered it metaphysically possible that the only created substance is a certain dog's soul. This suggests that perhaps Leibniz was committed to what we might call radical world-apart, that is, the thesis that for each created substance, it is metaphysically possible that it and God and no other substances exist. Given that God is not in any world, according to Leibniz, radical world-apart comes to this: for each created substance there is a possible world of which it is the only member. Conventional contemporary wisdom claims that Leibniz rejected radical world-apart. There are numerous objections to ascribing it to Leibniz, including an apparent inconsistency with universal expression. I do not know Leibniz's attitude toward radical world-apart. In this section various objections to ascribing it to Leibniz are canvased, closing with consideration of its relation to universal expression.

Some say that there are texts in which Leibniz outright asserted a contrary of radical world-apart. Consider the following from the *Theodicy*. Extolling the extraordinary breadth of God's wisdom with regard to the possibles, Leibniz wrote: "It [God's wisdom] even goes beyond finite combinations, it forms from them [the possibles] an infinity of infinities, i.e., an infinity of possible sequences of the universe, *each of which contains an infinity of creatures*" (*Theodicy* §225; emphasis mine). Strictly, what this passage claims is that there are infinitely many possible worlds, each having infinitely many members. But that is consistent with the thesis that there are also infinitely many possible worlds, each having finitely many members. Nothing in the passage (or its neighbors) strictly implies that none of the finite combinations, which God's wisdom is said to go beyond, constitutes a possible world.

In section 1 of chapter 4, we noted Leibniz's construction of possible worlds based on complete individual concepts. Following Mates, we noted that Leibniz preferred to parse talk of possible substances in terms of complete individual concepts. Following Mates, I tentatively assumed that a set of complete individual concepts constitutes a possible world just in case it is compossible and maximal.[89] Our focus now is on whether maximality really is required.[90] Consider a particular created individual substance, such as Arnauld. Consider an alleged possible world whose sole member is the complete individual concept of Arnauld. We know that set is not maximal, since the pair set containing Arnauld's concept and Leibniz's concept is compossible. So, if maximality is required, radical world-apart must be rejected. Considerable textual evidence points to maximality as a requirement for a possible world, much of it connected with passages in which Leibniz mentioned "the striving possibles."[91] Here is a typical passage: "Every possible demands existence, and, consequently, would exist unless prevented by another, which also demands existence and is incompatible with it," (G/7/194). There is a maximality principle at work here, but attention to context suggests that its application may be limited to the actual world. The quoted passage is immediately preceded by this: "Among truths of reason identicals are absolutely first truths, and among truths of fact there is this one, from which all experiential truths may be demonstrated a priori, namely . . . ." Leibniz was engaged in formulating a principle concerning what possible individuals exist in the actual world. The passage indicates that Leibniz took the actual world to be maximal. But, as we know, he took the actual world to be special in a number of respects; perhaps maximality is one of them.

Similar comments apply, I believe, to other passages where Leibniz appears to assume that possible worlds are maximal. Consider the following from "On Freedom": "If certain possibles never exist, then existing things are not always necessary; otherwise it would be impossible for other things to exist instead of them, and so all things that never exist would be impossible" (FC 178 [MP 106]). The argument of this passage seems to require the premiss that the world under discussion is maximal. Once again it seems reasonable to suppose that the world in question is the actual world, not just any possible world. The relevant distinction is contained in a passage from a letter from Leibniz to Des Bosses of 1706, which comes close to affirming radical world-apart. "That one substance exists alone is one of those things that does not agree with divine wisdom, and so will not come about, even if it could come about" (G/2/307).[92]

Maximality is much more than is required to show that Leibniz rejected radical world-apart. It will suffice to show that he held that the same individual substance cannot be in more than one possible world. A standard textual source for the latter claim is in the *Theodicy* §414: "If you posit a case that differs from the actual world only in one single definite thing and its consequences, a certain determinate world will answer you. Those worlds are all here, that is, in ideas. I will show you some where you will find, not quite the same Sextus that you have seen (that is not possible, he carries with him always what he will be), but Sextuses similar to him." We are familiar with Leibniz's metaphysical basis for the doctrine asserted in this passage, namely, superintrinsicalness. Superintrinsicalness has the consequence that any possible person with some primitive property that Arnauld lacked in the actual world would not be Arnauld. Hence, if Arnauld were to exist in two possible worlds—something radical world-apart requires of Arnauld—he would have to possess the same primitive properties in both worlds. When we consider our passage from the *Theodicy*, its lesson seems restricted in scope. If *f* is some primitive property Arnauld had, and you want to consider how things would have been had Arnauld lacked *f,* then you must consider worlds that lack Arnauld but possess Arnauld counterparts.

Put in terms of complete individual concepts, the lesson of *Theodicy* §414 seems to be that there is exactly one complete individual concept that does duty for Arnauld in any possible world in which Arnauld exists. Let that concept be C_A. There is some collection of complete individual concepts W such that C_A is a member of W and W is compossible and maximal. Presumably, W is (or is our proxy for) the actual world. Let D be some complete individual concept that is not a member of W. Hence, {D} ∪ W is not compossible. It is plausible to suppose that Leibniz took universal expression to have the consequence that for any complete individual concept E, if E is a member of W then {E, D} is not compossible. Let us suppose that he did. Then, if Arnauld's concept C_A is a member of any possible world W', other than W, then W' must be a proper subset of W. But singleton of C_A satisfies that condition. Hence, radical world-apart seems to survive its brush with *Theodicy* §414.

But perhaps it will not survive a brush with universal expression. According to that doctrine, a complete individual concept expresses a world it is in by expressing the other concepts (if any) in that world. This might incline us to ascribe the following principle to Leibniz: for any complete individual concept C and possible worlds W and W', if C expresses W and W', then W = W'. That principle would preclude radical world-apart. But should we ascribe this principle to Leibniz? That is the issue. Consider, once again, Arnauld's complete individual concept C_A and that unique compossible and maximal set W (presumably the actual world) of which C_A is a member, and {C_A}. Consider next Leibniz's complete individual concept C_L. C_L and C_A are both members of W. So C_A expresses C_L. So all the information contained in C_L is derivable from the information contained in C_A. This presents a problem only if it has the consequence that Leibniz exists in the possible world of which Arnauld is the only member. But here we need only invoke Leibniz's doctrine, expressed, for example, in *Necessary and Contingent Truths*, that existence is contained only in God's concept, not that of a created individual substance: "The possibility or notion of a created mind does not involve existence" (23 [MP 104]). So, we may suppose that on Leibniz's view, what is derivable from Arnauld's concept is not that Leibniz exists and is a Lutheran, but only that if Leibniz exists, then he is a Lutheran. Following this course, we would view expression as an intensional feature of substances, thus preserving radical world-apart.

7. DIVINE CONCURRENCE

For many students of Leibniz, paragraph 8 of the *Discourse* is where the real metaphysics begins. By choice of heading, Leibniz indicated that the main point of the theory of substance outlined in *DM* §8 and subsequent sections is to distinguish the actions of God from those of creatures. It becomes clear in the sequel that Leibniz's main point is to argue for his thesis of spontaneity, as opposed to Malebranche's occasionalism. But the heading for *DM* §8 might equally have indicated a forthcoming discussion of the topic of God's concurrence in human action. And *DM* §30 raises the question of "the action of God on the human will," but deflects it, recommending that in specific cases we not worry about God's determination of our will, but simply do our duty. Sound advice, I suspect; but those with a philosophical bent are likely to ignore it when leisure frees them from relevant "specific cases." Leibniz was one such. Since much of the material pertinent to this problem falls outside our texts and time period, my aim in this section is primarily to sketch problems of interpretation.

DM §8 commences by mentioning two views that Leibniz apparently intended to present as unacceptable extremes: occasionalism—"for there are some who believe that God does everything" (which Leibniz associated with Malebranche), and deism—"and others imagine that all he does is conserve the force that he has given to creatures" (which Leibniz associated with Durandus de Saint-Pourçain). Yet judicious selection from his own writings can make it seem as if he accepted both positions. Consider deism. In the texts that have been our primary concern, Leibniz wished to draw a sharp contrast between his views and those of Malebranche, particularly by emphasizing the differences between occasionalism and the thesis of spontaneity. Many passages in which Leibniz set out the thesis of spontaneity sound much like his summary of the position of Durandus in the *Theodicy*: "The concurrence of God with creatures . . . is only general and mediate; . . . God created substances and gives them the force they need, and after that he leaves them to themselves and does nothing but conserve them, without aiding them in their actions (*Theodicy* §27).[93]

But this cannot be his settled view. As stated, it simply will not fit with the way Leibniz presented these matters when his perspective was primarily theological. That perspective is exemplified in the following passage from *Necessary and Contingent Truths*: "We must examine in what way contingent things and particularly free substances depend in their choice and operation on the divine will and predetermination. I believe that it must be held as certain that there is as much dependence of things on God as is consistent with divine justice. Firstly, I assert that whatever perfection or reality is in things is continually produced by God, but that their limitation or imperfection belongs to them as creatures," (22 [MP 102]).

Consider, next, as apparent evidence of Leibniz's occasionalism, the following text written in 1677, in which Leibniz considered the proper interpretation of the (presumably correct) thesis that God cooperates in all our actions.

> Properly and accurately speaking, the correct thing to say is not so much that God concurs in an action, but rather that he produces it. For let us suppose that God concurs in some action in such a way that it is produced not only by God, but also in part by a man; from this supposition it follows that this particular concurrence of the man does not require the cooperation of God, which is contrary to hypothesis. For that particular concurrence is also an act; therefore, it follows in the end that all acts are produced in full by God, in the same way as are all creatures in the universe. He who produces half the thing twice over, produces the whole. Or, more accurately, he who produces half the thing, and, in turn, half of the remaining half, and, in turn, half of the remaining half of the preceding half—to infinity—produces the whole. This takes place in any act whatsoever, according to God's manner of operation. For let us suppose that God and a man concur in some act; it is necessary that God concur with this very concurrence of the man, and either it will proceed to infinity . . . or, rather, it will suffice to say from the beginning that God actually produces the act, even if it is the man who acts. (Grua 275)

This paragraph occurs in Leibniz's report of a conversation with the apostolic vicar to the Court of Hannover, Nicholas Steno. The full text appears to contain a number of arguments of Steno that Leibniz then set out to refute. We might think that the above argument falls into that category. But there is no refutation of it presented in the text, and, bluntly, it is too clever for Steno. Nonetheless, suppose we saw the argument as containing material for a reductio ad absurdum argument. What underlying principle might be the target? An obvious candidate would be the principle of divided effort, the thesis that there are actions of creatures in which some aspect is to be uniquely credited to the creature and some distinct aspect (presumably constituting the rest of the action in some sense) is to be credited to God. This principle was formulated and denied by St. Thomas in book 3, chapter 71, section 8 of the *Summa contra gentiles*. Its rejection was a commonplace thereafter.

My view is that Leibniz's mature position on concurrence involves accepting a version of the principle of divided effort just noted and, at the same time, accepting something resembling the conclusion of the argument cited, namely, the thesis that God produces everything that is real (that is, that has some perfection) in every action of every creature. A statement of Leibniz's mature doctrine concerning divine concurrence occurs in *Causa Dei*, an appendix to the *Theodicy*:

> In acting, things depend on God, since God concurs in the actions of things, insofar as there is something of perfection in their actions, which, at least, must emanate from God.

God's concurrence . . . is both immediate and special. It is immediate, because the effect depends on God not only because its cause originates in God, but also because God concurs no less nor more remotely in producing this effect than in producing its cause.

His concurrence is special, because it is directed not only at the existence and actions of a thing, but also at the manner and qualities of this existence, in so far as there is something of perfection in them, which always proceeds from God. (G/6/440 [Schrecker 115–116])[94]

The basic ideas of Leibniz's mature position may be found in a draft of a letter to Rémond of (November 1715 (see *ML* 478–480), his notes for a response to Lamy in November 1702 (G/4/588), and in the *Theodicy* (see §§377 and 392 and, especially, a piece Leibniz published in the *Mémoires de Trévoux* on §392). It occurs in Gerhardt (G/6/347–350) and in Huggard, pp. 389–392, under the title "Excursus on Theodicy §392." Essentially the same account of divine concurrence may be found in our time period in *De libertate, fato, gratia Dei* (Grua 306–322; see especially 314–316). The basic idea is this: God produces what there is of perfection in the states of creatures; creatures produce whatever there is of limitation in their own states. Obviously, in order to know what these ideas amount to, we need to grasp, in its depths, Leibniz's understanding of the perfection/limitation contrast, as applied to the states of created substances. We can at least grasp something of the intuition behind the distinction by noting Leibniz's favorite illustrative example-a heavily laden boat, moving with the current and solely by force of that current. The velocity of the boat is, in some sense, a function of two factors: (a) the force acting on the boat in virtue of the velocity of the current; and (b) the inertia of the boat itself in virtue of its weight. Both factors must be noted in a correct explanation of a change in the location of the boat, including the rate of that change.[95] Getting beyond illustrative examples to philosophical analysis of the perfection/limitation contrast is another matter.

Surely there appears to be tension between what we might call Leibniz's metaphysical exposition of creaturely action and what we might call Leibniz's theological exposition of creaturely action. On the deism-occasionalism scale, the former seems to be located near the deism end, the latter closer to the occasionalism end. There is no doubt that Leibniz believed that a single unified (and undoubtedly correct) theory of creaturely action is located under the appearances. I do not doubt it; but to believe it I would need to know more than I now know about the perfection/limitation account of the properties of created substances.

Chapter 8

❖❖❖❖❖❖❖❖❖

CONCLUDING REMARKS

In an insightful essay on the development of Leibniz's monadism, T. S. Eliot said of Leibniz: "His solicitude for the orthodoxy of his philosophy was not merely policy or timidity; his theological disputations are not merely a cover for logical problems."[1] It will be obvious to the reader of the preceding chapters that I agree with Eliot on this point. Some may suppose that more attention should be allocated to logical matters. That is perhaps true. As the concluding section of chapter 4 indicates, I think that the concept-containment account of truth—as a fundamental independent motivator of Leibniz's metaphysics—has been overrated. But there are motivations for Leibniz's metaphysical doctrines operating in our period that are broadly logical in character and that have not received the attention they deserve, here or elsewhere.

What I have in mind is Leibniz's effort to distinguish abstract entities from concrete individuals, and, within the class of concrete individuals, substances from nonsubstances. Much of the relevant material will soon appear publicly for the first time in forthcoming volumes of the Academy edition, covering Leibniz's philosophical writings in our period. I leave their study to others. In these concluding remarks I will note selected topics in Leibniz's philosophical theology where we might have benefited from Arnauld's probings, had he considered theological applications of the basic metaphysical structure Leibniz proposed, thus permitting the discussion to advance in the way Leibniz had expected it would.

There is the important matter of Leibniz's theological uses of superintrinsicalness. In chapter 6, section 3 I argued that Leibniz's commitment to superintrinsicalness is best understood in connection with his effort to secure persistence of basic individuals over time. I suggested that a basic motivation for his insisting on persistence was theological—an effort to secure moral agents with respect to whom God's justice and mercy can be exercised. On this interpretation, superintrinsicalness is required in order to guarantee the existence of some of the agents generating theodicean problems. By contrast, in chapter 4, section 4, I argued that superintrinsicalness is not an essential feature of any basic solution offered by Leibniz to a theodicean problem. These claims go against the grain of standard interpretations. They are highly speculative. Arnauld's probing, sedulously applied, would have helped set the record straight.

Leibniz claimed diverse theological advantages for the thesis that creation consists in God's selection of a world from an infinite set of possible worlds, each world being characterizable in terms of the complete individual concepts of the individual substances composing it. First, there are important theological problems that Leibniz believed were solved by the application of true metaphysical principles to this thesis. Thus, Leibniz claimed that the general problem of evil is solved by applying the principle of sufficient reason to creation, where creation is understood as outlined above. In chapter 3, section 4, we noted Arnauld's negative attitude toward similar reasoning in the case of Malebranche. It would have been to our benefit if Arnauld and Leibniz had engaged in full-scale debate on the relevant topics.

A second advantage Leibniz that claimed for his metaphysical structure is often overlooked-that the proposed metaphysical structure provides a framework in which competing theological views may be expressed and compared, and their claims adjudicated. A key ingredient supporting this claim is contained in the following passage from *Theodicy* §365. Speaking of the relation between God's decree at creation and the free action of some moral agent, Leibniz wrote: "The decree to give existence to this action no more changes its nature than the simple consciousness of it." The doctrine is dramatically affirmed in *Theodicy* §52. There, speaking of God's single total decree—Let this world be—Leibniz wrote: "It is clear that this decree changes nothing in the constitution of things, and that God leaves them just as they were in the state of pure possibility; that is to say that he changes nothing in their essence or nature, or even in their accidents, which are already represented perfectly in the idea of this possible world. Thus what is contingent and free remains so no less under the decrees of God than under his prevision."

Thus, Leibniz claimed that his basic metaphysical structure could be utilized to express the views of the Molinists, for example, who held that freedom consists in a liberty of indifference or equipoise that is inconsistent with universal causal determinism. Consider a Molinist possible world containing complete individual concepts that include actions done with liberty of indifference. Leibniz's key thesis has the consequence that in decreeing that such a world exist, and thereby bringing it about that the relevant complete individual concepts are instantiated, God in no way derogates from the liberty of indifference exercised by the creatures thereby made actual. This key thesis is the basis of Leibniz's response to some of Arnauld's criticisms.

Unfortunately, on this crucial topic we must make do without Arnauld's help. What is needed is a full-scale study of Leibniz's contributions to philosophical theology. Of the various books whose creation is recommended in this book, that is the one whose author I would like to be.

Appendix A

CATALOGUE OF THE CORRESPONDENCE

The table below includes all the philosophically significant material in the Leibniz-Arnauld correspondence. The column headings are to be understood as follows: "LBr pagination" refers to the numbers assigned to the relevant folio sheets found among Leibniz's papers in Hannover and catalogued by Eduard Bodemann in the late nineteenth century. "Mason number" refers to the Roman numeral assigned to the relevant item in the table of contents of H. T. Mason, ed. and trans., *The Leibniz-Arnauld Correspondence.* "Date new-style" refers to the date assigned to the relevant item in Georges Le Roy, ed., *Leibniz: Discours de metaphysique et correspondance avec Arnauld*, according to the calendar then prevailing in Catholic jurisdictions. "Gerhardt pagination" refers to the pagination in C. J. Gerhardt, ed., *Die philosophischen Schriften von G. W. Leibniz*, vol. 2. "RL pagination" refers to the pagination in Geneviève (Rodis-) Lewis, ed., *Lettres de Leibniz à Arnauld d'après un manuscrit inédit.*

❖ ❖ ❖

LBr pagination	Mason number	Date new-style	Gerhardt pagination	RL pagination	Author
46–47	I	11 Feb. 1686	11–14	—	Leibniz
48	II	13 March 1686	15–16	—	Arnauld
49–50; 51	III	12 April 1686	16–21	27–33	Leibniz
51	IV	12 April 1686	22–24	23–26	Leibniz
49v	V	15 April 1686	25	—	Leibniz
15–20; 52–57	VI	13 May 1686	25–34	—	Arnauld
59–60	IX	Draft for X	37–47	—	Leibniz
62–65	X[1]	14 July 1686	47–59	34–46	Leibniz
68–69	—[2]	Draft for XI	Unpublished	—	Leibniz
66–67	XI[3]	14 July 1686	59–63	47–51	Leibniz
108	XII	14 July 1686	131–132	—	Leibniz
21–23; 70–73	XIV	28 Sept. 1686	63–68	—	Arnauld
76–77	XVI	Draft for XVII	68–73	—	Leibniz
74–75	XVII	8 Dec. 1686	73–81	52–61	Leibniz
82	XVIII	8 Dec. 1686	81–83	—	Leibniz
24–26; 83–87	XIX	4 March 1687	84–90	—	Arnauld
78, 79, 81	—[4]	Draft for XX	Unpublished	—	Leibniz
88–91	XX	30 April 1687	90–102	62–75	Leibniz
29–31; 92–95	XXII	28 Aug. 1687	105–109	—	Arnauld
104–107	—	Draft for XXVI	Unpublished	—	Leibniz
98–103	XXVI	9 Oct. 1687	111–129	78–96	Leibniz
109	XXVII	14 Jan. 1688	132–134	97–100	Leibniz
110	XXVIII	23 March 1690	134–138	101–105	Leibniz

[1] Referred to herein as "the long letter of 14 July."
[2] A translation of this draft is in Appendix C.
[3] Referred to herein as "the short letter of 14 July."
[4] Folios 78, 78v, 81, and 81v constitute a complete draft for the letter of 30 April; 79 and 79v contain a separate draft for the material in the letter of 30 April at LA 98 and 99.

Appendix B

❖❖❖❖❖❖❖❖❖

SUGGESTIONS CONCERNING
TRANSLATIONS

Two translations from the original French have been used throughout this study: the Lucas and Grint translation of Leibniz's *Discourse on Metaphysics* and the Mason translation of his correspondence with Arnauld. The Lucas and Grint translation is based on Lestienne's edition of the *Discourse*. It contains the major variants and emendations. The Mason translation is based on the Gerhardt edition, which, in turn, is based on copies of the letters, and drafts thereof, retained and subsequently emended by Leibniz. Gerhardt included some, but not all, of Leibniz's drafts and alterations. In some cases he included material that Leibniz crossed out, and in a few he excluded material that Leibniz did not cross out. The full text, with appropriate critical apparatus, will be available for the first time in the critical edition being prepared by Dr. Reinhard Finster, to be published by Felix Meiner Verlag.

It is inevitable that translators will differ concerning matters of style and nuance. The suggestions for revision included below are restricted to those passages where it seems to me that the translations distort the sense of the texts translated, as well as three cases where the Gerhardt text contains misreadings of Leibniz's handwriting.

LUCAS AND GRINT

DM §9   Page 14: replace "subject" by "substance" in ". . . and that a subject can only begin by creation . . . ."

DM §12   Page 18, note a: replace "[that bodies are not substances in strict metaphysics (which was indeed the sentiment of the Platonics)] and that the whole nature" by "[that either bodies are not substances in strict metaphysics (which was indeed the sentiment of the Platonics)] or that the whole nature."

MASON

LA 27 (M 26)   Replace "I find it merely strange" by "I even find it strange."

LA 41 (M 44)   Replace "except however for freedom and contingency" by "without however eliminating freedom and contingency."

LA 43 (M 47)   Replace "Now, it is impossible to find another identity . . ." by "Now, it is impossible to find another reason . . . ."

LA 51 (M 57)   Replace "which are peculiar to him" by "which are peculiar to it."

LA 53 (M 60)   Replace "with the nature of substance and of individual entities" by "with the nature of substance and of indivisible entities." (Here Gerhardt misread Leibniz's handwriting.)

LA 75 (M 93)   Replace "thus crude souls" by "thus the souls of brutes."

LA 78 (M 96)   Replace "If man contains only a figured mass of infinite hardness (which I consider as no more consistent with divine wisdom than the void), he can not in himself . . ." by "If the atom contains only a figured mass of infinite hardness (which I consider as no more consistent with divine wisdom than the void), it cannot in itself . . . ." (Here Gerhardt misread Leibniz's handwriting.)

LA 93 (M 116)   Replace "since this movement is not susceptible of a similar explanation" by "since this movement is not susceptible of a simpler explanation."

LA 102 (M 128)   Replace "after which both parts and perhaps also dreams" by "after which both parhelia and perhaps also dreams." (Here Gerhardt misread Leibniz's handwriting.)

LA 125 (M 160)   Replace "since they too are devoid of consciousness or reflection" by "since in any case they are devoid of consciousness or reflection."

Appendix C

❖❖❖❖❖❖❖❖❖

THE DRAFT FOR THE SHORT LETTER OF 14 JULY 1686

The document translated below is a letter that Leibniz drafted for Arnauld but never sent, as Leibniz himself noted on the document. In its place Leibniz sent a letter dated 14 July 1686, which is found at LA 59–63 (RL 47–51). From June through early August 1686, Leibniz was extremely active, indeed agitated, on account of Arnauld's powerful response of 13 May 1686. Leibniz's writings in response to that letter include the following:

a. LA 37–47: draft for Leibniz's major reply to Arnauld. The draft was clearly intended as a draft; it is headed "Remarks on Arnauld's letter concerning my proposition that the individual concept of each person contains once for all everything that will ever happen to him."

b. LA 47–59 (RL 34–46): Leibniz's major reply to Arnauld's letter of 13 May.

c. LA 131–132: a letter to Ernst dated 14 July 1686 requesting that Ernst himself ask Arnauld whether he really believed Leibniz's position to be wrongheaded, and, if so, whether he really believed that one who accepted Leibniz's position could not be tolerated in the Catholic church. It seems clear to me that Leibniz then held faint hope that his major reply (b) would change Arnauld's mind about the falsity of Leibniz's position; his hope was that Arnauld would grant that Leibniz's position was not anathema to the Church. He was making a last-ditch stand to salvage what he could of his reunion project.

d. LA 103 (see also A/1/4/404–406): a letter to Ernst with the same point as (c). In a state bordering on desperation, Leibniz wrote: "Whatever the situation, I will be content if he at least considers that these opinions, even if they should be very much mistaken, contain nothing directly contrary to the definitions of the Church."

e. LA 59–63 (RL 47–51): a second letter to Arnauld dated 14 July 1686. This letter, sent in place of the version translated below, contains an outright plea for Arnauld's *nihil obstat*. It also contains a review of Leibniz's activities in jurisprudence, silver mining, geology, history, geometry, algebra, and a little metaphysics.

f. The draft translated below. It is similar to (e) up to LA 60; it diverges at the sentence beginning "Je ne parle qu'avec peine de la manière . . ." ("I speak only with sorrow of the manner . . ."). What follows is an extraordinarily straightforward presentation of the basic elements of Leibniz's thought at the time.

My translation presents the manuscript (LBr 68, 68v, 69, and 69v), without including a display of emendations and items suppressed. Finster's edition of the
correspondence will include a full presentation of the manuscript.

The material speaks for itself. One small textual matter is worth noting. The term
entelechy is used in the last paragraph to refer to a substantial form. Careful scrutiny
of the handwritten text suggests that *entelechy* was added at some time subsequent to
the initial drafting of this unsent draft. My hypothesis is that when Leibniz cogitated
on the matter of publishing the correspondence, drafts, as well as copies actually
sent, were spruced up.

[Folio 68] But I see that in order to show you my conceptions, it is necessary to get on
higher ground and commence with first principles or the elements of truths. Thus, I
conceive that every true proposition is immediate or mediate. An immediate proposition is one that is true in itself—namely, when the predicate is expressly included
in the subject—and these sorts of truths I call identicals. Mediate propositions are
all those other propositions where the predicate is contained virtually in the subject
in such a way that the proposition finally can be reduced to truths [68v] that are
identicals by an analysis of the subject or actually by an analysis of the predicate as
well as the subject. And that is what Aristotle and the Scholastics intended by saying:
predicatum inesse subjecto [the predicate is in the subject]. That is also what this axiom
comes to: there is nothing without a cause, or, rather, there is nothing for which a
reason cannot be given; that is, every truth, of right or of fact, can be proved a priori
by showing the connection of the predicate and the subject, although as often as not
it falls to God alone to know this connection distinctly, especially in matters of fact,
which finite minds know only a posteriori and by experience.

Now, what I have just said is, in my opinion, the nature of truth in general, otherwise I would not know what truth is; for our experiences are marks but not causes of
truth, and truth must have some general nature, which belongs to it in itself without
relation to us. Now, I can conceive nothing better for this purpose, nor more in conformity with the sentiments of men, and even of all philosophers, than what I have
just explained. But it seemed to me that the consequences, which extend further than
is thought, have not been considered sufficiently. Now, since every truth that is not
an identical has its reason or its a priori proof, this must be held not just for eternal
truths, but also for truths of fact. The only difference is that in the case of eternal
truths, the connection between the subject and the predicate is necessary and depends on the possibility or impossibility of essences, or indeed on the understanding
of God; and in the case of truths of fact or existence, this connection is contingent
and depends in part only on the will of God, or some other rational creature. Eternal
truths are demonstrated on the basis of ideas or definitions of terms. Contingent
truths do not have demonstrations, properly speaking, but they must have their a
priori proofs or reasons, which let us know with certainty why the matter turned out
one way rather than another. And in order to provide these reasons, it is necessary
in the end to go back again to the will of a free cause, and primarily to the decrees
of God, of which the most general is the will to make known his wisdom and his
power to the extent that creatures are susceptible to them. In my opinion, this is
the principle of all existent things or truths of fact. For God chooses the best from

an infinity of possibles. It is in this that the reconciliation of freedom and reason or certitude consists. For God will not fail to choose the best because he is Sovereign Wisdom; but he cannot but choose freely, because what he chooses is not necessary and does not include existence in its essence or concept, independent of the decrees of God, since the contrary is possible also, otherwise it would include in itself a contradiction.

Supposing, therefore, that in the case of propositions of fact, the predicate is included in the subject, although, by a connection depending on free decrees of God, it is clear that the concept of each person or other individual substance includes, once for all, everything that will ever happen to it, for this person may be considered [69] as the subject, and the event as the predicate. Now we have established that every predicate of a true proposition is included in the subject, that is, that the concept of the subject must include that of the predicate. Furthermore, it follows that what philosophers commonly call extrinsic denominations must likewise be demonstrable from the concept of the subject, but in virtue of the general connection of everything, which the common people do not know; for people do not understand that, for example, the least motion of the smallest particle in the universe affects the entire universe, although less obviously in proper proportion, since the large and the small differ only proportionally. Finally, it follows from this great principle that every individual substance, or every complete being, is like a world apart, which includes in itself all the events of all the other substances, not by an immediate action of one on the other, but from the concomitance of things and in virtue of its own concept, because God has made it in the beginning and conserves it, or still produces it continually with a perfect relation to all remaining creatures.

In fact, the concept of an individual substance, or complete being, is nothing else but that—namely, a concept sufficiently complete so that one can deduce from it everything that can be attributed to the same subject. And that is what is lacking in incomplete concepts. For, to take an example, the concept of being a king is incomplete, and can be attributed to some subject without everything that can be said of that same subject being deducible from it; for in order to be a king, it does not follow, for example, that one is a conqueror. But the concept of Alexander the Great is complete, for it is the individual concept of that person that includes everything that can be attributed to the subject, and everything that distinguishes him from every other individual. It also follows that every individual can be conceived as a lowest species (*species plane infima*) and that it is not possible that there are two individuals who resemble each other perfectly, or who differ *solo numero*, which is what St. Thomas has already maintained with respect to angels, and I myself find it necessary to maintain it for all individual substances. But it is essential to take the specific difference, not following common usage, according to which it is absurd to say that two men differ with respect to species, but according to the usage of mathematicians who hold that two triangles or two ellipses that are not congruent differ with respect to species. Now, although I agree that a perfect resemblance takes place in the case of incomplete concepts—for example, two figures perfectly congruent can be conceived—nevertheless, I maintain, and I deduce it manifestly from principles mentioned above, that this cannot occur in the case of substances.

One of the most notable consequences of these principles is the explication of the manner according to which substances have commerce among themselves, and particularly how the soul is aware of what happens in the body and, in return, how the body follows the wishes of the soul. Descartes is content to say that [69v] God has willed that the soul receive some sensation following certain movements of the body and that the body receive some movements following certain sensations of the soul, but he has not wanted to undertake to explain it. His disciples have had recourse to the universal cause, and have insisted that God produces sensations in the soul suitable to the movements in the body, but that is to have recourse to a miracle. But now here is the explication which is not hypothetical, but, in my opinion, demonstrative. For since an individual substance includes everything that will ever happen to it, it is obvious that my subsequent state is a consequence (although contingent) of my preceding state, and that this state will always agree with those of other created beings, according to the hypothesis of concomitance explained by this: God, who is the cause of everything, acts by resolutions which have a perfect connection among themselves. Consequently, there is no need to have recourse to bodily impression, which is the common hypothesis of physical causes, nor to a particular action of God different from that with which he continually conserves everything, following the laws that he has established, which is the hypothesis of occasional causes, since concomitance alone suffices for everything.

If love of my own thoughts does not lead me astray, I do not think that it would be easy to say something stronger, in order to establish the immortality of the soul in an entirely invincible way. For unless God destroys it, nothing can, since nothing acts on it, except itself. And what is more, it follows that the soul will always retain traces of everything that ever happens to it, although it would not always have occasion to remember them. The traces are absolutely independent of the body, like everything else that happens in the soul, which is, in effect, like a mirror of the universe and even a particular expression of the divine omnipotence and omniscience, because it expresses everything, although some more clearly than others, and everything accommodates to its will, although some in a manner less refractory than others.

But what will we say about individual substances that are not intelligent or animated? I admit I do not know enough to answer that question, any more than the one concerning the soul of beasts. These are questions of fact that are difficult to resolve. In any case, if bodies are substances, they necessarily have in them something that corresponds to the soul and that philosophers have insisted on calling substantial form. For extension and its modifications cannot make up a substance according to the concept that I have just given, and if there is only that in bodies, then it can be demonstrated that they are not substances, but rather true phenomena, like the rainbow. Hence, in case bodies are substances, then substantial forms necessarily must be reestablished, although, as the Cartesians say, it is true that the forms, which must be admitted into general physics, change nothing in phenomena, which would always be explicable without requiring recourse to the form, any more than to God or some other general cause, since it is necessary in particular cases to reduce matters to particular reasons, that is, to applications of the mathematical and mechanical laws that God has established. This entelechy or principle of the actions and passions of bodies, which is called the form, lacking memory or consciousness, will not have what constitutes the same person in the moral sense, which is something capable of punishment and reward; that is reserved for souls that are rational and intelligent, who have very great privileges. It can be said that intelligent substances or persons express God rather than the universe, whereas bodies express the universe rather than God. For God is himself an intelligent substance who communicates with persons more particularly than with other substances and who forms with them a society, which is the republic of the universe, of which he is the monarch. This republic of the universe is the most perfect and the most felicitous possible. It is the masterpiece of the designs of God, and it can truly be said that all other substances are created primarily in order to contribute to this burst of glory with which God makes himself known to minds.

Notes

CHAPTER 1: INTRODUCTION

1. On the former date, see Leibniz's letter to Foucher (G/1/420). On the latter, see Barber, *Leibniz in France*, p.258. Barber cites a notice in the *Nouvelles littéraires* of 1708 announcing Leibniz's (unfilled) intention to publish the Arnauld correspondence with the forthcoming *Theodicy*.

2. Mates, "Individuals and Modality in the Philosophy of Leibniz," pp.83–84.

3. Castañeda, "Leibniz's Concepts and Their Coincidence *Salva Veritate*," p.382.

4. Russell, *A Critical Exposition*, p.vi.

5. Ibid., pp.xiii–xiv.

6. Mates, "Individuals and Modality in the Philosophy of Leibniz," p.109.

CHAPTER 2: THE INTERMEDIARY

1. See also two letters to Malebranche dated 22 June 1679 and 27 Dec. 1694: A/2/1/477f. and G/1/353. References to *Theodicy* are as follows: a section number without prefix refers to the section numbers in the main, three-part investigation of the justice of God and so forth. Citations of the preliminary discourse are by section number, with the prefix "Prel. Dis."

2. A/1/3/243.

3. A/1/3/246.

4. What Leibniz had in mind with respect to transubstantiation will be outlined later in this chapter.

5. MK 80. It should be noted that Stuart Brown makes good use of the *Systema* in *Leibniz*, his recent study for the Philosophers-in-Context series, published by the University of Minnesota Press.

6. See, for example, *Theodicy*, Prel. Dis. 23–26. For an excellent discussion of Leibniz on the mysteries, see Marcelo Dascal's article "Reason and the Mysteries of Faith: Leibniz on the Meaning of Religious Discourse," in his *Leibniz*.

7. See, for example, *DM* §16.

CHAPTER 3: THE GREAT ARNAULD

1. Jacques, *Années d'exil*, p.34.

2. Ibid., p.376.

3. Ibid., p.444.

4. Abercrombie, *The Origins of Jansenism*, p.321.

5. See *OA*/17/180–187.

6. In the letter of 1692, Arnauld noted that his careful examination of St. Thomas's views had taken place seven or eight years earlier.

7. See also Arnauld's letter to Bossuet of July 1693 (*OA*/3/662–664).

8. *OA*/10/614–624.

9. In an unpublished paper, Cranston Paull has challenged my claim that Leibniz was a determinist and a compatibilist with respect to human freedom. Some of his evidence is based on a very plausible analysis of Leibniz's reasoning in the paper *Necessary and Contingent Truths*, where Leibniz claimed that "free substances" sometimes "act, as it were, by a private miracle" (C 20 [MP 100]).

10. In the *Theodicy* (§47), Leibniz distinguished the position of St. Thomas from that of the new Thomists, citing Bañez and Alvarez as new Thomists. See, for example, Dominico Bañez, *Scholastica commentaria in primam partem Summae Theologicae Sancti Thomae Aquinatis.*

11. The only work in my ken devoted entirely to Arnauld's treatment of the global theme is Jean Laporte, *La doctrine de Port-Royal*, vol. 2, *Exposition de la doctrine (d'après Arnauld)*, part 1, *Les vérités de la grâce*. It is learned, but partisan. By contrast, the article "Jansenisme" by J. Carreyre in the *Dictionnaire de théologie catholique* (vol. 8, part 1, pp.318–530) is a model of selfless, objective scholarship. I also recommend the following articles in the dictionary: "Liberté," "Concours divin," "Prémotion physique," and "Molinisme." I am grateful to two philosophers at the University of Notre Dame, Alfred Freddoso and Thomas Flint, who helped me with these matters.

12. For a helpful introduction to the *Traité*, followed by a blow-by-blow account of the Malebranche-Arnauld debate focusing on the *Traité*, I recommend Ginette Dreyfus's introduction to *Malebranche: Traité de la Nature et de la Grâce*, subtitled *Introduction philosophique, notes et commentaire du texte de 1712, texte de l'édition originale de 1680*. (I mention the subtitle in order to distinguish this volume from vol. 5 of *Oeuvres complètes*, which has the same title, editor, publisher, place, and date.) For a comparison of the *Traité* with Leibniz's *Discourse on Metaphysics* and, more generally, intellectual relations between Malebranche and Leibniz, I recommend André Robinet's marvelous study *Malebranche et Leibniz: Relations personnelles*. Robinet presents Leibniz's reading notes on the *Traité*, compares the content of the *Traité* with the *Discourse on Metaphysics*, and notes approvingly Gueroult's hypothesis that Leibniz "had the *Traité de la Nature et de la Grâce* under his eyes when he composed the *Discours de Metaphysique*" (p.139). I also recommend Leroy Loemker's article "A Note on the Origin and Problem of Leibniz's *Discourse* of 1686," reprinted in Leclerc, *The Philosophy of Leibniz*.

13. Gouhier, *Cartesianisme et Augustinisme au XVIIᵉ siècle*, p.127.

14. AT/7/208 (CSM/2/146).

15. AT/7/214 (CSM/2/150).

16. AT/7/216 (CSM/2/152).

17. See AT/7/247–248 (CSM/2/172) for Descartes's acceptance.

18. For Arnauld's letter, see AT/5/184–191; for Descartes's solution to the first problem, see AT/7/248–256 (CSM/2/173–178). For a penetrating discussion of the issues, see Nadler, "Arnauld, Descartes, and Transubstantiation."

19. "Semblances" here translates the Latin *species*.

20. *OA*/38/89–176.

21. AT/4/166–168. Translated and edited by Anthony Kenny in *Descartes: Philosophical Letters*, pp.156–158.

22. See the discussion in chap. 2.

23. See A/2/1/175. The basic ideas involved are to be found in the sections on transubstantiation in drafts for the *Catholic Demonstrations*; see, for example, A/6/1/508–512 (L 115–118).

24. For an example of Arnauld's ridicule of scholastic explanations via forms, see *OA*/38/142–143; and, for Leibniz, note his well-known remark: "However much I agree with the Scholastics in this . . . metaphysical explanation of the principles of bodies, I am as corpuscular as one can be in the explanation of particular phenomena" (LA 58).

25. *La logique* 320 (DJ 322).

26. See, for example, *OA*/38/136–176.

27. Fine-tuning (a), (b), and (c), which follows, would require that considerable attention be given to the notion of a state of a substance. These principles should be understood so that agent causality is not excluded.

28. *OM*/1/46 (LO 5).

29. *OM*/3/19 (LO 548).

30. *OM*/3/22 (LO 549). The French is: "L'homme ne se donne point aussi de nouvelles modifications qui modifient ou qui changent *physiquement* [my emphasis] sa substance." The "physiquement" carries a load of theory here.

31. *OM*/3/20 (LO 548).

32. For Leibniz's criticism of Malebranche's consent theory, which is along these lines, see his letter to Lelong of March 1712 (*ML* 423).

33. *Dissertation*, chap. 1 (*OA*/38/688). Of course, Malebranche rejected this characterization of his account of freedom. For Malebranche's response, see sections 11, 12, and 13 of chapter 12 of *Réponse à une dissertation de M. Arnauld . . . (OM*/7/565–568). These pages constitute one of the best presentations of Malebranche's account of consent.

34. Interestingly, Arnauld went on to argue that there is a plausible argument for the supposition that as things now stand, human beings lack the relevant power. In virtue of the Fall, he wrote, "our soul does not know what must be done in order to move our arm by means of animal spirits." This principle—if the soul does not know the mechanism for bringing about a state of affairs, then it cannot be the real cause of that state of affairs—was employed by Malebranche in article 10, Méditation 6 of *Méditations chrétiennes et metaphysiques (OM*/10/62), to which Arnauld referred approvingly. Arnauld then suggested that perhaps in the state of innocence (prior to the Fall) the human soul had the relevant knowledge and power, that the elect would have it after resurrection, and that angels now do (*OA*/38/690–691).

35. Mason, *Leibniz-Arnauld Correspondence*, p.xviii.

36. Loemker, "Note," p.233.

37. Couturat, "Sur la metaphysique de Leibniz," pp.20–21.

38. See Brody, "Leibniz's Metaphysical Logic," and Jarrett, "Leibniz on Truth and Contingency."

39. In this section the Dickoff-James translation is at its least literal, with unfortunate results, in my opinion.

40. Discourse 2, §1.

41. Discourse 2, §54.
42. Third Elucidation, §22.
43. Discourse 1, addition to §12.
44. Discourse 1, §13.
45. *Summa theologicae,* part 1, Question 19, Article 3, Reply 5.

CHAPTER 4: FREEDOM AND CONTINGENCY

1. In philosophy and theology, innocence is almost always relative. Even here at its most innocent beginnings, philosophical and theological problems lurk. Leibniz frequently noted one way in which we acquire an idea of temporal duration: we have the thought that something x is f, and that that very same x is non-f, and that the preceding thoughts are not contradictory. The notion of the passage of time saves us from contradiction. We suppose that x is f at t and non-f at t', where t' is later than t, for example (see *LH* IV 7C Bl. 71–72). This suggests that the properties in an individual concept need to be indexed to time. In what follows, we may suppose that has been done.

2. Note that what Leibniz said here implies that there is *a* complete concept of an abstraction—for example, of a species—not that *the* concept of an abstraction is complete. Much will be made of that distinction in what follows. The term here translated "complete concept" is *notion accomplie,* not the more usual *notion complète.* But little should be made of the merely verbal point. Thus, in the draft for the short letter of 14 July (translated as Appendix C in this book), Leibniz said that "la notion d'Alexandre le Grand est accomplie" (see LBr 69).

3. Material for solving this problem occurs in section 2 of this chapter.

4. See, for example, *DM* §31 and LA 19, 20, 41, 51, 52, and 53.

5. Gerhardt has "it is not enough that . . ." ("ce n'est assez . . ."). Based on the letter Arnauld received, Rodis-Lewis has "it is enough for me that . . ." ("ce m'est assez . . ."). I have examined Leibniz's copy with great care and found it illegible. Obviously he meant "it is enough for me."

6. In chap. 7, I consider whether rejecting maximality as a requirement is inconsistent with other Leibnizian doctrines, and conclude that it does not appear to be.

7. In section 2 of this chapter, the notion of an essential property is characterized without reference to possible worlds, hence, in a more Leibnizian way.

8. C 17 (MP 96). Cf. Grua 270–271 and *General Inquiries* 374 (P 64).

9. See *Necessary and Contingent Truths* 18 (MP 98).

10. See, for example, *LH* IV 7C Bl.70, tentatively dated 1683–1685 in the *Vorausedition*: "the world is the composite of all *created* things" (emphasis mine). Cf. Grua 396.

11. See Alvin Plantinga, "Leibniz's Lapse," in *The Nature of Necessity.*

12. See LA 40, 41, and 51.

13. Leibniz also said little by way of a general characterization of (a), that is, a world-plan. Fortunately, in the case of the actual world, according to Leibniz, one characterization of its plan is available—to create the best possible world.

14. Leibniz made this point frequently. Aside from LA 51 and G/7/312 (MP 78–79), see G/4/518 (L 493), G/2/262 (L 533), and G/4/533–554, where Leibniz wrote in notes for a reply to Bayle: "When I said that each monad, soul, mind has received a particular law, it must be added that it is only a variation of the general law that rules the universe."

15. A highly abstract account of the various types of laws of nature may be found in *Necessary and Contingent Truths* 19–20 (MP 99–100).

16. *La logique* 39 (DJ 31).

17. For a popular statement of Leibniz's project, under the designation "the General Characteristic," see G/4/184–189 (L 221–225). For more detail, see "On a Rational Language" (*LH* IV 7B, 3 Bl. 5), "On Term and Proposition" (*LH* IV 6, 12f Bl. 16), "Grammatical Thoughts" (*LH* IV 7B, 3 Bl. 25–26), "On the Philosophical Language" (*LH* IV 7B, 3 Bl. 40–49), and "Rational Language" (G/7/28–30).

18. See also C 243 (P 12)—where Leibniz is somewhat tentative about the prospects of avoiding abstractions completely—note in addition *LH* IV 7C Bl. 101, and *LH* IV 7C Bl. 109–110. Presumably, "Modesty is a virtue" gets replaced by something like "All modest persons, insofar as they are modest persons, are virtuous persons."

19. Actually, the construction of the rational language was intended by Leibniz as frosting on a cake that combined metaphysical and logical considerations. Papers representing much of Leibniz's work on this topic are appearing in the *Vorausedition* for the first time. For a helpful study of some of these materials bearing on the points at issue here, I recommend an article by Donald Rutherford, "Truth, Predication and the Complete Concept of an Individual Substance."

20. See C 243, 286, and 432.

21. Cf. LA 52–53.

22. LA 20, 37, 42, 45, 49, and 53.

23. Leibniz sometimes distinguished between a strict concept of an individual —i.e., a concept including only primitive properties of that individual—and various flabby concepts of that individual, all equivalent, in some important sense, to its (one and only) strict concept. For details, see my paper "Truth and Sufficient Reason in the Philosophy of Leibniz," pp.215–216. See also section 5 of this chapter.

24. Remarks similar to those in the previous footnote apply here.

25. For a discussion of some of these, see section 9 of this chapter.

26. In the draft for the letter of 14 July at LA 38–39, and in the letter itself at LA 49, Leibniz stated that "the concept of a species includes only eternal and necessary truths." In order to obtain this result, we need to consider the quantifier in (5) as ranging over possible as well as actual individuals. This requirement undoubtedly would complicate Leibniz's program of replacing talk about possible individuals by talk about actual individuals and concepts.

27. A more accurate account would include a reference to time: x has f essentially at t just in case x has f at t, and it is metaphysically impossible that x exists at t and yet lacks f at t. In *De libertate creaturae et electione divina* (preliminary date 1686 in the *Vorausedition*), Leibniz wrote: "Actually, whatever does not belong to a thing perpetually does not even belong to it necessarily at the time it belongs to it, but only accidentally, by decree, divine or human" (Grua 383). Let us say that x has f perpetually just in case x has f at every time at which it exists. Leibniz seems committed to the thesis that any property an individual has essentially, it also has perpetually. It may even be that Leibniz also accepted the converse, so that he thought that all and only the perpetual properties of an individual are its essential properties. This has suggested to some that Leibniz's notion of an essential property is basically temporal rather than modal. I disagree. The matter is discussed briefly in section 6 of this chapter.

28. In our immediate texts; see LA 42 and 53, and *DM* §30. For other texts in our time period, see Grua 314 and *Specimen* (G/7/311 [MP 78]).

29. In the copy retained by Leibniz, the relevant passage begins, "God was free to create . . ."—a genuine farrago. Arnauld set matters straight in his letter of 13 May; see LA 27.

30. See LA 27.

31. See *Necessary and Contingent Truths* 24 (MP 104).

32. These definitions ignore fine detail. Thus, in Grua 270–271 and elsewhere, Leibniz seems to require that both p and q be contingent in order for q to be hypothetically necessary relative to p. I think the point is this: he wanted to distinguish absolute from hypothetical necessity, so the cases that interested him were ones in which q, although contingent, is hypothetically necessary relative to some p. There are also some peculiarities in the behavior of hypothetical necessity as herein defined, relative to a "possible-in-its-own-nature" operator that is involved in the possible-in-its-own-nature defense (see section 7 of this chapter). There are also texts (*New Essays* 178–179 and *Necessary and Contingent Truths* 21–22 [MP 102]) that suggest a notion of physical hypothetical necessity.

33. I take it that Arnauld and Leibniz would both hold that the propositions "Adam exists" and "God decides to create Adam" are logically equivalent.

34. Leibniz claimed that God selects an entire world, all at once (so to speak), in the *Theodicy* §84, in *De libertate, fato, gratia Dei* (Grua 314), and in Grua 341, 343, 345, and 371.

35. We may assume that Arnauld's example, to which Leibniz referred, is the following conditional: If Arnauld exists, then a nature capable of thought exists.

36. Leibniz was careful to distinguish necessity of the *consequent* from necessity of the *consequence;* see Grua 306.

37. See, for example, LBr 59, LA 37, and, of course, LA 51.

38. See LA 46, 51, and 56.

39. See LA 28.

40. The original here translated as "in general terms—i.e., in terms of essence, or a species concept, or an incomplete concept" is given in Latin, one of Leibniz's verbal cues that a significant point is involved. The Latin is "sub ratione generalitatis seu essentiae seu notionis specificae sive incompletae"; hence the name "sub ratione generalitatis strategy."

41. Those who believe that Leibniz accepted superessentialism are inclined to see the sub ratione generalitatis strategy as specifying a nonmodal sense of "essential property" that Leibniz employed. See the closing remarks of section 6.

42. Concept D entails property f just in case it is not possible that there is an x such that x falls under D and yet x lacks f. Whether (12) captures Leibniz's intent turns in part on what exactly he intended by the *seu* ("or") in the phrase "essence or species concept." Proposition (12) requires that each essence concept be a species concept.

43. This is just the kind of passage that can mislead about the scope of hypothetical necessity in Leibniz's scheme. Consider an example Leibniz first used and then suppressed in *DM* §13: Peter's denial of Christ. Leibniz claimed that the *connection* between Peter and the property of denying Christ is contingent. Leibniz was *not* claiming that "Peter denies Christ" is hypothetically necessary relative to "Peter exists." The claim is more like this: the conditional "If Peter exists, then Peter denies Christ" is hypothetically necessary relative to certain background information about Peter conjoined with certain free decrees of God, that is, laws of nature.

44. Grua 348; the doctrine of infinite analysis provided the way out of the circle.

On this point, see Robert Adams, "Leibniz's Theories of Contingency," to which I am very much indebted. See also De Twisse, *Scientia media* (Arnhem, 1639), a defense of Calvin and Anglicanism, with criticisms of Suarez, among others; Leibniz's reading notes are presented in Grua 347–359.

45. The sources are abundant. A sample would include *Discourse* §§30 and 31, LA 42, 45, and 53; *Specimen* (G/7/311 [MP 78]); *De libertate, fato, gratia Dei* (Grua 314); *Confessio* (A/6/3/148); and *Theodicy* §414.

46. For the passage Leibniz was paraphrasing, see LA 33.

47. The summary just quoted is the summary sent to Arnauld. In summaries retained by Leibniz, he subsequently struck "since this free action is contained in his concept . . . ."

48. For texts from our period, in addition to DM §30, see *De libertate, fato, gratia Dei* (Grua 314), *Specimen* (G/7/311–312 [MP 78]), *Primary Truths* 520 (MP 89), *Necessary and Contingent Truths* 24 (MP 105), *On Freedom* (FC 182–183 [MP 109–110]), and *De libertate creaturae et electione divina* (Grua 382–383).

49. In addition to the text quoted, see Grua 371, *Theodicy* §§52 and 84, and *Causa Dei* §42 (Schrecker 122–123).

50. See *Theodicy* §9.

51. Proposition (4) is intended to express Leibniz's idea that the connection between him and his journey to Paris is intrinsic; (3), to deny that it is necessary.

52. Section 6 of this chapter contains references to various efforts to equate Leibniz's distinction between accidental and essential properties with a distinction between temporary and perpetual properties, as well as other more subtle accounts proposed by those who ascribe superessentialism to Leibniz.

53. The symbol → represents material implication; >, subjunctive implication. We leave subtleties concerning temporal indicators aside here.

54. Various colleagues have made useful comments about possible ways to fill out the details of the mentioned programs, including Ermanno Bencivenga, Dale Brant, David Cowles, and Paul Graves.

55. The passage in brackets was added in the margins.

56. See also LA 51 in the actual letter of 14 July.

57. The evidence on this point is equivocal. The passage last quoted is preceded by the following equivocal claim: "There exists an infinite number of laws, some peculiar to one world, some to another" (LA 40). This might lead us to suppose that no two worlds have the same laws; but it does not say that.

58. For a marvelous discussion of these matters, see Loeb, *From Descartes to Hume*, pp.274–291.

59. See also A/6/3/520, from the Paris notes.

60. Letter to Morell, 1698. See also Grua 364–365; *Principles of Nature and Grace* §9 (G/6/602–603 [MP 200]); and *Monadology* §47.

61. Leibniz sometimes made a distinction between what is primitive absolutely and what is primitive relative to us. Usually he stated explicitly that the alphabet of human thoughts, grand a venture as it may be, will have to settle for the latter; see, for example, C 220–221.

62. It is a mark of his genius that, although the idea of such a catalogue sounds like a fantasy, Leibniz employed the idea, assigning arbitrary "characteristic numbers" to concepts, in order to devise a test for the validity of Aristotelian syllogisms. With some restrictions, it works. For a description of the system, see my paper "Truth and Sufficient Reason in the Philosophy of Leibniz," pp.221–224.

63. See A/6/3/490–491.

64. It is unfortunate that "intrinsic" is used in connection with two entirely different ideas, both of which are important to us. The notion of having a property intrinsically is a different notion from that of a property being intrinsic, or being an intrinsic denomination.

65. Adams, "Primitive Thisness and Primitive Identity," p.7.

66. Note that the weak thesis of intrinsic foundations is a strong thesis. It is here termed weak in relation to a still stronger version that is forthcoming.

67. For assertions of the thesis, see *Primary Truths* 521 (MP 90), *Specimen* (G/7/311 [MP 78]), and C 8 (MP 133), where Leibniz characterized the denial of purely extrinsic denominations as "a consideration which is of the greatest importance in all philosophy, and in theology itself."

68. Compare Benson Mates, *The Philosophy of Leibniz*, chap. 12, "Relations and Denominations," and Robert Adams, "Phenomenalism and Corporeal Substance in Leibniz," p.255, n.2.

69. Truths about God's relation to W are excluded.

70. See Grua 309 and 311, *DM* §13, and LA 39 and 52.

71. *OM/8/703–704*.

72. Can we find any passages from our time period where Leibniz held that some entity has a property perpetually, but not necessarily—where the notion of necessity is clearly that of metaphysical necessity? I think we can. In *De libertate, fato, gratia Dei*, Leibniz struggled with the following problem: since God knows every proposition from all eternity, and every eternal thing depends on the one eternal substance, namely, God, how can there be contingent propositions? (See especially Grua 309–312.) It is a presupposition of the problem, as posed by Leibniz, that there are propositions that have the property of being true perpetually, although they do not have the property of being true necessarily (in the relevant sense of the word). Hence, Leibniz believed that there are entities that have certain properties perpetually without having those properties necessarily. But, of course, the entities in question—propositions—are not substances; so this is not a clear-cut counterexample to the thesis that Leibniz held that all the perpetual properties of a substance are essential to that substance.

73. See, particularly, "Leibniz and the Doctrine of Inter-World Identity," pp.50–53.

74. Ibid., p.53.

75. Grua 287–291.

76. Grua 289 and LH I 20, Bl. 344; unfortunately, the clause commencing "even if" is lacking in Grua.

77. The "in itself" in brackets was subsequently struck.

78. Robert Adams, "Leibniz's Theories of Contingency," p.254.

79. Passages mentioning this comparison are found in the following works from our time period: *Specimen* (G/7/309 [MP 75]), *General Inquiries* 388 (P 77), *Necessary and Contingent Truths* 17–18 (MP 97), G/7/200 (Schrecker 13), Grua 303–304, FC 183–184 (MP 110).

80. C 1–3. A continuation of the paper, not contained in Couturat, occurs in Grua 325–326. Grua suggests a date of 1689, apparently based primarily on the evidence that the manuscript is written on Italian paper. That evidence certainly suggests 1689 as the earliest likely date, since Leibniz first traveled in Italy in that year.

81. In *De contingentia* (Grua 302–306), while expounding the alleged analogy, Leibniz explicitly mentioned Euclid's contribution.

82. The manuscript of *General Inquiries* contains the date 1686, written in Leibniz's hand. To the best of my knowledge, this is the only solid evidence that Leibniz possessed the doctrine of infinite analysis at the time of the correspondence with Arnauld. But, as these things go, that is pretty good evidence.

83. With the exception of "reductions to identicals," the terminology is mine. My suggestion is that the ideas are Leibniz's. In particular, I suggest that the notion of proof employed in *General Inquiries* vacillates among the three, and that Leibniz was aware of it.

84. See, for example, $G/7/300$–301 (L 226), $G/7/44$, C 513 (MP 7), Grua 287, $G/7/295$ (MP 14), and C 402 (MP 94).

85. The extent to which *General Inquiries* is a working draft is made clear by the following: at paragraph 40 (C 369 [P 59]), Leibniz effectively defined a true proposition as one reducible to an identical proposition. Ninety-three paragraphs later we have the material from C 388 (P 77), noted above, in which reduction to identicals is presented as the mark of necessary truths.

86. See, for example, *De contingentia* (Grua 305), C 1–2, *Necessary and Contingent Truths* 17–18 (MP 97), and *On Freedom* (FC 181 [MP 108–109]). By contrast, Leibniz waffled with respect to the notion of an a priori proof. Thus, in *Specimen* he stated that every truth has an a priori proof, although only necessary truths are reducible to identicals ($G/7/309$ [MP 75]). This leaves us wondering what Leibniz then took an a priori proof to be. At LH IV 7C, Bl. 73–74, in a note in the margin, Leibniz argued that no contingent truth has an a priori proof because no contingent truth can be demonstrated.

87. Gregory Brown and Mark Kulstad noted numerous problems with this example. Note that C_s and UC_s decompose to the same primitives. On some plausible readings of Leibniz's salva veritate principle, this has the consequence that $C_s = UC_s$; other principles, plausibly attributed to Leibniz, have the consequence that C_s and UC_s are at least logically equivalent concepts. Either way it would appear that p and q are logically equivalent propositions on the basis of principles plausibly attributed to Leibniz. But since q is an identity, p must be a necessary truth. Something has gone wrong. Perhaps my example is off-target; just as likely, some of the logical principles plausibly attributed to Leibniz need adjustment for the case of infinite analysis. The fact is that problems set in long before we reach such esoteric matters. The notion of analysis employed—roughly substituting on the basis of definitions— makes sense when applied to concepts of abstractions, but is desperately in need of clarification when applied to complete individual concepts.

88. I suggest that various passages from *General Inquiries*—for example, 371 (P 61), 374 (P 63–64), and 388 (P 77)—are best understood by bearing in mind the distinctions among reductions to identicals, nonterminating but converging proof sequences, and meta-proofs. For more detail, see my article "Truth and Sufficient Reason in the Philosophy of Leibniz," from which some of this material is taken.

89. For support for (3), see $G/7/44$, *Necessary and Contingent Truths* (C 18 [MP 98]), and *On Freedom* (FC 181 [MP 108]).

90. See, for example, *Necessary and Contingent Truths* (C 18 [MP 97]) and C 272–273. For more detail, see my "Truth and Sufficient Reason in the Philosophy of Leibniz."

91. In *DM* §13 and LA 62, Leibniz asserted that every true proposition has an

a priori proof, but he did not explicitly identify an a priori proof with a reduction to identicals. As noted above, that identification is explicit in the draft for the short letter of 14 July, but that letter was not sent to Arnauld.

92. G/3/582 (L 664).

93. I refer to the strange line of thought—it can hardly be called an argument —concerning the need for an a priori reason for saying that a certain person (as it turns out, Leibniz) in Paris at some time and a certain person (again, Leibniz) subsequently in Germany, are one and the same entity. See LA 42–43 (draft) and LA 53 (letter of 14 July). In postponing consideration of this line of reasoning, we do not run the risk of missing the source of Arnauld's concession. There is no evidence that Arnauld was in the least moved by it.

94. Fabrizio Mondadori, "Reference, Essentialism, and Modality in Leibniz's Metaphysics," p.90.

95. Couturat, *La logique de Leibniz*, pp.208–218.

96. For more detail on these matters, see my "Truth and Sufficient Reason in the Philosophy of Leibniz," pp.232–234 and p.242, n.52.

97. See the discussion at the close of section 4 of chap. 3.

98. We may take the account attributed to Arnauld in section 3 of this chapter to be "the standard account."

99. See C 391 (P 80).

100. For a first-crack suggestion, see my "Truth and Sufficient Reason in the Philosophy of Leibniz," pp.241–242, n.47.

101. For Leibniz's efforts on this score in our time period, see C 51–52 (P 19), C 69, and C 85.

102. For a brilliant, textually informed treatment of Leibniz's pre-*Discourse* reflections on the substance-attribute relation, see Mercer, "The Origins of Leibniz's Metaphysics."

103. Grua 390.

104. The "individual" in brackets does not occur in Arnauld's copy of the letter; it is an above-the-line insertion in Leibniz's copy.

105. We may assume throughout this discussion that all references to properties are actually to primitive properties; see section 5 of this chapter.

106. See, particularly, LA 20 and 52–53.

107. See LBr 63; the relevant passage occurs in the margin, where it is crossed out.

CHAPTER 5: SUBSTANCE

1. Among the metaphysical theses that I have in mind are these: where x is a created individual substance, Leibniz held in the *Discourse* and/or correspondence that x has a complete concept; x remains numerically the same over time; each state of x contains traces of all that x has been and marks of all that x will be; the identity of indiscernibles holds of x; x is incorruptible and ingenerable; x is indivisible; x expresses the entire universe; the hypothesis of concomitance holds of x; whatever happens to x is a consequence of its concept; and x has true (substantial) unity. For references, see section 3 of this chapter.

2. The terminology here is mine, not that of Leibniz.

3. The passage in question is not only in the margin, it is written with different ink from that used in the main body of the letter. These facts have suggested to some

that the passage was added later. It may have been, but the material occurs in the main text of the unpublished draft for the letter of 9 Oct. 1687; see LBr 105.

4. There are numerous passages in the correspondence whose natural interpretation implies that souls are individual substances. But there are surprisingly few where Leibniz asserted outright that souls are individual substances. One such is at the beginning of the draft for the letter of 8 Dec.; see the last two lines of LA 68.

5. See also Leibniz's letter of 4 Nov. 1715 to Rémond (G/3/657), where primary matter is regarded as an incomplete entity, that is, an abstraction.

6. The term *entelechy* occurs in various items of the correspondence, drafts (published and unpublished) as well as copies of letters retained by Leibniz. It does not occur in any letter received by Arnauld. I believe that every occurrence is an addition made after completion of the correspondence with Arnauld.

7. For typical uses of "the substance of" in the *Discourse* and correspondence, see the heading for *DM* §12, LA 72, 98, and 124.

8. Articles 34–36 of the *Discourse* concentrate on the distinction between spirits and nonspiritual souls. According to *DM* §34, nonspiritual souls, lacking reflection, also lack moral qualities and, hence, are not persons. According to *DM* §36, whereas all substances express their world, spirits express God as well, since God is a spirit.

9. See Leibniz's letter of 1699 to Thomas Burnett (G/3/260) for a clear statement of the doctrine of infinite descent.

10. The conditions listed in the last three sentences are crucial; they serve to fully differentiate the corporeal substance theory from the monadological theory.

11. Third reply, Question 1. See St. Thomas Aquinas, *Quaestiones de anima*, and the translation by James H. Robb.

12. Some such scenario is recommended by Daniel Garber in his brilliant article "Leibniz and the Foundations of Physics: The Middle Years."

13. Grotefend, *Briefwechsel*, p.225.

14. Those who are confident that the fair copy was amended by Leibniz with the corporeal substance theory in mind may see one substance in concreto here (Alexander the Great) and one substance in abstracto (the great man's soul).

15. This is a rare case where the usually reliable Lucas and Grint translation goes astray. The "either" that starts the bracketed passage is missing; the "or" that completes the bracketed passage is replaced by "and." The result is a galimatias.

16. Thus the fair copy—with some apparent reluctance—rejects the spiritual theory. What theory of substance it accepts is less clear.

17. For the draft, see LA 41–43; for the letter itself, see LA 57.

18. LA 58.

19. LA 58. In the version received by Arnauld, the last clause of the quoted passage is: "and that corresponds in some way to what is called the soul" (RL 45).

20. Leibniz's claim that corporeal substances, although extended, are not divisible is discussed in chap. 6.

21. LA 65. In the copy of Arnauld's letter retained by Leibniz, this passage is underlined, which was a standard method of indicating quotation, or something near to quotation; apparently, exact replication was not required.

22. For Arnauld's queries, see LA 65–68.

23. See LA 77. In the draft for the short letter of 14 July, Leibniz had already characterized these questions as being "questions of fact that are difficult to resolve" (LBr 69v). Malpighi, Swammerdam, and Leeuwenhoek are cited by Leibniz in the letter of 19 Oct.; see LA 122–123.

24. This passage is a draft for the first paragraph of LA 98.

25. In Arnauld's response of 4 March 1687, he employed the expression "true unity" in place of Leibniz's "substantial unity" (LA 85); Leibniz subsequently followed suit. Neither expression occurs in the *Discourse*, but the idea does under the rubrics "ens per se" (*DM* §10) and "unum per se" (*DM* §34).

26. See RL 54. The words in brackets were added in the margin, but they are contained in the copy Arnauld received.

27. See RL 70. The words in brackets were added in the margin, but they are contained in the copy Arnauld received.

28. See LA 121 and 126. The latter passage occurs in a summary not contained in the copy received by Arnauld, suggesting to some that it is a later addition. I doubt it; exactly the same language occurs in the body of the unpublished draft for that letter. (See LBr 105.)

29. See LA 118 and LBr 104.

30. See Arnauld's criticisms at LA 106–107.

31. The italicized expressions occur in the copy received by Arnauld (see RL 87). In the copy retained by Leibniz, these expressions are struck and replaced by "entelechy" and "entelechies," respectively.

32. See section 1 of this chapter.

33. See especially G/2/267 and G/2/256.

34. See G/2/506 (L 617).

35. This argument is the principal subject of *DM* §12. It occurs in the correspondence at LA 77, 97–98, and 118; in *Specimen* (G/7/314–315 [MP 81–82]); in *Primary Truths* 522–523 (MP 92); and in a letter from Leibniz to Foucher (G/1/392).

36. Other sources of this identification in the neighborhood of our time period are *LH* IV 1, 14c (1683); the *New System* of 1695 (G/4/479 [MP 116–117]); and *Specimen dynamicum* of 1695 (GM/6/236–237 [L 436–437]).

37. In Leibniz's mature metaphysics, primitive active force is clearly identified with the tendency of a substance to pass from one perception to another, in accordance with its developmental law. See, for example, a letter from Leibniz to De Volder in 1705 (G/2/275).

38. In *Specimen dynamicum*, Leibniz wrote: "Active force . . . is of two kinds, namely, primitive, which is in all corporeal substances per se . . . , or derivative, which is exercised in various ways through a limitation of primitive force resulting from the conflict of bodies among themselves" (GM/6/236 [L 436]). In the correspondence with De Volder, Leibniz put the matter this way: "Primitive [active] force is the law of the series, as it were, while derivative force is the determinate value that distinguishes some term in the series" (G/2/262 [L 533]). Laws of nature, then, pertain to derivative active force. The developmental law of a substance, noted in section 1 of chapter 4, is here identified with its primitive active force, which, as noted in the previous note, is not construed as a physical item in the correspondence with De Volder.

39. See DM §18, LA 97–98, 115, 133, 137; and *Specimen* (G/7/314 [MP 82]).

40. For a discussion of the relevant issues, see Gueroult, *Leibniz: Dynamique et metaphysique*, particularly chapter 7. It should be noted that the relevant identification of those objects at rest and those in motion, based on force, is not open to human beings, according to Leibniz. Indeed, in the *Phoranomus* Leibniz noted the equivalence of various hypotheses concerning relative motion, and added, "Not even an

angel could discern, in mathematical rigor, which of several such bodies is at rest, and is the center of motion of the others" (C 590).

41. Leibniz made the same point concerning shape in the following texts from our period: *Specimen* (G/7/314 [MP 81]); *Primary Truths* (522 [MP 92]); letter to Foucher of 1687 (G/1/392); and *LH* IV 1, 14c Bl. 11 (1683).

42. Texts with a similar flavor can be found outside our period—for example, a reply to Bayle in 1702 (G/4/568 [L 583]) and a letter to Sophie in 1706 (G/7/563).

43. This argument was formulated and then struck from a piece entitled "Dans les corps il n'y a point de figure parfait," probably dating from 1686, according to the *Vorausedition*. (See L. A. Foucher de Careil, *Leibniz: Lettres et opuscules inédits* [Hildesheim: Georg Olms, 1975], pp.244–246.) The major argument employed therein goes as follows: in virtue of the fact that infinitely many bodies act on each body at each instant, and those actions constantly vary, "there is no body that has any shape during some time, however small it may be." Then comes the premiss that carries the load: "Now I believe that what exists only in a moment has no existence, since it begins and ends at the same time." The rest is easy inference. It would be worthwhile to formulate this principle exactly and compare it with an exact formulation of the major principle employed in the draft for the letter of 30 April (see LBr 81v) to show that since motion is a successive being, "it can never exist, no more than time." I leave this project to others. Other useful statements of the "since motion is a successive being, it never really exists" principle are to be found in a letter to Pellisson (*ML* 281) and in a letter to Jaquelot (G/3/457).

44. Adams, "Phenomenalism and Corporeal Substance in Leibniz," p.226.

45. I have concentrated on Leibniz's views concerning shape, primarily because they have not received the attention they deserve. I believe that a close examination of Leibniz's remarks on motion in our period supports a similar conclusion; namely, that a realistic interpretation simply does not accord with the texts. See *Specimen* (G/7/313 [MP 79]) and LA 69–70, where the code words "in metaphysical precision" and "in the last analysis" tell us that what we are getting is the inside story.

46. See, for example, section 13 of *On Nature Itself* (G/4/513 [L 505]).

47. Leibniz's central argument for this thesis is outlined in section 1 of chap. 6.

48. See McGuire, " 'Labyrinthus Continui'."

49. On this point, see the important study by Glenn A. Hartz and J. A. Cover, "Space and Time in the Leibnizian Metaphysics."

50. Leibniz's account of what we take to be intersubstantial causation in terms of reciprocal changes in degree of confusion of perception is an example of what I mean by a replacement analysis, where a purportedly metaphysically muddled concept is replaced, rather than strictly analyzed, by a metaphysically acceptable concept. See *DM* §15.

CHAPTER 6: SUBSTANTIAL FORMS

1. See, for example, *DM* §18, LA 97–98 and 133, and *Specimen* (G/7/314–315 [MP 81–82]).

2. See *Brevis demonstratio* (GM/6/117–123 [L 296–301]), published in 1686.

3. In *DM* §21, Leibniz argued that if extension were the essence of corporeal substance, then the laws of motion would be other than what they are. Daniel Garber has noted that Leibniz's argument at *DM* §21 seems to presuppose that motive

force is an intrinsic feature of corporeal substances. See Garber, "Leibniz and the Foundations of Physics," p.124, n. 174.

4. See *Specimen dynamicum* (G/6/237 [L 437]).

5. I am indebted to a discussion of these matters with John Etchemendy. The difficulties of providing a rational basis for the relevant thesis were brought home to me by David Cowles.

6. The argument occurs in numerous other texts from our time period; see, for example, *Specimen* (G/7/314 [MP 81]); *LH* IV 7C Bl. 105–106, 109–110, 111–114; and *LH* IV 7B Bl. 13–14.

7. See LA 86.

8. LA 107.

9. Cf. Jonathan Bennett, *Kant's Dialectic*, pp.174–175.

10. See, for example, Leibniz's letter of 9 Oct. 1687 (LA 119), where the expression "phenomenal or notional unity" is introduced in connection with the idea of *one* rainbow, one *flock*.

11. See, for example, the draft for the letter of 30 April (LBr 81), the letter itself (LA 96), and the letter of 9 Oct. (LA 118).

12. See *Primary Truths* 522 (MP 91).

13. It might be supposed that a close study of Cordemoy's argument for atomism, to which Leibniz frequently referred approvingly, would shed light on Leibniz's own reasoning here. Leibniz's reading notes on the relevant sections of Cordemoy's work are included in the first appendix to Clair and Girbal, *Gerauld de Cordemoy*. Frankly, I think the light is shed in the other direction.

14. By a grounded decomposition set D of an aggregate A, I mean a decomposition set D for A, every element of which is a nonaggregate.

15. Schmidt 478–484. It is assigned a probable date of 1685 in the *Vorausedition*.

16. Schmidt 481. In the third sentence, Schmidt has "aut eodem toto" (or in the same whole). The *Vorausedition* has "aut eodem loco" (or in the same place). The latter makes sense; the former does not.

17. LA 87.

18. Similar remarks may be found in the correspondence at LA 76 and 98.

19. Cf. R. S. Woolhouse, "Leibniz and the Temporal Persistence of Substances," pp.84–85.

20. The doctrine of marks and traces occurs in *DM* §§8 and 29, and in the correspondence at LA 39, 47, 57, 78, 98, and 126, among other passages. In a letter to De Volder in 1703, Leibniz formulated the doctrine of marks and traces and said of it: "This is the most certain nature of every substance" (G/2/251 [L 530]).

21. Developmental laws for possible worlds and individuals were discussed in section 1 of chap. 4.

22. This passage is from Leibniz's response in 1698 to Bayle's criticisms of the *New System*; see G/4/518 (L 493).

23. This passage is from a letter to De Volder written in 1704; see G/2/263–264 (L 534–535).

24. The relevant doctrine is found in the *Discourse* §§14, 16, 32, 33; in the correspondence at LA 47, 57, 69, 75, 115, 136; and in *Specimen* (G/7/312 [MP 79]).

25. See LA 115.

26. See section 3 of chap. 5 for references to supporting texts.

27. See Loeb, *From Descartes to Hume*, §35. Similar ideas are contained in Robert Adams's paper "Predication, Truth, and Transworld Identity in Leibniz."

28. Leibniz often claimed that the denial of substantial forms led to Spinoza; see a letter to Alberti (G/7/444) and *On Nature Itself* (G/4/508 [L 502]).

29. The doctrine involved here occurs in numerous texts. See, for example, *Monadology* §19 and *Principles of Nature and Grace* §4. Brian Skelly focused my attention on these texts and the related problem of interpretation.

30. See G/4/558 (L 577).

31. The quoted passage is from the draft for the long letter of 14 July. Essentially the same formulation occurs in the letter itself; see LA 57.

32. God's "ordinary concourse" is the subject of section 7 of chap. 7.

33. Leibniz's conception of the miraculous is compared with Malebranche's in section 4 of chap. 7.

34. See esp. pp.264–274.

35. See the discussion of ordinary concourse in section 7 of chap. 7, where something is said about the terminology employed to formulate the relevant doctrine.

CHAPTER 7: ACTION

1. The characteristic scholastic language of immanent versus transeunt causation does not occur in the letters as received by Arnauld, nor in the published drafts. But in the unpublished draft for the letter of 30 April 1687, Leibniz utilized the terminology. See LBr 78.

2. The "way out, which is surely ingenious" described by Leibniz in this passage is what I mean by the "change the direction, but not the quantity of motion" view, which Leibniz herein attributed to Descartes.

3. On this topic, see Garber, "Mind, Body," p.130, n.35.

4. Whatever the origin of the "change the direction, but not the quantity of motion" view, Leibniz enjoyed expounding it and then criticizing it. In addition to LA 94 and G/4/497 (MP 129–130), see *Theodicy* §59, *New Essays* 224, and *Monadology* §80.

5. G/3/45–46 (letter to Bayle, 1687).

6. For Leibniz's derivation of the conservation of direction of motion, see GM/6/496–500; for a superb explanation of this matter, see Garber, "Mind, Body."

7. The usual references are to Francisco Suarez *Disputationes metaphysicae* XII, ii, 4 and XVIII, i–iii. Sometimes Leibniz's criticisms were aimed at the application of the influx theory to the case of sense perception. In that case, the culprit was the *species intentionales* and the usual references to Suarez are to *De anima*, book 3, chap. 1 and book 4, chap. 2. Although Leibniz was not taken with Suarez's contribution on this topic, he respected Suarez as a metaphysician. As an example of his respect, see *New Essays* 431, where Leibniz noted a series of topics, such as the continuum, contingency, and the principle of individuation, on which Suarez and other Scholastics made comments. Leibniz concluded: "There is still gold in this dross."

8. See LBr 70.

9. Loeb, *From Descartes to Hume*, p.312.

10. On these matters, I am much indebted to Jonathan Bennett, *A Study of Spinoza's Ethics*; see, particularly, his accounts of dualism (pp.41–50) and parallelism (pp.127–151).

11. Ibid., p.41.

12. Ibid., p.47.

13. See section 2 of chap. 5.

14. We have already discussed the problems surrounding this premiss in this context.

15. LBr 70.

16. Bayle's criticism is contained in article H of the entry "Rorarius" in Bayle's *Dictionnaire historique et critique* (1697 edition). Leibniz responded in 1698; see G/4/517–524 (L 492–497). Bayle augmented his criticism in the 1702 edition of the *Dictionnaire*, in article L of the Rorarius entry. Leibniz's notes for a response are detailed and useful; see G/4/524–554.

17. See LA 113–114.

18. Bayle actually employed a different example—a dog illicitly enjoying eating his master's bread and then struck with a stick, with attendant pain. See *Pierre Bayle: Oeuvres diverses: Choix d'articles tirés du Dictionnaire historique et critique*, 2: 977 (translated by Richard Popkin as *Historical and Critical Dictionary*, pp.237–238).

19. See Leibniz's remarks at Grua 358.

20. In a note published with *Specimen*, Leibniz referred to a substance as "the occasional cause of its actions that are transeunt" (G/7/313 [MP 81]).

21. In order for (i) to serve its intended purpose here, the coming into being or the ceasing to be of either a mode or a substance should be construed as an alteration. As noted in chapter 3, section 3, Malebranche's theory of human freedom, based on the notion of consent to desire, requires that although consents are in some sense states of a substance, they do not require causes.

22. See *OM*/2/309 (LO 446).

23. See *OM*/2/313 (LO 448).

24. See, for example, *OM*/10/49–50, *OM*/7/514–515, and *OM*/12/155–161 (Doney 153–159). I believe that a careful analysis of Malebranche's efforts to establish a relevant principle excluding overdetermination will show that they lean on the first argument for the conclusion that God is the only real cause. See, for example, *OM*/2/316 (LO 450).

25. *ML* 412.

26. See *ML* 479–480. The relevant passage occurs in Leibniz's draft of a letter to Rémond of 4 November 1715 (G/3/656–660); it is marked for exclusion and is not printed in Gerhardt. Referring to a work by Du Tertre, claiming to refute Malebranche, Leibniz wrote: "It seems that the author of the Refutation has not adequately answered the argument taken from continual creation, which seems to deny all action to creatures. I have responded to that argument thus in the *Theodicy*, that in the matter of continued existence, God produces only the perfections of things, but that the imperfection or new limitation attached thereto is a consequence of the preceding state, limited to the creature, and that thus there is truly what theologians call a concourse."

27. See, for example, *OA*/39/242.

28. In order to capture the intent of Malebranche's mature thought, we would need to put restrictions on the content of G, as well as its form, in order to insure that the generalization G is causal in nature. Clearly, the relevant notion of causality would not be what Malebranche referred to as real or true causality.

29. See chap. 3, section 3.

30. See, for example, *OM*/7/527, 576; and *OM*/8/655.

31. See, for example, *OM*/3/213 (LO 662–663), *OM*/4/77, and *OM*/5/66–67.

32. Many students of Malebranche have missed the full force of Arnauld's objection on this point, but not Louis Loeb; see *From Descartes to Hume*, pp.198–199, n. 8.

33. See *ML* p.392.

34. Ibid. The passage on which Leibniz commented is in chap. 151, part 2 of Bayle's *Réponse aux questions d'un provincial* (*Oeuvres diverses*, 3:812).

35. For other examples, see *OM*/3/89 (LO 589), *OM*/5/61, and *OM*/8/651–655.

36. See, for example, *OM*/7/594, *OM*/8/758–759, and *OM*/12/267 (Doney 267).

37. The relevant notion of causality would not be what Malebranche referred to as real or true causality. It would be the common notion that Malebranche attempted to capture with the notion of occasional causality.

38. On this point, as on many others, Malebranche deserves better from his commentators than he has received.

39. The same fivefold scheme may be found in Malebranche's replies to Arnauld's criticisms. See, for example, *OM*/8/705ff., where Malebranche stated that there are apparently other types of laws unknown to us.

40. See, for example, *OM*/5/30.

41. See, for example, *OM*/1/215–216 (LO 102) and *OM*/2/227 (LO 733). It must be borne in mind that what seventeenth-century thinkers called "animal spirits" were taken to be spirits in the sense in which Scotch whiskies are spirits; they were not taken to be spiritual, but rather material.

42. See, for example, *OM*/3/49–50 (LO 559). This category pertains to Malebranche's theory of thought—the notorious "vision in God."

43. See, for example, *OM*/5/197–206.

44. See, for example, *OM*/5/70–71, 96–98; and *OM*/7/547–553.

45. *OM*/8/705.

46. For details, see the addition to article 17, second discourse of the *Traité* (*OM*/5/76–88). This feature of Malebranche's system led Fénelon sarcastically to summarize Malebranche's "solution" as follows: "If God had not given us a savior, all men could be saved by his general will to give them his grace in abundance; it is precisely because we have a savior that so many souls perish" (*Oeuvres de Fénelon*, 3:269).

47. By "necessary condition" I mean a causally necessary condition, where the notion of causality is the common notion, not what Malebranche referred to as real or true causality.

48. See *OA*/38/695.

49. See *OM*/8/658.

50. The same point is made in the eighth elucidation to the *Search after Truth*; see *OM*/3/97–98 (LO 594).

51. A passage in the last elucidation to the *Traité* is a good example. There (*OM*/5/204) Malebranche clearly stated that "a body is never moved, unless another strikes it"; but he prefaced his remarks by saying that consideration was then restricted to "the purely material world."

52. See G/3/355.

53. In our texts, this argument by elimination is to be found at *DM* §33; LA 46–47 and 57–58; and LBr 69–69v.

54. See, for example, Leibniz's draft for a letter to Basnage (1706): "It seems that I can also say that my hypothesis is not gratuitous, since I believe that I have shown that there are only three hypotheses possible, and that mine alone is both intelligible and natural, but it can even be proved a priori" (G/3/144).

55. But on occasion Leibniz developed an argument for the premiss that one of

the three accounts must obtain. Consider this passage from a letter of 30 June 1704 to Lady Masham: "One cannot find another hypothesis than these three in all. For either the laws of bodies and of souls are interfered with, or they are conserved. If these laws are interfered with (which must come from something outside), it must be that either one of these two things interferes with the other, and that is the hypothesis of influence, which is common in the schools; or it is a third thing that interferes with them, that is, God, in the hypothesis of occasional causes" (G/3/355).

56. See, for example, G/4/510 (L 502–503).

57. In connection with Leibniz's argument, the following curiosity arises. After explaining his theory of spontaneity to l'Hospital in a letter of 22 July 1695, Leibniz wrote: "Arnauld had believed at first glance that this might endanger grace and favor the Pelagians. But having received my explanation, he discharges me of that accusation" (GM/2/24). In general, I have found Leibniz's accounts of his exchange with Arnauld accurate and entirely fair. In the present case, I have no idea what passage in the letters from Arnauld Leibniz had in mind.

58. See LA 92.

59. Here are some other sources containing helpful statements of it: letter to l'Hospital, 1695 (GM/2/298–9); letter to Basnage, 1696 (G/3/122); letter to Lady Masham, 1705 (G/3/341); *Considerations on Vital Principles and Plastic Natures*, 1705 (G/6/541 [L 587]); and *Theodicy* §61.

60. Since the cue ball is not God, the point is obvious in the case of Malebranche. To make it obvious in the case of Leibniz, imagine the game played with obliging hedgehogs, i.e., corporeal substances.

61. Typically, while the idea of a distinction between the rigorous conception of real causality and an ordinary conception of quasi-causality remained fixed in Leibniz's thinking, the terminology took a beating. Thus, in *Primary Truths* we have: "Every created individual substance exerts *physical* action on, and is acted on by all others. . . . Strictly, it can be said that no created substance exerts *metaphysical* action on another" (C 521 [MP 90]). And in the *Theodicy*, at §59: "Many moderns have recognized that there is no *physical* communication between the mind and the body, although *metaphysical* communication always subsists."

62. We need to take heed of our proviso on extended causal histories noted in section 2 of this chapter—namely, that a history begins with some post-creation event. Otherwise, Leibniz's own conservation principles would be inconsistent with his beliefs about creation.

63. For a marvelous discussion of Leibniz's sophisticated attitude toward materialism, see Margaret Wilson's article "Leibniz and Materialism."

64. Cf. R. S. Woolhouse, "Leibniz's Reaction to Cartesian Interaction."

65. I am indebted to Daniel Fouke for his help on these points.

66. See G/1/358–359.

67. See G/1/360–361.

68. See, for example, Leibniz's draft for a letter to Basnage, G/3/144.

69. It is probably best to consider Leibniz's claims about the relationships holding among (a), (b), (c), and (d); and then to consider what role Leibniz attributed to God in these matters.

70. Jalabert, "Leibniz et Malebranche," pp.287–288.

71. The same point is made in Leibniz's copy of his letter to Arnauld of 8 Dec. 1686 (see LA 75), but the relevant sentence does not occur in the letter received by Arnauld.

72. See Ian Hacking, "A Leibnizian Theory of Truth," p.193.

73. This should be taken with a grain of salt; there is hardly any doctrine in Leibniz's system about which he did not make an analogous claim.

74. See Mates, "Leibniz on Possible Worlds," and Rescher, *Leibniz*, esp. chaps. 2 and 5.

75. These same paragraphs in the *Discourse* contain the thesis that spirits express God as well. As noted in chap. 5, *DM* §36 contains the idea that expressing "God rather than the world" distinguishes spirits from other souls.

76. Essentially the same characterization of expression (or representation—I take them to be the same) may be found in a letter to Foucher 1686 (G/1/383); the same characterization of perception occurs in *Specimen* (G/7/317 [MP 85]). For detailed discussion of various problems connected with these suggested definitions, see two articles by Mark Kulstad: "Leibniz's Conception of Expression" and "Some Difficulties in Leibniz's Definition of Perception."

77. See Kulstad, "Leibniz's Conception of Expression," p.57.

78. A similar restriction occurs in a series of definitions that Grua considers to be from 1679; see Grua 538 and 540. In other texts, Leibniz distinguished between cases of expression having a basis in nature and those that are arbitrary. He utilized the relation between a word and what it refers to as an example of the latter. See G/7/264 (L 208).

79. *Oeuvres diverses, Volumes supplémentaires* I, 2:977.

80. See, for example, G/4/522 (L 496) and *New Essays* 53.

81. See, for example, *DM* §8; LA 41 and 57; *Primary Truths* (521 [MP 90]); and the draft for the short letter of 14 July (LBr 69).

82. See LA 112.

83. See LA 74.

84. *DM* §§14 and 15 forge a link between accommodation construed in terms of the quality of perception (measured on the confused-distinct scale), and accommodation construed in terms of satisfaction of desires. Here the distinction between the weak thesis of universal expression and the strong thesis of universal perception may be relevant. Developing an account of accommodation based on those notions might lead to a basis for an "accommodation measure" for each possible world. In this case, the question on which I have focused—whether universal expression implies universal accommodation—would be seen to be uninteresting. As a sample of the sort of reconstruction I have in mind—in the perception case—I recommend Robert Brandon's article "Leibniz and Degrees of Perception."

85. See LA 70.

86. See *DM* §§6 and 7; *Specimen* (G/7/312 [MP 78–79]); and *ML* 222.

87. On these matters I am especially indebted to discussions with Mark Kulstad and Donald Rutherford.

88. See LA 115.

89. See Mates, *The Philosophy of Leibniz*, p.73.

90. In a passage where Leibniz set out to carefully delineate his views on possible worlds, he wrote: "There are as many possible worlds as there are series of things that can be posited not implying a contradiction" (Grua 390). There is no hint of maximality here.

91. On the topic of the striving possibles, see David Blumenfeld's penetrating discussion in "Leibniz's Theory of the Striving Possibles."

92. The last clause is "etsi fieri possint," which could also be translated "although

it could come about."

93. Cf. *Theodicy* §381, where Leibniz ascribed to Durandus the deistic alternative of *DM* §8.

94. In asserting that God's concurrence is both immediate and special, Leibniz meant to disassociate himself from the position of Durandus, according to which God's concurrence is only mediate and general.

95. This example is employed in connection with Leibniz's account of the provenance of actions in the *Summary of the Theodicy*, Objection V (G/6/383 [Huggard translation, pp.384–385]); in *Causa Dei* (G/6/450 [Schrecker 129–130]); in *Theodicy* §30, where it is explicitly used to explain Leibniz's way of avoiding both deism and occasionalism; and in the footnote to *Theodicy* §392, previously noted.

CHAPTER 8: CONCLUDING REMARKS

1. T. S. Eliot, "The Development of Leibniz's Monadism," *The Monist* 26 (1916):534–556; reprinted as Appendix 1 of *Knowledge and Experience in the Philosophy of F. H. Bradley*. The quoted passage occurs on p.182 of the book, which is a slightly revised version of Eliot's doctoral dissertation. Eliot did not return to Harvard to defend the dissertation.

Bibliography

❖❖❖❖❖❖❖❖❖

The bibliography below is divided into three sections. The first contains relevant texts and translations. The second contains various bibliographic aids. The third contains those items from the vast secondary literature that directly influenced me while I was preparing this book. Each year the last issue of *Studia Leibnitiana* contains bibliographic information concerning Leibniz literature—texts, secondary works, reviews—published in the preceding year.

TEXTS AND TRANSLATIONS

Aquinas, St. Thomas. *On the Unity of the Intellect against the Averroists*. Translated by Beatrice H. Zedler. Milwaukee: Marquette University Press, 1968.

——. *Quaestiones de anima*. Edited by James H. Robb. Toronto: Pontifical Institute of Medieval Studies, 1968.

——. *Questions on the Soul*. Translated by James H. Robb. Milwaukee: Marquette University Press, 1984.

——. *Tractatus de unitate intellectus contra Averroistas*. Edited by L. W. Keeler, S. J. Rome: Gregorian University, 1936.

Arnauld, Antoine. *The Art of Thinking*. Translated by James Dickoff and Patricia James. Indianapolis: Bobbs-Merrill, 1964.

——. *Oeuvres de Messire Antoine Arnauld, Docteur de la Maison et Société de Sorbonne*, 43 vols. Paris: 1775–1783. Reprint. Brussels: Culture et Civilisation, 1967.

Arnauld, Antoine, and Pierre Nicole. *La logique, ou L'art de penser*. Edited by Pierre Claire and François Girbal. Paris: J. Vrin, 1981.

Bayle, Pierre. *Historical and Critical Dictionary*. Translated by Richard H. Popkin. Indianapolis: Bobbs-Merrill, 1965.

——. *Oeuvres diverses*. Introduction by Elizabeth Labrousse. Hildesheim: Georg Olms, 1964–1982.

Cordemoy, Gerauld de. *Oeuvres philosophiques*. Edited by Pierre Clair and François Girbal. Paris: Presses Universitaires de France, 1968.

Descartes, René. *Oeuvres de Descartes*. Edited by Charles Adam and Paul Tannery. Paris: 1897–1913. Reprint. Paris: J. Vrin, 1964–1975.

——. *Philosophical Letters*. Translated and edited by Anthony Kenny. Oxford: Clarendon Press, 1970.

————. *The Philosophical Writings of Descartes*. Translated by John Cottingham, Robert Stoothoff, and Dugald Murdoch. Cambridge: Cambridge University Press, 1985.

Fénelon, François. *Oeuvres de Fénelon*. Versailles: J. A. Lebel, 1820.

Leibniz, Gottfried Wilhelm. *Der Briefwechsel des Gottfried Wilhelm Leibniz in der Königlichen öffentlichen Bibliothek zu Hannover*. Edited by Eduard Bodemann. Hannover, 1895. Reprint. Hildesheim: Georg Olms, 1966.

————. *Briefwechsel zwischen Leibniz, Arnauld und dem Landgrafen Ernst von Hessen - Rheinfels*. Edited by C. L. Grotefend. Hannover: 1846.

————. *Confessio philosophi*. Translated by Yvon Belaval. Paris: J. Vrin, 1970.

————. *Confessio philosophi*. Translated by Otto Saame. Frankfurt am Main: Vittorio Klostermann, 1967.

————. *Discours de metaphysique*. Edited by Henri Lestienne. Paris: J. Vrin, 1970.

————. *Discours de metaphysique et analyse détaillée des lettres à Arnauld*. Edited by Emile Thouverez. Paris: Belin Frères, 1910.

————. *Discours de metaphysique et correspondance avec Arnauld*. Edited by Georges LeRoy. Paris: J. Vrin, 1970.

————. *Discours de metaphysique et Monadologie*. Edited by André Robinet. Paris: J. Vrin, 1974.

————. *Discourse on Metaphysics*. Translated by Peter G. Lucas and Leslie Grint. Manchester: Manchester University Press, 1961.

————. *Escritos filosoficos*. Edited and translated by Ezequiel de Olaso. Buenos Aires: Editorial Charas, 1982.

————. *Fragmente zur Logik*. Translated by Franz Schmidt. Berlin: Akademie-Verlag, 1960.

————. *Generales inquisitiones de analysi notionum et veritatum/Allgemeine Untersuchungen über die Analyse der Begriffe und Warheiten*. Translated by Franz Schupp. Hamburg: Felix Meiner, 1982.

————. *Gottfried Wilhelm Leibniz's General Investigations Concerning the Analysis of Concepts and Truths*. Translated by Walter H. O'Briant. Athens: University of Georgia Monographs no. 17, 1968.

————. Leibniz-Archiv, Niedersächsische Landesbibliothek, Hannover. Leibniz Briefwechsel: no. 16 (Arnauld).

————. *The Leibniz - Arnauld Correspondence*. Translated by H. T. Mason. Manchester: 1967. Reprint. New York and London: Garland, 1985.

————. *Die Leibniz - Handschriften der öffentlichen Bibliothek zu Hannover*. Edited by Eduard Bodemann. Hannover, 1895. Reprint. Hildesheim: Georg Olms, 1966.

————. *Leibniz und Landgraf Ernst von Hessen - Rheinfels: Ein ungedruckter Briefwechsel über religiose und politische Gegenstande*. Edited by Christoph Rommel. 2 vols. Frankfurt am Main: Literarische Anstalt, 1847.

————. *Lettres de Leibniz à Arnauld d'après un manuscrit inédit*. Edited by Geneviève (Rodis-)Lewis. Paris, 1952. Reprint. New York and London. Garland, 1985.

————. *Logical Papers*. Edited and translated by G. H. R. Parkinson. Oxford: Clarendon Press, 1966.

————. *Malebranche et Leibniz: Relations personnelles*. Edited by André Robinet. Paris: J. Vrin, 1955.

————. *Mathematische Schriften*. 7 vols. Halle, 1849–1863. Reprint. Hildesheim: Georg Olms, 1963.

———. *Monadology and Other Philosophical Essays*. Translated by Paul Schrecker and Anne Martin Schrecker. Indianapolis. Bobbs-Merrill, 1965.

———. *New Essays on Human Understanding*. Translated by Peter Remnant and Jonathan Bennett. Cambridge: Cambridge University Press, 1981.

———. *Opuscules et fragments inédits de Leibniz*. Edited by Louis Couturat. Paris, 1903. Reprint. Hildesheim: Georg Olms, 1966.

———. *Philosophical Papers and Letters*. Edited and translated by Leroy E. Loemker. 2d ed. Dordrecht: D. Reidel, 1969.

———. *Philosophical Writings*. Edited and translated by Mary Morris and G. H. R. Parkinson. London: Dent, 1973.

———. *Die philosophischen Schriften von G. W. Leibniz*. Edited by C. J. Gerhardt. 7 vols. Berlin, 1875–1890. Reprint. Hildesheim: Georg Olms, 1965.

———. *Sämtliche Schriften und Briefe*. Edited by the German Academy of Science. Darmstadt, Leipzig, and Berlin: Georg Olms and Akademie Verlag, 1923–.

———. *Textes inédits*. Edited by Gaston Grua. 2 vols. Paris, 1948. Reprint. New York and London: Garland, 1985.

———. *Theologisches System*. Translated by Carl Haas. Tübingen, 1860. Reprint. Hildesheim: Georg Olms, 1966.

Malebranche, Nicholas. *Entretiens sur la metaphysique* (Dialogues on metaphysics). Translated by Willis Doney. New York: Abaris Books, 1980.

———. *Oeuvres complètes de Malebranche*. Edited by André Robinet. Paris: J. Vrin, 1958–1984.

———. *The Search after Truth/Elucidations of the Search after Truth*. Translated by Thomas Lennon and Paul J. Olscamp. Columbus: Ohio State University Press, 1980.

———. *Traité de la Nature et de la Grâce*. Edited by Ginette Dreyfus. Paris: J. Vrin, 1958.

BIBLIOGRAPHIC AIDS

Müller, Kurt, and Albert Heinekamp. *Leibniz - Bibliographie: Die Literatur über Leibniz bis 1980*. Frankfurt am Main. Vittorio Klostermann, 1984.

Müller, Kurt, and Gisela Krönert. *Leben und Werk von G. W. Leibniz: Eine Chronik*. Frankfurt am Main. Vittorio Klostermann, 1969.

Ravier, Emile. *Bibliographie des oeuvres de Leibniz*. Paris, 1937. Reprint. Hildesheim. George Olms, 1966.

Schrecker, Paul. "Une bibliographie de Leibniz." *Revue philosophique de la France et de l'étranger* 1938: 324–346.

Totok, Wilhelm. *Handbuch der Geschichte der Philosophie. Vol. 4. Frühe Neuzeit: 17. Jahrhundert*. Frankfurt am Main: Vittorio Klostermann, 1981.

SECONDARY LITERATURE

Abercrombie, Nigel. *The Origins of Jansenism*. Oxford: Oxford University Press, 1936.

Abraham, William E. "Complete Concepts and Leibniz's Distinction between Necessary and Contingent Propositions." *Studia Leibnitiana* 1969: 263–279.

———. "Predication." *Studia Leibnitiana* 1975: 1–20.

Adam, Antoine. *Du mysticisme à la révolte: Les Jansenistes du xvii⁰ siècle*. Paris. Fayard, 1968.

Adams, Robert Merrihew. "Leibniz's Theories of Contingency." In Hooker, *Leibniz*, pp. 243–283.

———. "Phenomenalism and Corporeal Substance in Leibniz." In French, Uehling, and Wettstein, *Contemporary Perspectives*, pp. 217–257.

———. "Predication, Truth, and Transworld Identity in Leibniz." In Bogen and McGuire, *How Things Are*, pp. 235–283.

———. "Primitive Thisness and Primitive Identity." *The Journal of Philosophy* 76, no. 1 (Jan. 1979): 5–26.

Aiton, E. J. *Leibniz: A Biography*. Bristol and Boston: Adam Hilger, 1985.

Allen, Diogenes. "Mechanical Explanations and the Ultimate Origin of the Universe According to Leibniz." *Studia Leibnitiana*, special issue no. 13 (1983).

Alquie, Ferdinand. *Le Cartesianisme de Malebranche*. Paris. J. Vrin, 1974.

Armogathe, J. R. *Theologia Cartesiana: L'explication physique de l' Euchariste chez Descartes et dom Desgabets*. The Hague: Martinus Nijhoff, 1977.

Baker, Lynne Rudder. "Was Leibniz Entitled to Possible Worlds?" *Canadian Journal of Philosophy* 15, no. 1 (March 1985): 57–74.

Bañes, Dominico. *Scholastica commentaria in primam partem Summae Theologicae Sancti Thomae Aquinatis*. Madrid and Valencia. Biblioteca de Tomistas Espanoles, 1934. Reprint. Dubuque, Iowa: Wm. C. Brown Reprint Library, n.d.

Barber, W. H. *Leibniz in France, from Arnauld to Voltaire: A Study in French Reactions to Leibnizianism, 1670–1760*. Oxford: Oxford University Press, 1955. Reprint. New York and London: Garland, 1985.

Baruzi, Jean. *Leibniz et l'organisation religieuse de la terre*. Paris: Felix Alcan, 1907. Reprint. Aalen: Scientia Verlag, 1975.

———. "Du 'Discours de metaphysique' à la 'Theodicée'." *Revue philosophique de la France et de l'étranger* 1946: 391–409.

Baucher, J. "Liberté." In *Dictionnaire de théologie catholique*, vol. 9: 660–703.

Becco, Anne. *Du simple selon G. W. Leibniz*. Paris: J. Vrin and Editions du C.N.R.S., 1975.

Beck, Lewis White. *Early German Philosophy*. Cambridge: Harvard University Press, 1969.

Belaval, Yvon. *Leibniz critique de Descartes*. Paris: Gallimard, 1960.

———. *Leibniz: Initiation à sa philosophie*. Paris: J. Vrin, 1975.

———. *Etudes leibniziennes*. Paris: Gallimard, 1976.

Bennett, Jonathan. *Kant's Analytic*. Cambridge: Cambridge University Press, 1966.

———. *Kant's Dialectic*. Cambridge: Cambridge University Press, 1974.

———. *A Study of Spinoza's Ethics*. Indianapolis: Hackett, 1984.

Blumenfeld, David. "Leibniz's Theory of the Striving Possible." *Studia Leibnitiana* 1973: 163–177.

———. "Leibniz on Contingency and Infinite Analysis." In *Philosophy and Phenomenological Research* 45, no. 4 (June 1985): 483–514.

———. "Superessentialism, Counterparts, and Freedom." In Hooker, *Leibniz*, pp. 103–123.

Bogen, James, and James E. McGuire, eds. *How Things Are: Studies in Predication and the History of Philosophy and Science*. Dordrecht: D. Reidel, 1985.

Bouillier, Francisque. *Histoire de la philosophie cartésienne* 3d ed. Paris: Delagrave, 1868.

Brandon, Robert. "Leibniz and Degrees of Perception." *Journal of the History of Philosophy* 19 (1981): 447–479.

Broad, C. D. *Leibniz: An Introduction*. Cambridge: Cambridge University Press, 1975.

Brody, Baruch. "Leibniz's Metaphysical Logic." In Kulstad, *Essays*, pp. 43–55.

Brown, Gregory. " 'Quod ostendendum susceperamus': What did Leibniz Undertake to show in the Brevis Demonstratio?," *Studia Leibnitiana*, special issue no. 13 (1984): 122–137.

Brown, Stuart. *Leibniz*. Minneapolis: University of Minnesota Press, 1984.

Brunner, Fernand. *Etudes sur la signification historique de la philosophie de Leibniz*. Paris: J. Vrin, 1951.

Burgelin, Pierre. *Commentaire du Discours de metaphysique de Leibniz*. Paris: Presses Universitaires de France, 1959.

Burkhardt, Hans. *Logik und Semiotik in der Philosophie von Leibniz*. Munich: Philosophia Verlag, 1980.

Capek, Milic. "Leibniz on Matter and Memory." In Leclerc, *Philosophy of Leibniz*, pp. 78–113.

Carreyre, J. "Jansenism." In *Dictionnaire de théologie catholique*, vol. 8, part 1: 318–529.

Castañeda, Hector. "Leibniz's Concepts and Their Coincidence *salva veritate*." *Noûs* 1974: 381–398.

Clatterbaugh, Kenneth C. *Leibniz's Doctrine of Individual Accidents*. *Studia Leibnitiana*, special issue no. 4 (1973).

Cognet, Louis. *Le Jansenisme*. Paris: Presses Universitaires de France, 1961.

Couturat, Louis. *La logique de Leibniz*. Paris: Presses Universitaires de France, 1901. Reprint. Hildesheim. Georg Olms, 1969.

———. "Sur la metaphysique de Leibniz." *Revue de metaphysique et de morale* 10 (1902).

Curley, E. M. "The Root of Contingency." In Frankfurt, *Leibniz*, pp. 69–97.

Dascal, Marcelo. *Leibniz: Language, Signs, and Thought*. Amsterdam and Philadelphia. John Benjamins, 1987.

———. *La semiologie de Leibniz*. Paris: Aubier Montaigne, 1978.

Dicker, Georges. "Leibniz on Necessary and Contingent Propositions." *Studia Leibnitiana* 1982: 221–232.

Dreyfus, Ginette. *La volonté selon Malebranche*. Paris: J. Vrin, Paris, 1958.

Earman, John. "Perception and Relations in the Monadology." *Studia Leibnitiana* 1977: 212–230.

Eisenkopf, Paul. *Leibniz und die Einigung der Christenheit*. Munich: Verlag Ferdinand Schoningh, 1975.

Eliot, T. S. *Knowledge and Experience in the Philosophy of F. H. Bradley*. London: Faber and Faber, 1964.

Fitch, Gregory. "Analyticity and Necessity in Leibniz." *Journal of the History of Philosophy* 1979: 29–42.

Fleming, Noel. "On Leibniz on Subject and Substance." *The Philosophical Review* 96 (1987): 69–95.

Flint, Thomas. "Two Accounts of Providence." In Morris, *Divine and Human Action*, pp. 147–181.

Frankel, Lois. "Leibniz's Principle of Identity of Indiscernibles." *Studia Leibnitiana* 1981: 192–211.

———. "Being Able to Do Otherwise: Leibniz on Freedom and Contingency." *Studia Leibnitiana* 1984: 45–59.

Frankfurt, Harry G., ed. *Leibniz: A Collection of Critical Essays*. New York: Doubleday, 1972.

French, Peter A., Theodore E. Uehling, Jr., and Howard K. Wettstein, eds. *Contemporary Perspectives on the History of Philosophy.* Midwest Studies in Philosophy, vol. 8. Minneapolis: University of Minnesota Press, 1983.

Frins, V. "Concours divin." In *Dictionnaire de théologie catholique*, vol. 3: 781–796.

Furth, Montgomery. "Monadology." *The Philosophical Review* 76 (1967). Reprinted in Frankfurt, *Leibniz.*

Gabbey, Alan. "Force and Inertia in Seventeenth-century Dynamics." *Studies in the History and Philosophy of Science* 1971: 1–67.

Gale, George. "Leibniz's Dynamical Metaphysics and the Origin of the Vis Viva Controversy." *Systematics* 11 (1973): 184–207.

———. "On What God Chose: Perfection and God's Freedom." *Studia Leibnitiana* 1976: 69–87.

———. "The Physical Theory of Leibniz." *Studia Leibnitiana* 1970: 114–127.

Garber, Daniel. "Leibniz and the Foundations of Physics: The Middle Years." In Okruhlik and Brown, *Natural Philosophy*, pp. 27–130.

———. "Mind, Body, and the Laws of Nature in Descartes and Leibniz." In French, Uehling, Wettstein, Op.cit.: 105–133.

———. "Motion and Metaphysics in the Young Leibniz." In Hooker, *Leibniz*, pp. 160–184.

Garrigou-Lagrange, R. "Prémotion physique." In *Dictionnaire de théologie catholique*, vol. 13: 31–77.

Gilson, Etienne. *Etudes sur le rôle de la pensée médiévale dans la formation du système cartésien.* 4th ed. Paris: J. Vrin, 1975.

———. *Index scolastico-cartésien.* Paris: J. Vrin, 1979.

Gouhier, Henri. *Cartésianisme et Augustinisme au xviiᵉ siècle.* Paris: J. Vrin, 1978.

———. *La philosophie de Malebranche et son expérience religieuse.* 2d ed. Paris: J. Vrin, 1948.

Grimm, Robert. "Individual Concepts and Contingent Truths." *Studia Leibnitiana* 1970: 200–223.

Grua, Gaston. *Jurisprudence universelle et theodicée selon Leibniz.* Paris: Presses Universitaires de France, 1953. Reprint. New York and London: Garland, 1985.

Gueroult, Martial. *Leibniz: Dynamique et metaphysique.* Paris: Aubier-Montaigne, 1967.

———. *Malebranche.* 3 vols. Paris: Aubier, 1955–1959.

Hacking, Ian. "A Leibnizian Theory of Truth." In Hooker, *Leibniz*, pp. 185–195.

———. "Why Motion Is Only a Well-founded Phenomenon." In Okruhlik and Brown, *Natural Philosophy*, pp. 131–150.

Hart, Alan. "Leibniz on Spinoza's Concept of Substance." *Studia Leibnitiana* 1982: 73–86.

Hartz, Glenn, and J. A. Cover. "Space and Time in the Leibnizian Metaphysics." *Noûs* 1988: 493–519.

Heinekamp, Albert. *Das Problem des Guten bei Leibniz.* Bonn: H. Bouvier, Bonn, 1969.

Holland, A. J., ed. *Philosophy: Its History and Its Historiography.* Dordrecht: D. Reidel, 1985.

Hooker, Michael, ed. *Leibniz: Critical and Interpretive Essays.* Minneapolis: University of Minnesota Press, 1982.

Hunter, Graeme. "Leibniz and the 'Super-Essentialist' Misunderstanding." *Studia Leibnitiana* 1981: 123–132.

Iltis, Carolyn. "Leibniz and the Vis Viva Controversy." *Isis* 62 (1971): 21–35.

Ishiguro, Hide. *Leibniz's Philosophy of Logic and Language*. Ithaca: Cornell University Press, 1972.

———. "Pre-established Harmony versus Constant Conjunction: A Reconsideration of the Distinction between Rationalism and Empiricism." *Proceedings of the British Academy* 63 (1977): 239–263.

Jacques, Emile. *Les années d'exil d'Antoine Arnauld (1679–1694)*. Louvain: Publications Universitaires de Louvain and Editions Nauwelaerts, 1976.

Jalabert, Jacques. "Création et harmonie préétablie selon Leibniz." *Studia Leibnitiana* 1971: 190–198.

———. *La théorie leibnizienne de la substance*. Paris: Presses Universitaires de France, 1947. Reprint. New York and London: Garland, 1985.

———. "Leibniz et Malebranche." *Les études philosophiques* 1981: 279–292.

———. *Le Dieu de Leibniz*. Paris: Presses Universitaires de France, 1960. Reprint. New York and London: Garland, 1985.

Jarrett, Charles E. "Leibniz on Truth and Contingency." In Jarrett, King-Farlow, and Pelletier, *New Essays*, pp. 83–100.

Jarrett, Charles E., John King-Farlow, and F. J. Pelletier, eds. *New Essays on Rationalism and Empiricism. Canadian Journal of Philosophy*, supplementary volume 4 (1978).

Jolly, Nicholas. *Leibniz and Locke: A Study in the New Essays on Human Understanding*. Oxford: Clarendon Press, 1984.

———. "An Unpublished Leibniz Manuscript on Metaphysics." *Studia Leibnitiana* 1975: 161–189.

Kabitz, Willy. *Die Philosophie des jungen Leibniz*. Heidelberg: Carl Winter, 1909. Reprint. Hildesheim: Georg Olms 1974.

Kauppi, Raili. *Über die Leibnizsche Logik*. Acta Philosophica Fennica, fasc. 12. Helsinki, 1960. Reprint. New York and London: Garland, 1985.

Kneale, Martha. "Leibniz and Spinoza on Activity." In Frankfurt, *Leibniz*, pp. 215–237.

Kulstad, Mark "Leibniz's Conception of Expression." *Studia Leibnitiana* 1977: 55–76.

———. "Some Difficulties in Leibniz's Definition of Perception." In Hooker, *Leibniz*, pp. 65–78.

Kulstad, Mark, ed. *Essays on the Philosophy of Leibniz*. Rice University Studies, vol. 63, no. 4 (1977).

Lalande, André. *Vocabulaire technique et critique de la philosophie*. 15th ed. Paris: Presses Universitaires de France, 1985.

Laporte, Jean. *La doctrine de Port-Royal. Vol. 2. Exposition de la doctrine (d'après Arnauld). Part 1. Les vérités de la Grâce*. Paris: Presses Universitaires de France, 1923.

———. *Etudes d'histoire de la philosophie française au xvii siècle*. Paris: J. Vrin, 1951.

Layman, Ronald. "Transubstantiation: Test Case for Descartes's Theory of Space." In Lennon, Nicholas, and Davis, *Problems*, pp. 149–170.

Leclerc, Ivor. "Leibniz and the Analysis of Matter and Motion." In Leclerc, *Philosophy*, pp. 114–132.

Leclerc, Ivor, ed. *The Philosophy of Leibniz and the Modern World*. Nashville: Vanderbilt University Press, 1973.

Lennon, Thomas M. "La logique janseniste de la liberté." *Revue d'histoire et de philosophie religieuses* 1979, no. 1: 37–44.

———. "Occasionalism and the Cartesian Metaphysic of Motion." *Canadian Journal of Philosophy*, supplementary volume no. 1, part 1 (1974): 29–50.

———. "Occasionalism, Jansenism and Scepticism: Divine Providence and the Order of Grace." *The Irish Theological Quarterly* 45, no. 3 (1978): 185–190.

Lennon, Thomas, John M. Nicholas, and John W. Davis, eds. *Problems of Cartesianism*. Kingston and Montreal: McGill, Queen's University Press, 1982.

Lenzen, Wolfgang. "Zur extensionalen und 'intensionalen' Interpretation der Leibnizschen Logik." *Studia Leibnitiana* 1983: 129–148.

Loeb, Louis E. *From Descartes to Hume*. Ithaca: Cornell University Press, 1981.

Loemker, Leroy E. "A Note on the Origin and Problem of Leibniz's *Discourse* of 1686." *Journal of the History of Ideas* 8 (Oct. 1947): 449–466.

———. *Struggle for Synthesis*. Cambridge: Harvard University Press, 1972.

Machamer, Peter. "The Harmonies of Descartes and Leibniz." In French, Uehling, and Wettstein, *Contemporary Perspectives*, pp. 135–142.

Machamer, Peter K., and Robert G. Turnbull, eds. *Motion and Time, Space and Matter: Interrelations in the History of Philosophy and Science*. Columbus: Ohio State University Press, 1976.

Maher, Patrick. "Leibniz and Contingency." *Studia Leibnitiana* 1980: 236–242.

Mates, Benson. "Individuals and Modality in the Philosophy of Leibniz." *Studia Leibnitiana* 1972: 81–118.

———. "Leibniz on Possible Worlds." In B. van Rootselaar and J. F. Staal, eds. *Logic, Methodology and Philosophy of Science*. Vol. 3. Amsterdam: North-Holland, 1968. Reprinted in Frankfurt, *Leibniz*, pp. 335–364.

———. *The Philosophy of Leibniz: Metaphysics and Language*. Oxford: Oxford University Press, 1986.

McCracken, Charles J. *Malebranche and British Philosophy*. Oxford: Clarendon Press, 1983.

McGuire, James E. " 'Labyrinthus Continui': Leibniz on Substance, Activity, and Matter." In Machamer and Turnbull, *Motion and Time*, pp. 290–326.

———. "Phenomenalism, Relations, and Monadic Representation: Leibniz on Predicate Levels." In Bogen and McGuire, *How Things Are*, pp. 205–233.

McRae, Robert. *Leibniz: Perception, Apperception, and Thought*. Toronto: University of Toronto Press, 1976.

———. "Miracles and Laws." In Okruhlik and Brown, *Natural Philosophy*, pp. 171–181.

Meijering, Theo. "On Contingency in Leibniz's Philosophy." *Studia Leibnitiana* 1978: 22–59.

Mercer, Christia. "The Origins of Leibniz's Metaphysics and the Development of his Conception of Substance." Ph.D. diss., Princeton University, 1989.

Miel, Jan. *Pascal and Theology*. Baltimore: The Johns Hopkins University Press, 1969.

Mondadori, Fabrizio. "Leibniz and the Doctrine of Inter-World Identity." *Studia Leibnitiana* 7 (1975): 21–57.

———. "The Leibnizian 'Circle'." In Kulstad, *Essays*, pp. 69–96.

———. "Reference, Essentialism, and Modality in Leibniz's Metaphysics." *Studia Leibnitiana* 5 (1973): 74–101.

———. "Solipsistic Perception in a World of Monads." In Hooker, *Leibniz*, pp. 21–44.

————. "Understanding Superessentialism." *Studia Leibnitiana* 1985: 162–190.

Morris, Thomas V., ed. *Divine and Human Action: Essays in the Metaphysics of Theism.* Ithaca: Cornell University Press, 1988.

Mouy, Paul. *Les lois du choc d'après Malebranche.* Paris: J. Vrin, 1927.

Nadler, Steven M. *Arnauld and the Cartesian Philosophy of Ideas.* Princeton: Princeton University Press, 1989.

————. "Arnauld, Descartes, and Transubstantiation: Reconciling Cartesian Metaphysics and Real Presence." *Journal of the History of Ideas* 1988: 229–246.

Naert, Emilienne. *Mémoire et conscience de soi selon Leibniz.* Paris: J. Vrin, 1961.

Nason, John W. "Leibniz's Attack on the Cartesian Doctrine of Extension." *Journal of the History of Ideas* 7 (1946): 447–483.

O'Briant, Walter H. "Leibniz's Preference for an Intensional Logic." *Notre Dame Journal of Formal Logic* 8, no. 3 (July 1967): 254–256.

Okruhlik, Kathleen. "The Status of Scientific Laws in the Leibnizian System." In Okruhlik and Brown, *Natural Philosophy,* pp. 183–206.

Okruhlik, Kathleen, and James Robert Brown, eds. *The Natural Philosophy of Leibniz.* Dordrecht: D. Reidel 1985.

Parkinson, G. H. R. *Leibniz on Human Freedom. Studia Leibnitiana* special issue no. 2 (1970).

————. *Logic and Reality in Leibniz's Metaphysics.* Oxford: Oxford University Press, 1965. Reprint. New York and London: Garland, 1985.

————. "Science and Metaphysics in Leibniz's 'Specimen Inventorum'." *Studia Leibnitiana* 1974: 1–27.

Parkinson, G. H. R., ed. *Truth, Knowledge and Reality: Inquiries into the Foundations of Seventeenth-Century Rationalism. Studia Leibnitiana* special issue no. 9. Wiesbaden: Franz Steiner Verlag, 1981.

Plantinga, Alvin. *The Nature of Necessity.* Oxford: Oxford University Press, 1971.

Popkin, Richard H. "Leibniz and the French Sceptics." *Revue internationale de philosophie* 1966: 228–248.

Radner, Daisie. *Malebranche: A Study of a Cartesian System.* Amsterdam: van Gorcum Assen, 1978.

Ree, Jonathan, Michael Ayers, and Adam Westoby. *Philosophy and Its Past.* Atlantic Highlands, N.J.: Humanities Press, 1978.

Remnant, Peter. "Descartes: Body and Soul." *Canadian Journal of Philosophy* 9 (1979): 377–386.

Rescher, Nicholas. *Leibniz: An Introduction to His Philosophy.* Totowa, N.J.: Rowman and Littlefield, 1979.

————. *Leibniz's Metaphysics of Nature.* Dordrecht: D. Reidel, 1981.

Robinet, André. *Architectonique disjonctive automates systémiques et idéalité transcendantale dans l'oeuvre de G. W. Leibniz.* Paris: J. Vrin, 1986.

————. "Le 'Discours de metaphysique' dans la vie de Leibniz." *Revue internationale de philosophie* 1966: 165–173.

————. "Leibniz face à Malebranche." In *Leibniz: Aspects de l'homme et de l'oeuvre.* Paris: Aubier-Montaigne, 1968.

————. "La signification du Discours de metaphysique de Leibniz." *Revue de metaphysique et de morale* 1960: 195–198.

————. *Système et existence dans l'oeuvre de Malebranche.* Paris: J. Vrin, 1965.

(Rodis-) Lewis, Geneviève. "Augustinisme et Cartésianisme à Port-Royal." In E. J.

Dijksterhuis et al. *Descartes et le Cartésianisme hollandais*. Paris: Presses Universitaires de France, 1950.

———. "La critique leibnizienne du dualisme cartésien." *Revue philosophique de la France* 136 (1946): 473–485.

———. *Individualité selon Descartes*. Paris: Librairie Philosophique J. Vrin, 1950.

———. *Nicholas Malebranche*. Paris: Presses Universitaires de France, 1963.

Rondet, Henri. *Gratia Christi*. Paris: Beauchesne, 1948.

Rorty, Richard, J. B. Schneewind, and Quentin Skinner, eds. *Philosophy in History*. Cambridge: Cambridge University Press, 1984.

Ross, G. MacDonald. *Leibniz*. Oxford and New York: Oxford University Press, 1984.

Russell, Bertrand. *A Critical Exposition of the Philosophy of Leibniz*. London: George Allen and Unwin, 1900. 2d ed., 1937.

Rutherford, Donald. "Truth, Predication and the Complete Concept of an Individual Substance." *Studia Leibnitiana*, special issue no. 15 (1987): 130–144.

Scheffler, Samuel. "Leibniz on Personal Identity and Moral Personality." *Studia Leibnitiana* 1976: 219–240.

Schepers, Heinrich. "Zum Problem der Kontingenz bei Leibniz: Die beste der möglichen Welten." In *Collegium Philosophicum* Stuttgart, 1965: 326–350.

Sedgwick, Alexander. *Jansenism in Seventeenth-Century France*. Charlottesville: University Press of Virginia, 1977.

Serres, Michel. "Etablissement, par nombres et figures, de l'Harmonie préétablie." *Revue internationale de philosophie* 1966: 216–227.

Sleigh, R. C., Jr. "Leibniz on the Two Great Principles of All Our Reasoning." In French, Uehling, and Wettstein, *Contemporary Perspectives*, pp. 193–216.

———. "Truth and Sufficient Reason in the Philosophy of Leibniz." In Hooker, *Leibniz*, pp. 209–242.

Vacant, A., E. Mangenot, and E. Amann, eds. *Dictionnaire de théologie catholique*. Paris: Librarie LeTouzey et Ane, 1903–1950.

Vanstennberghe, E. "Molinisme." In *Dictionnaire de théologie catholique*, vol. 10: 2,094–2,187.

Watson, Richard A. *The Breakdown of Cartesian Metaphysics*. Atlantic Highlands, N.J.: Humanities Press, 1987.

———. "Transubstantiation among the Cartesians." In Thomas M. Lennon, John M. Nicholas, and John W. Davis, eds. *Problems of Cartesianism*. Kingston and Montreal: McGill, Queen's University Press, 1982.

Westfall, Richard S. *Force in Newton's Physics*. London: Macdonald, 1971.

Wilson, Margaret. "Leibniz and Locke on 'First Truths'." *Journal of the History of Ideas* 1967: 347–366.

———. "Leibniz and Materialism." *Canadian Journal of Philosophy* 1974: 495–513.

———. "Leibniz's Dynamics and Contingency in Nature." In Machamer and Turnbull, *Motion and Time*, pp. 264–289.

———. "Possible Gods." *The Review of Metaphysics* 1979: 717–733.

Woolhouse, R. S. "Leibniz and the Temporal Persistence of Substances." In Parkinson, *Truth*, pp. 84–96.

———. "Leibniz's Principle of Pre-Determinate History." *Studia Leibnitiana* 1975: 207–228.

———. "Leibniz's Reaction to Cartesian Interaction." *Proceedings of the Aristotelian Society*, n.s. 86 (1985–1986): 69–82.

————. "The Nature of an Individual Substance." In Hooker, *Leibniz*, pp. 45–64.

————. "Pre-established Harmony Retuned: Ishiguro versus the Tradition." *Studia Leibnitiana* 1985: 204–219.

Yost, R. M., Jr. *Leibniz and Philosophical Analysis*. University of California Publications in Philosophy, vol. 27. Berkeley and Los Angeles, 1954. Reprint. New York and London: Garland, 1985.

Index

❖❖❖❖❖❖❖❖❖

Garber, Daniel (*continued*)
tation of extension, 209; on motive force,
211–12; on conservation of direction of
motion, 213
Gerhardt, C. J., 7, 8, 191
Girbal, François, 212
God: and creation, 13, 87; his will and
contingency, 67; theodicean concerns,
68–69; and the possible-in-its-own-
nature defense, 82–83; his causality,
134–36; argument for his existence from
accommodation, 180
Gouhier, Henri, 31
Grace, doctrine of: Leibniz on, 20; Jansen-
ism and, 28–29; realm of, according to
Malebranche, 159, 215
Graves, Paul, 205
Grint, Leslie, 8, 191
Grotefend, C. L., 7, 8
Grounding principle, 121–24
Grua, Gaston, 8, 217
Gueroult, Martial, 210

Hacking, Ian, 172, 217
Harmony, pre-established. *See* Concomi-
tance, principle of
Hartz, Glenn A., 211
Heinekamp, Albert, 8
History of philosophy, exegetical versus
philosophical, 2–6
Hollandine, Louise, 24
l'Hospital, Guillaume François de, 131, 151,
165, 169, 216
Human beings, paradigms of corporeal
substances, 105, 107

Identicals, 84–85
Identity: and superintrinsicalness, 71; and
truth, 90; of substance over time, 109,
121, 132; and aggregates, 124; and sub-
stantial forms, 126
Identity of indiscernibles: principle of in
DM, 10; characterized, 72; and substance,
109
Impetus, 118
Indestructibility, 106, 109
Individuals, possible, 50
Indivisibility: and souls, 104; and corporeal
substances, 106, 109
Infinite analysis: doctrine of, sec. 8, chap. 4;
characterized, 12; and modal notions,
70; and the proportion analogy, 84; and
Euclid's algorithm, 84; and contingency,
85

Innocent X, pope, 27
Innocent XI, pope, 28
Intrinsic denominations. *See* Properties:
primitive
Intrinsic foundations: weak thesis characterized, 75–76; strong thesis characterized,
77; Leibniz's attitude toward, 78

Jacques, Emil, 34
Jalabert, Jacques, 172
Jansen, Cornelius, 26
Jansenism: and *Augustinus*, 27; and Port
Royal, 27; allegedly heretical theses of,
27; and the "Peace of the Church," 28;
doctrine of efficacious grace, 28–29
Jaquelot, Isaac, 173, 212
Jarrett, Charles, 41

Kenny, Anthony, 201
Kripke, Saul, 8
Krönert, Gisela, 22
Kulstad, Mark: on infinite analysis, 207; on
expression and perception, 174, 217

Lamy, François, 163, 168
Language, the rational: as a logically per-
fect language, 54; and the concept-
containment account of truth, 55
Laporte, Jean, 200
Laws, developmental: of worlds and indi-
viduals, 52–53; and spontaneity, 129; and
primitive active force, 210
—of nature: and natures, 79, 162; and ac-
commodation, 178–79; and derivative
active force, 210
Leeuwenhoek, Anton van, 105, 209
Lelong, J., 169
Le Roy, Georges, 189
Lestienne, Henri, 7, 101, 191
Lewis, David, 71
Lewis, Geneviève. *See* Rodis-Lewis, Gene-
viève
Locke, John, 3
Loeb, Louis, 214; on identity over time,
132; on the dualistic framework, 144; on
"concept packing," 205
Loemker, Leroy, 40, 200
Louis XIV, 26–28
Lucas, Peter, 8, 191

McGuire, James E., 211
Mackie, J. L., 2
Malebranche, Nicholas, 11; Arnauld's criti-
cisms of, 30; on freedom, 37–38, 201; on